JAPAN'S PRISONERS OF CONSCIENCE

This book is a narrative account of the criminal prosecution of three peaceful protesters in Japan during the Iraq War that tells the inside story of their arrests and trial and examines the larger issues raised by the case.

Based on interviews with defendants, lawyers, and eyewitnesses and other Japanese language sources, the book carries rich descriptions of the individuals at the heart of the story, including the charismatic leader of the "Tachikawa Tent Village" who has been protesting since U.S. military forces were stationed in her hometown in the early postwar era. Authored by an attorney who has researched and written on Japanese legal issues for more than three decades and was the plaintiff in a suit that made constitutional history by opening Japan's courts to free reporting, this book offers expert insights into the forces that affect the right to freedom of political speech in Japan.

Illustrating the sharp political conflict that has deeply affected Japan's defense policy for decades, this book will be of great interest to scholars and students of Comparative Law, Peace Studies, Japanese Society, and Modern Asian History.

Lawrence Repeta has served as a lawyer, business executive, and law professor in Japan and the United States. He retired from the Meiji University (Japan) law faculty in 2017. He is best known in Japan as the plaintiff in a suit that opened Japan's criminal trials to free reporting. He has served on the board of directors of the Japan Civil Liberties Union and Information Access Clearinghouse Japan, non-governmental organizations that advocate for the protection of individual rights and government transparency.

"Little known outside Japan, and not well remembered within the country, in Repeta's capable hands the tale of victories, reversals, and limited vindication of the defendants offers a clear-eyed warning of the challenges to free speech faced by Japanese society today."

Andrew Gordon, Lee and Juliet Folger Fund Professor of History, *Harvard University, United States*

"This meticulous account of a major civil liberties case provides unparalleled insight into the operation of Japan's criminal justice system. This book is a must read for all students of Japan's Constitution."

Tom Ginsburg, Leo Spitz Professor of International Law, Ludwig and Hilde Wolf Research Scholar, Professor of Political Science, *University of Chicago, United States*

"This superb book details the abuse of police power to suppress dissent during the Iraq War. The author leads readers into Japan's courtrooms and delivers rich descriptions of the lawyers and supporters who rallied to defend three antiwar activists jailed and prosecuted after they criticized the Self-Defense Forces deployment to Iraq."

Jeff Kingston, Director of Asian Studies and Professor of History, *Temple University, Japan*

"Repeta presents a tapestry of stories about trials that have received little or no attention in the West, but are critical to understanding how the courts function in politicized cases."

Colin P.A. Jones, Professor, *Doshisha Law School, Japan*

JAPAN'S PRISONERS OF CONSCIENCE

Protest and Law During the Iraq War

Lawrence Repeta

Routledge
Taylor & Francis Group
LONDON AND NEW YORK

Designed cover image: Photograph courtesy of Yutaka Osawa

First published 2023
by Routledge
4 Park Square, Milton Park, Abingdon, Oxon OX14 4RN

and by Routledge
605 Third Avenue, New York, NY 10158

Routledge is an imprint of the Taylor & Francis Group, an informa business

British Library Cataloguing-in-Publication Data
A catalogue record for this book is available from the British Library

Library of Congress Cataloging-in-Publication Data
Names: Repeta, Lawrence, 1951- author.
Title: Japan's prisoners of conscience: protest and law during the Iraq war/Lawrence Repeta.
Description: New York, NY: Routledge, [2023] |
Includes bibliographical references and index.
History"–Provided by publisher.
Identifiers: LCCN 2022025220 (print) | LCCN 2022025221 (ebook) |
ISBN 9781032046297 (hbk) | ISBN 9781032046266 (pbk) |
ISBN 9781003193999 (ebk)
Subjects: LCSH: Prisoners–Japan. | Iraq War, 2003-2011–Moral and ethical aspects–Japan. | Protest movements–Japan.
Classification: LCC HV9813 .R47 2023 (print) | LCC HV9813 (ebook) |
DDC 364.60952–dc23/eng/20220902
LC record available at https://lccn.loc.gov/2022025220
LC ebook record available at https://lccn.loc.gov/2022025221

ISBN: 978-1-032-04629-7 (hbk)
ISBN: 978-1-032-04626-6 (pbk)
ISBN: 978-1-003-19399-9 (ebk)

DOI: 10.4324/9781003193999

Typeset in Bembo
by Deanta Global Publishing Services, Chennai, India

For Miki

CONTENTS

ACKNOWLEDGMENTS

I am very grateful to the individuals who made time for interviews and shared source materials and photographs from their files, especially the Tent Village members and their attorneys. Their enthusiastic commitment to freedom of political expression gives life to the constitutional promise. The courage of Tent Village members and other protesters in peacefully expressing opinions that criticize government policy is a lesson to all on the rights and duties of citizens in a democracy. Without their fortitude in challenging the Self-Defense Force deployment and fighting court battles to the very end—and their efforts to preserve a documentary record of their experience—there would be no story to tell. I must also acknowledge my debt to the many Japanese mentors who provided the guidance that prepared me to attempt this work and others.

I am also indebted to Dan Rosen, Jeff Kingston and Colin P. A. Jones for their expert reviews of the complete text. Their countless suggestions smoothed the path for readers to come.

I am also grateful to Mac Jeffery and Ken Straiton for their assistance in gathering photographs and preparing them for publication.

Finally, there are no words sufficient to express my gratitude to my wife, Miki, who provided assistance and loving support throughout the years when I worked on this project. She served as an invaluable guide as I struggled to understand the Japanese source materials, communicate with individuals in Japan, and pull everything together into a coherent whole.

FIGURES

INTRODUCTION

Amnesty International was launched in 1961 after British human rights lawyer Peter Benenson spoke out on behalf of two Portuguese students sentenced to prison for raising their glasses to toast freedom during the authoritarian Salazar regime, a time of severe repression in Portugal. Today Amnesty is one of the world's largest and most highly respected international human rights organizations, with millions of members worldwide.

Benenson's letter describing the plight of the students was published by a major London newspaper under the title "The Forgotten Prisoners."[1] He labeled these victims of political repression "Prisoners of Conscience" and defined them as "Any person who is physically restrained (by imprisonment or otherwise) from expressing (in any form of words or symbols) an opinion which he honestly holds and which does not advocate or condone personal violence." Benenson asked readers to write their own letters showing support for the students. A few weeks later, he gathered with six others, including several members of Parliament, to found the new human rights group "Amnesty International."[2]

Since then, Amnesty has identified countless "prisoners of conscience" imprisoned by authoritarian regimes throughout the world. Until the spring of 2004, however, the organization had never applied the term to anyone imprisoned in Japan, a country with a progressive democratic Constitution that expressly guarantees freedom of thought and speech.

This book tells the story of two men and a woman who were the first Japanese designated prisoners of conscience by Amnesty International. They were arrested and detained in police jails in a Tokyo suburb for 75 days after they distributed flyers that sharply criticized their government's decision to support the United States in its war in Iraq.

Amnesty staff members at the London headquarters were initially puzzled when Japanese colleagues requested the designation for the three suspects. Japan rightfully enjoys a reputation as a society where individual freedoms are ordinarily well protected. But the case arose at a time of conflict over the fundamental tenets of Japan's postwar Constitution. Article 9 of that Constitution renounces war as a sovereign right and the "threat or use of force as means of settling international disputes." It also prohibits the maintenance of military forces for this purpose. So Prime Minister Jun'ichiro Koizumi's orders to deploy small contingents of Japan's "Self-Defense Forces" to the Middle East—the first formal deployment of Japanese military forces to an active war zone since 1945—was highly controversial.

Many Japanese believed that the deployment was a clear violation of Article 9. The three messengers who delivered the antiwar flyers that led to their arrests represented this common belief.

Japan's dominant political leaders have repeatedly declared their opposition to the limits imposed on military action by Article 9 and to other provisions of the Constitution. They say the Constitution was imposed on Japan by a foreign military force and does not match the "history, tradition and culture" of their country, so the document must be thoroughly revised. Alongside their condemnation of Article 9, they oppose the strong individual rights protections that reflect what they label "the western theory of natural rights." These leaders declare that the individualism at the heart of the Constitution causes severe damage to communal and family norms and can lead to the breakdown of society. They single out free speech protection as an especially troublesome obstacle to achieving the superior goal of maintaining public order.[3]

Because political leaders hold beliefs like these, open criticism of government policy enjoys only a tenuous existence. By vigorously criticizing the Koizumi Administration's Iraq War policy, the three individuals at the heart of this story placed themselves in peril. When they were put behind bars, the stage was set for a confrontation between their claims to free speech and the government's demand for public order.

The case would provide a challenging test for Japan's courts and their commitment to the principles declared in the Constitution.

A NOTE ON STYLISTIC CONVENTIONS

The text follows the standard practice in employing macrons to vowels for Japanese sounds that are drawn out. For example, *hyōgen no jiyū*, the term for "freedom of expression," requires such extended sounds. Macrons are not usually applied for very well-known words, such as place names (Tokyo, Osaka, etc.). I extended this exception to the family name Kato and to family names that begin with an extended "o" sound. For example, we have "Osawa" and "Onishi" rather than Ōsawa and Ōnishi. I also chose to show given names first with family names to follow as is standard in English publications rather than the Japanese practice, which is the reverse.

ACRONYMS

ASDF	Air Self-Defense Forces
DPJ	Democratic Party of Japan
GSDF	Ground Self-Defense Forces
ISC	Intelligence Security Corps
JCP	Japan Communist Party
JSP	Japan Socialist Party
LDP	Liberal Democratic Party
MEXT	Ministry of Education
MOFA	Ministry of Foreign Affairs
MSDF	Maritime Self-Defense Forces
NPA	National Personnel Authority
NPEL	National Public Employees Law
SDF	Self-Defense Forces
SDP	Social Democratic Party

PROLOGUE

The Prime Minister Speaks (December 2003)

Prime Minister Jun'ichiro Koizumi began 2004 with a formal visit to the Yasukuni Shrine. During his 2001 campaign for the nation's highest office, he pledged to visit the shrine at least once per year. He faithfully honored this pledge during his more than five years in office. But throughout his long tenure, this would be the only year that he arranged his visit for the New Year holiday, a time when Shinto shrines all over the country are crowded with people paying respects to the gods who, according to tradition, created the Japanese islands and look after the people. In other years, the Prime Minister selected less conspicuous times to visit.

Because the Yasukuni Shrine venerates the spirits of the war dead, including wartime Prime Minister General Hideki Tojo and others executed after the Tokyo War Crimes Trials, it is widely seen as a symbol of Japanese militarism. Every visit by a Japanese Prime Minister provokes a storm of criticism from Beijing, Seoul, and Pyongyang—and sometimes even a mild rebuke from Washington. Japan's business and political leaders, some from the Prime Minister's own party, recommended against these visits, but Koizumi brushed aside their cautions.

On January 1, 2004, he went in style. According to a wire service report, he was "[d]ressed formally in *hakama* pleated skirt and traditional *kimono* bearing his family crest," and he

> walked solemnly into the shrine, which was surrounded by hundreds of well-wishers to mark the New Year's Day. He bowed deeply at the main chamber before being escorted inside by a Shinto priest and spent a few minutes paying his respects out of sight from the media.[1]

The visit carried a very special meaning that year. On December 9, 2003, the Cabinet formally approved a basic plan for the dispatch of Japan's Self-Defense

DOI: 10.4324/9781003193999-1

Forces (SDF) to Iraq. The deployment marked a major milestone in Japan's postwar history, the first formal deployment of armed military forces to an active war zone since 1945. The Prime Minister appeared on primetime television that evening to deliver a stirring address to the nation regarding his orders to deploy Japan's Self-Defense Forces in the Iraq war zone.

He assured his countrymen that the SDF would not engage in combat, but would solely be involved in "humanitarian and reconstruction assistance." He did not describe the intense pressure applied by the Bush administration to put Japanese "boots on the ground" in Iraq, but he left no doubt that his action was calculated to please Washington.

> As I have long stated, in order to ensure the peace and security of Japan and achieve greater prosperity, we must continue to enhance the Japan-US alliance, while simultaneously cooperating with the international community. ... I believe now is the time indeed when we are to be tested, not only in our words, but in our deeds, as we act to maintain both the US-Japan alliance and international coordination. Japan cannot alone secure its own peace and security. It was for this reason we concluded the Japan-US Security Treaty and why we must accord the Japan-US alliance the importance it deserves.[2]

In Koizumi's view, in order for Japan to be "a trustworthy ally of the United States," it was required to deploy military forces. The first concrete step in this mission occurred on December 26 with the departure of an Air Self-Defense Force (ASDF) advance team of 48 members for Kuwait, where they prepared the ground for an ASDF operating base. The team boarded a C-130 "Hercules" transport aircraft at the ASDF base at Komaki, just outside the city of Nagoya, for the long flight. The Prime Minister dutifully traveled to the Komaki base to express his gratitude for the service of the small contingent and his wishes for their safe return.[3] The first deployment of Ground Self-Defense Forces (GSDF) took place on January 16 when an advance team arrived in Kuwait.

Article 9 of Japan's Constitution required that the Koizumi Administration take extreme care in shaping the SDF mission. Adopted in the immediate aftermath of Japan's defeat in World War II, it declares that "the Japanese people forever renounce war. ... and the threat or use of force as a means of settling international disputes." Under a July 2003 law and a plan approved by the Cabinet, GSDF activities were to be limited to humanitarian and reconstruction assistance involving medical services, water supply, and rehabilitation and maintenance of schools and other public facilities in southeastern Iraq, an area thought to be at a safe distance away from combat taking place in other parts of the country.

Despite the stated limitations, many people believed the deployment violated Article 9. As the troops departed, small groups gathered outside SDF bases to protest.[4]

1

"RAISE YOUR VOICES WITH US!"

(1945–2004)

On January 17, 2004, the day after the first GSDF contingent landed on Iraqi soil, residents of an apartment complex located on the western outskirts of Tokyo found single-page flyers from an antiwar group among the various items that came through their mail slots. The complex was made up of eight four-story apartment buildings; each building provided homes to 24 families.[1] These apartments looked no different from thousands of drab, anonymous structures found nearly everywhere around Tokyo, but in one respect, they were special: The residents were members of the Self-Defense Forces and their families. The buildings were located just outside the border of the Tachikawa GSDF base, home to the only airfield maintained by the Self-Defense Forces within metropolitan Tokyo. Residents of the buildings targeted by the activists were assigned to the GSDF helicopter squadron and other SDF units that operated from the Tachikawa base. The flyers called upon residents to join the antiwar activists in raising their voices against the Iraq deployment.

The authors of these flyers were members of a tiny group that styled itself the "Tachikawa Self-Defense Force Monitoring Tent Village" ("Tent Village"). The January delivery was the fourth in a series of five monthly flyers planned for the winter of 2003–4. Each flyer started with a catchy headline followed by a page of text that reported recent developments on the ground in Iraq or Kasumigaseki, the seat of Japan's national government. Each one finished with a simple plea to SDF members to call a hotline where they could be counseled on how to decline orders to the war zone or otherwise oppose Japan's march to war. Finally, the phone number and address of the nearby Tent Village office appeared at the bottom.

The first flyer, delivered on October 12, was titled, "What will be the result of the Iraq deployment?" It set out the basic case for opposing the war:

DOI: 10.4324/9781003193999-2

> In launching a preemptive attack, the United States started an illegal war in violation of all international law. The U.S. government justified the invasion with claims that Saddam Hussein possessed 'weapons of mass destruction' and was allied with Al-Qaeda, but evidence for these claims has yet to be found.[2]

U.S. President George W. Bush appeared in Tokyo just a few days after the October flyer in order to pressure Japan's Prime Minister to speed up preparations for deployment of Japanese forces to Iraq.[3] Koizumi had yet to formally announce that SDF forces would be deployed to Iraq, though his "alliance-first" rhetoric left little doubt about his commitment. Readers of the flyer were also told that resistance to the war was growing in the United States and that by opposing the war, they would be joining thousands of American soldiers and family members who had formed a nationwide organization for that purpose. Then there was a brief self-introduction.

> Here in Tachikawa we have demonstrated against war and against the bases and we have even called for the dissolution of the Self Defense Forces. These ideas may be different from your own. But we are united in the belief that no SDF member should kill anyone and no SDF member should be killed. Japan's Constitution renounces the "threat or use of force as a means of settling international disputes." Unless we stop the flow of events, it could lead to disaster.

Subsequent flyers would attack the Prime Minister's assertions that there was nothing to worry about because SDF forces sent to Iraq would be adequately protected and would be sent only to safe areas of the country. "Even in an area that appears to be safe," one flyer said, "once it is occupied with forces allied with the Americans, it will come under attack. For the residents of such an area, the SDF will be viewed as 'gods of death' (*shinigami*) [emphasis added]. For an army of aggression, no place is safe."[4]

The January 17 flyer was delivered by three Tent Village members who quietly strode the corridors of the apartment buildings, slipping their missives into mail slots as they passed. It was titled "Let's Think Together and Raise Our Voices Against Deployment of the SDF to Iraq!" The text reported that Saddam Hussein had been captured, but this seemed to make little difference on the ground—Iraqi attacks on occupation forces continued. As American companies secured contracts to rebuild Iraq and take over oil fields, it became clear that the claim of "weapons of mass destruction" was just a baseless pretext for the invasion. The war was another opportunity for the rich to get richer.

The January 17 message also reported a number of suicides among U.S. troops and a recent rebellion among Bulgarian troops deployed to assist the Americans. It quoted Defense Agency Director Shigeru Ishiba's remark that SDF forces in Iraq should fire upon unidentified vehicles that approached their positions.

Members of the Tent Village regularly used a small van to approach the gates of the Tachikawa Self-Defense Force base. Was Ishiba suggesting that peaceful citizens like themselves be shot, too? In its final flourish, the flyer declared, "Before deciding that 'orders are orders,' think about the meaning of each one. If you disagree with this deployment, raise your voices together with us!"

To outside observers, the goal of persuading SDF members to reject orders to deploy to the Middle East or otherwise support the war effort may have seemed quixotic at best, but the silent messengers were committed activists and the flyer deliveries were only one element of an ongoing campaign that included small protest marches, loudspeaker speeches at the Tachikawa base's main gate, and distribution of flyers at the Tachikawa train station. They even tried to hand out flyers to SDF personnel as they departed the base, but few had the interest (or courage) to accept them in broad daylight. The Tent Village activists were not deterred by the cold response to their entreaties; they walked in the footsteps of many who had preceded them, for the region had a long tradition of anti-military activism.

Tachikawa

The city of Tachikawa is located about 20 miles east of central Tokyo, at the western edge of the Kanto plain. The great value of a wide-open plain so close to the great city had been obvious for hundreds of years. Leaders of the Tokugawa era saw this plain as an abundant source of food for the growing Edo metropolis. Commencing with projects launched at the end of the 17th century, the Tokugawa government made significant investments in river control and land reclamation in the region, so when it collapsed and was replaced by the Meiji government in the 19th century, the land supported a productive farming society.[5]

The strategic value of the area changed when Japan's leaders learned of Western advances in military technology symbolized by the arrival of Commodore Perry's "black ships" in Tokyo Bay in 1853. They understood that the country would have to modernize rapidly or face possible invasion and colonization like much of Asia. Samurai with swords were out and conscripted soldiers with modern western weapons were in. Japan's new army needed space, and the wide-open plain around Tachikawa, so close to Tokyo, was a very good fit. In the 1870s, the Meiji government began to acquire significant blocks of this land to provide space for its growing military forces.[6]

The military value of the Tachikawa area increased dramatically with the advent of the air age. The Tachikawa plain was ideal for the construction of airfields and operation of early versions of military aircraft. Tachikawa provided an important base for Japan's fledgling air force and a major site for military aircraft manufacture, which began in the 1920s. According to one scholar, "the Tachikawa Air Base quickly became the most important airbase in Japan, a hub for aeronautical research and exchange with other nations that were also developing their aviation technologies, including France, Germany, and England."[7]

When Japanese forces invaded the Asian mainland in the 1930s, weapons production was ramped up and Tachikawa became a military boomtown. At its peak, Tachikawa Aircraft Company employed more than 30,000 workers. Hitachi employed another 10,000 next door and other military contractors were nearby. Thousands of military aircraft were produced at Tachikawa during the war years.[8] These planes delivered death throughout East Asia as the Emperor's forces expanded his empire.

Of course, the farmers were still there. As envisioned by the 17th century Tokugawa planners, they continued to play a big role in feeding the people of Tokyo. They continued, but they had to make room for the growing military presence. In the words of historian Dustin Wright, "the productive forces of the region were shifted from the production of agricultural commodities to the production of empire."[9]

The Tachikawa story took a disastrous turn in the final stages of the war as Allied air forces executed a massive bombing campaign across the Japanese islands. American bombers arrived over Tachikawa in clear skies on February 17, 1945, bombsights focused on the aircraft assembly plants. In Wright's description, "The bombers dropped an immense payload on the Tachikawa engine assembly plant, essentially rendering it inoperable, while other U.S. fighter planes strafed trains and Japanese aircraft on the runway."[10]

The attack was a success. Production facilities were severely damaged and would no longer play a significant role in the war. To ensure that these facilities remained inoperable, bombers returned on April 4, April 24, and then again near the war's end on August 2.[11]

The farmers who had made room for the military buildup found themselves living next door to very high-value targets that burst into a flaming inferno when struck by the American bombers. This was particularly true of residents of the Sunagawa district, adjacent to facilities that produced military aircraft. Many fled or escaped to bomb shelters, but inevitably some were left behind and died in their homes. Many workers were found dead in factory rubble, and homes of local residents were destroyed.[12] Families who had farmed the land for generations became victims because their homes were located close to the military facilities nearby. Survivors would curse the war, mourning the loss of loved ones and family homes.

This kind of suffering provided the inspiration for broad public support for Article 9 of Japan's Constitution, which forever renounced war. Over the nearly six decades that followed, no Japanese troops had killed or been killed at war. Now the Prime Minister was declaring that he would send Japanese troops to an active war zone for the first time since those terrible days. Like peace activists all over Japan, members of the Tachikawa Tent Village were committed to doing all they could to sound the alarm and call upon their fellow citizens to oppose the move.

Occupation

After Japan's surrender and demobilization in 1945, the U.S. military took over the existing Tachikawa military base and continued to operate it for the next 25 years. The Tachikawa story took another wrenching turn as the city was transformed into one of the most notorious "base towns" in East Asia, with thousands of sex workers, easy availability of illegal drugs, noise from frequent takeoffs and landings, street crimes, and other problems.[13] Local residents had no choice but to persevere. Worse, from 1945 through 1955, the Americans expanded the boundaries of their base into the surrounding countryside no fewer than four times.[14] When another expansion was proposed into Sunagawa, an area that bordered the northern edge of the base that had suffered most from the wartime bombing ten years before, the locals chose to fight. The farmers saw this as a life-or-death struggle, for loss of farmland meant loss of community and way of life.[15] In the fall of 1956, farmers and their allies in student groups, labor unions, and others fought "pitched battles in the muddy farm plots of Sunagawa"[16] against police charged with evicting them in order to extend the Americans' runway. At times, as many as 6,000 protesters gathered to protect the land against further encroachment. Approximately 1,000 people were injured, many seriously. The protests continued into 1957 until the Americans gave up, abandoning the planned extension. The success of this battle, commonly known as the "Sunagawa Struggle," would inspire Japanese anti-base and antiwar protesters from that time forward.[17]

FIGURE 1.1 Today a stone monument to peace commemorates the site of the "Sunagawa Struggle." (Photograph by the author, 2019)

The Sunagawa Struggle was a pre-cursor to the massive protests against the extension of the U.S.-Japan Security Treaty in 1960 and then against the Vietnam War and other contentious issues in the late 1960s. Similar demonstrations arose in industrialized countries around the world, but in Japan, the presence of more than 100 U.S. military facilities staffed by about 40,000 U.S. military personnel who were accompanied by another 50,000 dependents provided additional cause for conflict. In Tachikawa, the anti-base sentiment was so deeply rooted that local voters elected a young activist who ran under the slogan "Let's get rid of the base and make our city a nice place to live!" to the Tachikawa City Council in 1966. He would remain in that post for three decades.[18]

The U.S. government listed Tachikawa airfield as one of 14 "major facilities" in Japan during the Vietnam War era.[19] Like other big U.S. bases in Japan, Tachikawa directly supported military operations in Southeast Asia. As the war escalated in 1967, the U.S. command again sought to expand the base. Masses of protesters rose up once more that summer.[20] Demonstrations continued throughout 1967 and 1968. Protesters even dug trenches around the base in their effort to block expansion. In December, protesters persuaded a local landowner to construct a tower on his property just at the edge of the Tachikawa runway to obstruct landings. A few days after construction was completed, the U.S. command canceled the plan to extend the runway.[21] The protesters had won again. In 1969, the Americans gave up not only on base expansion but on the Tachikawa base itself, announcing that they would consolidate operations at the nearby Yokota air base and return the Tachikawa facility to Japan. But the date of that return was not fixed and local residents were anxious about future use of the property.

The Formation of "Tent Village"

The American war in Southeast Asia continued, with hundreds of thousands of American troops on the ground in South Vietnam and intensive bombing of targets in both the North and the South. Mass protests in Japan reached a peak in late 1969, as the U.S.-Japan Security Treaty came up for renewal and Prime Minister Eisaku Sato flew to Washington for talks with President Richard Nixon. The resulting communique, issued on November 21, 1969, promised that Okinawa would be returned to Japan in 1972.[22] Recovery of Okinawa, which had been operated as a U.S. military colony since 1945, was the biggest political issue of the day, with universal support among the Japanese people.[23] Along with the proposed return of Okinawa and the resumption of the Paris Peace Talks in 1969, improved police tactics and other factors diminished the vitality of the protests. Although the war continued, by the early 1970s antiwar protests in Japan were dying down.

In Tachikawa, the U.S. decision to give up the base was certainly good news for the community. However, the future of the huge tract in the center of the city was uncertain. Some residents organized to demand conversion of the land to civilian use—a "Committee for Peaceful Use" was even formed to discuss future plans. These pie-in-the-sky dreams were quashed, however, when a senior official of Japan's Defense Agency[24] named Noboru Minowa appeared in Tachikawa in late 1972 to report the national government's decision: Ground Self-Defense Force units and other national government facilities would be located on the site.[25] Japanese law requires civilian control of the military. Minowa was a medical doctor and a member of the Diet from Hokkaido who had been appointed as the second-highest ranking official in the Defense Agency that year. He took on the unpleasant task of delivering the news to the mayor of Tachikawa and other local officials who had hoped for a different result.

The decision to convert the former U.S. military property into an SDF base triggered the formation of the "Tent Village," named after a cluster of tents set up on a strip of land abutting the base property that served as a base for antiwar protests.[26] By 1973, the Americans were gone. The focus of this new group was not a foreign military force, but Japan's own. One Tent Village activist would later write

> I remember the day I realized I would have to "find words to cast at the SDF officers." Rain was falling. Transfer of the main SDF force was complete. When we went out to protest, SDF guards were lined up before us, pelted by the rain. In the past, during the "Sunagawa Struggle" when we protested expansion of the US military base, the police were there to protect the U.S military. When we yelled "Yankee Go Home!" the words had real meaning.
>
> What should we say now? Can we yell "Go Home!" to the young SDF members before us? They are Japanese, just like me.[27]

Tent Village members soon found the words and commenced daily broadcasts through a 200-watt loudspeaker hidden behind a hut in the "village." Their mission was to monitor Japan's own military force. Along with a strong majority of Japan's constitutional scholars and other experts, they firmly believed that the mere existence of the Self-Defense Forces violated the Constitution. They continued with protest marches and began publishing a newsletter.[28]

For its part, the national government took full advantage of the recovered land. On one side of the property, the runway was converted for use by GSDF helicopters; a long string of government buildings was planned for the other. In a concession to local residents, a large piece of the property would be converted into a public park, but this also brought conflict: The park was to be named after the Emperor and local activists were opposed not only to war but to the imperial institution as well.[29]

As years passed and Japan avoided participation in foreign wars, interest in protesting at SDF bases died down. As for Tent Village, by the time the three messengers set off to deliver their flyers in 2003, regular membership had declined to fewer than ten individuals. But somehow the group was able to maintain an office and conduct regular antiwar marches and other events. At the end of 2002, it even published a 46-page pamphlet that commemorated the group's 30-year history.[30]

When Prime Minister Koizumi considered deployment of the SDF to the Middle East in 2003, small groups of protesters gathered at SDF bases around Japan. Like other activists, Tent Village members discussed what they could do to block the deployment. They decided on the flyer campaign at an offsite gathering that summer. According to their plan, teams of two or three messengers successfully executed deliveries at the SDF apartments in October, November, and December.

The Flyer Deliveries

Like the Tent Village members themselves, SDF officers and residents of the apartments were well aware that the expected deployment had become a matter of grave national concern, especially after the Cabinet resolution of December 9. Four days after the Prime Minister appeared on national television to explain the decision, another Tent Village flyer appeared in residents' mail slots. This one called the war a terrible mistake. It cited the deaths of two Japanese diplomats on November 29 among other evidence that showed conditions in Iraq had seriously deteriorated since the American president had declared "Mission Accomplished" on May 1. It called on SDF members to reject orders to Iraq and once again introduced the hotline for confidential counseling.

Japan's Defense Agency itself owned the apartment buildings where this took place and the building managers were SDF officers. The flyers had caught their attention and that of the state security police. Sometime after the December 13 delivery, they decided to act.

On December 18 and 19, 2003, building managers posted A-3 and A-4 size paper notices at entrances to the property and at individual buildings. The notices prohibited entry to the property by any unauthorized person and also prohibited the distribution of flyers or other promotional activity or product sales as well as unauthorized parking. On December 22, managers filed a complaint with the local police against the unauthorized intrusions by the Tent Village activists. They also distributed notices to the residents themselves, requesting them to call the police emergency line (110) and notify Tachikawa base authorities if they spotted anyone delivering "anti-SDF" flyers in the buildings.[31]

When the next delivery occurred on January 17, 2004, the building managers were ready. Two Tent Village messengers met at 11:30 a.m. nearby and then proceeded to their assigned buildings. After completing deliveries at three buildings, one of them, a 46-year-old middle school cook named Toshiyuki Obora, climbed the stairs to the fourth floor of his last building of the day. There he was confronted by an airman who happened to be home when Obora passed by and noticed the sound of the flyer sliding through his mail slot. The airman telephoned the police according to instructions. Then, quickly

FIGURE 1.2 A Self-Defense Force apartment building where Tent Village activists delivered antiwar flyers in 2003 and 2004. (Photograph by Yutaka Osawa, 2004)

descending to the ground floor, he caught up with Obora and demanded that he stop distributing flyers. Obora said that he had no intention to annoy anyone and asked the airman's opinion about the messages in the flyers. The airman responded that he had no interest in exchanging opinions. He pointed to a notice on a nearby signboard and declared that distributing flyers in the building was prohibited. Obora said he understood and departed. The airman called the police again.

Meanwhile, a second airman confronted Tent Village member Nobuhiro Onishi at a different building, saying

> We've been told to report you. This is the place where we live. We can't have just anyone coming in here. Don't do this anymore. You can see the notices posted on the gate and the building entrance. You're committing trespass.[32]

When Onishi pointed out that he'd seen others delivering commercial flyers in the building, the airman responded that there was no objection to commercial flyers, it was the flyers "criticizing the SDF Iraq deployment" that were the problem.

Then the airman directed Onishi to pick up all the flyers he'd distributed in the building and followed him as he did so.

Tent Village members discussed the situation at their next regular meeting. They confirmed that all flyers clearly showed Tent Village contact information, but there had been no direct communication from building managers or other SDF officers. They decided to stay alert but to go ahead with the next delivery scheduled on February 22. On that day, just two members made the deliveries and they went off without a hitch.

2

POLICE INVESTIGATE THE "TRUE NATURE" OF TENT VILLAGE

(February–March 2004)

The police struck at dawn on Friday, February 27.

Teams armed with search and arrest warrants pounded on doors and demanded access at six locations. In addition to an apartment maintained by Tent Village, they appeared at the homes of five members. The squads conducted searches and seized computers, diaries and calendars, files, and other materials. After the searches were complete, the three members who had distributed flyers on January 17 were arrested on suspicion of criminal trespass.

The police also alerted television crews to the early morning raid so the public could watch the forces of law and order in action. A *Kyodo* reporter who served on a committee that studied the effects of news media practices on human rights severely criticized the behavior of the television crews invited to report the event:

> On the day of the arrests, Fuji Television and TBS (Tokyo Broadcasting System) camera crews were in place in front of the Tent Village office from early morning. Their reports strictly followed the line set by the police reflecting the viewpoint of the state security division. They reported the actual names of the suspects included in the police announcement and followed the standard "crime report" format, disclosing ages, addresses and other information concerning the suspects. Fuji Television in particular, showed a scene where one TV member was being led away by the police; incredibly, they blurred the facial images of police officers while providing a clear close-up of the Tent Village member, even taking the trouble to show the scene in slow motion.
>
> Although TBS did protect the identities of the suspects, they wrapped up their report with this statement: "On high alert against possible terror attacks at a time when Self-Defense Forces have been deployed to Iraq,

DOI: 10.4324/9781003193999-3

> the Tokyo Metropolitan Police Department is seeking to clarify the true nature of this group."[1]

This was surely one of the easiest police investigations conducted anywhere in the world that year. The Tent Village had been operating in the open for more than three decades. Throughout that long period, the group had not been involved in violent activity. Tent Village members saw themselves as ordinary citizens with the passion and courage to speak out. They were outraged at the attempt to paint them as possible terrorists. At the time of the arrests, Tent Village barely survived, with fewer than ten members. It was a threat to no one. There was nothing to justify the heavy-handed police action.[2]

The three suspects, two men and a woman, were confined in local police jails. Among them, the most senior of the three, 46-year-old Toshiyuki Obora, had joined a Tent Village study group as a college student in 1978 and became a formal member the following year.

Early in the morning of February 27, Obora was suddenly awakened by a phone call that reported the police had launched a raid on the Tent Village office. Before he could get his clothes on, he discovered half a dozen state security police at his door. They showed him a search warrant, but he did not foresee what would follow. After searching his apartment for about three hours, an officer said, "Actually, we have another warrant—one for your arrest."[3]

The second male suspect, 30-year-old Nobuhiro Onishi, also made his first contact with Tent Village as a college student, about 15 years after Obora. In 2001 or 2002, he began to attend weekly meetings and pay dues and became a key Tent Village member. Onishi was identified by plainclothes police at the Tachikawa train station on the morning of February 27 and arrested as he tried to board a cab.

The third suspect, Sachimi Takada, the lone female, was the same age as Onishi. She was the most recent recruit to Tent Village, first acquainted with other members when she participated in a local autumn festival in 1999 or 2000. At the time of the arrests, she resided in the small apartment that also served as the Tent Village office.

Police arrived at the Tent Village apartment just after 6:30 a.m. Takada heard the chime and someone pounding on the door. She tried to turn over and go back to sleep, but the clamor was too much. When she got up to look through the peephole, she saw the corridor was filled with police, both in uniform and street clothes. One of them yelled, "This is the Tachikawa police! Open the door! If you don't open it, we'll break it down!"

Takada found her phone and quickly called another member. There was no answer, so she left a frantic message. Just then the police pushed the door open, breaking the chain. Takada told them to stop unless they could show a search warrant. When they did, she saw the words, "Trespass on January 17, 2004." She remembered distributing flyers on that date but did not recall trespassing anywhere. As in Obora's case, the police delayed showing her the arrest warrant until after their search was complete.[4]

When the police were done with the Tent Village apartment, Takada was subjected to a body search by a female officer in a separate room. Then it was time to go. The police led her into the corridor and then down the stairs. When they reached the building entrance, she was startled by several television cameras pointed in her direction. She later wrote, "I felt like they were pointing guns at me."[5]

Takada was initially taken to the Tachikawa Police Station, a big facility with over 400 officers, but in the afternoon, she was transferred to the Tokyo Metropolitan police jail just across the street. Even though the jail was so near, she was tightly bound in handcuffs and a body belt and loaded into the same police wagon that carried her from the Tent Village apartment.[6] Upon arrival, she was searched again and placed in a cell with other detainees. She was assigned the number 666 to use in place of her name. Her clothes were confiscated, and she was required to purchase replacements.[7]

In synchronized raids the police struck the residences of five Tent Village members in addition to the group's small office in a fifth-floor apartment overlooking the SDF base.[8] In each case, the police arrived without warning and demanded entry. They confiscated materials at all six locations and arrested the residents at three.

The most senior Tent Village member was 66-year-old Katsuko Kato. She was awakened by the ringing of her telephone. The excited voice she heard was that of Takada screaming, "Kato-san, come to the office right away!" Kato immediately called other members, but none responded. Then the pounding on her own door began.[9]

The search of all six locations followed a pattern. Ten or more police arrived, and six entered each apartment to conduct the search while the others stood guard outside. The scope of the search described in the warrant was very broad, including not only material related to the January 17 flyer delivery but more general material related to the Tent Village itself that described its history and organization. Kato and others would cite the breadth of the search and seizure as evidence that the true police motive was not to prosecute three individuals for trespassing but to investigate and harass Tent Village.[10]

Like the others, she watched while police officers gathered files, notebooks, calendars, and her personal computer. When they were done, they handed her a list of the material to be carted away. Kato tried to conceal her personal calendar and some other items by holding them in a handbag at her side, asserting that because the police had no warrant for a body search, they could not see them. They laughed and emptied the bag anyway.[11]

Katsuko Kato was one of the original Tent Village members, the only one still active when the police struck three decades after the group's founding. Aside from serving as the primary historian and spokesperson for Tent Village, Kato was active in other causes and is the author of numerous essays and two books. At the time of the police raid, Kato was at work on a book based on her father's experience in China during the war years. Her computer was filled with messages exchanged with sources in China. Now that it was in the hands of the police, she lost access to her hard-earned research. She notified her Chinese translator not to send messages until a new e-mail account was established.

Kato's computer was gone, but she still had a fax machine and a phone. Like others, she sent out as many messages as she could to report the police raid. She didn't yet know about the arrests or how many places had been searched, but she feared the worst.[12]

She would later view the police raids and arrests in historical context: "We know from Japan's past that when the troops go off to war, the people at home lose their freedom. Now it was happening again."[13]

"Anti-Military Broadcasts" and Other Protests

After the initial shock, Tent Village members and their friends quickly mobilized. Some chose the most direct means to protest the arrests—a march to the police station with signs and a bullhorn. A group of 40 braved the cold to appear before the Tachikawa Police Station on the night of the arrests to holler out their outrage. Later that night, 30 gathered in the Tent Village office to discuss a response, spilling out of the crowded space into the corridor outside.[14] There was a strong consensus that the arrests were a threat to all peace activists, labor activists, and anyone else who relied on leafleting to broadcast their messages. They would have to fight to preserve these rights. Some were labor activists who had experienced arrests and police intimidation. They told the others what to expect.[15]

The sense that the arrests were very serious, there could be more to come, and this was a genuine threat was widely shared. In order to fight the police action they would have to get their story into the news media, find lawyers, and raise money. This was a daunting challenge for a group of ordinary citizens with no organization or funding behind them.[16]

On the following day, a Saturday, the remaining TV members performed what they called an "anti-military broadcast" (*hangun hōsō*) at the main gate to the Tachikawa SDF base. This involved driving their light van to the gate with loudspeakers blasting their voices over the fence and toward the SDF members on the other side. Such broadcasts had been a standard Tent Village ritual going back to the founding of the group in the 1970s. In recent years, the broadcasts were delivered at least once per month. They usually parked the Tent Village truck near the front gate and continued their appeals to SDF members for ten minutes or more before the police arrived to shoo them away. On the day after the arrests, however, the police were ready. The activists barely delivered five minutes of their speech before the police were on them. They moved the truck and there were no arrests.[17]

FIGURE 2.1 Tent Village members make an "anti-military broadcast" from their van at the SDF Tachikawa base main gate. (Photograph by Yutaka Osawa, 2004)

There was a regularly scheduled protest at the Tachikawa train station on Sunday. The station is a major hub used by tens of thousands every day. Tent Village supporters set up protest signs outside the entrance and handed out flyers and expressed thanks to the passersby who would take one. When they were finished at the train station, they marched the short distance to the police station to formally deliver a flyer in the form of a constitutionally protected petition.[18]

Like protesters all over Japan, they relied on Article 16 of the Constitution, which expressly guarantees the right of every person to petition the government. Over the years Tent Village members had delivered countless similar petitions at the SDF facilities in Tachikawa. In each case, a guard or officer on duty formally accepted the petition. To add to the formality of the little ceremony, Tent Village members read their petitions aloud, sometimes employing a bullhorn to spread their message. Now that their colleagues sat in jail, they followed the same practice to demand their release.

Small protests outside the jail cells, at the train station, and elsewhere, would continue in the days to come.[19]

The protesters' chants and shouted messages outside the Tachikawa jails may have reinforced the morale of the three detainees, who could sometimes hear the racket, but did little to get the word out to the larger community. With their three mates sitting in jail cells, the remaining Tent Village members did their best to spread the word, but when their homes were searched, their personal computers and files had been taken away. Limited to phone calls and fax messages, the members' range did not extend very far.

Katsuko Kato sent multiple fax messages to news outlets with no response. Frustrated when the news media showed no interest, she feared the arrests would be ignored by the world at large.[20]

FIGURE 2.2 Peace activists deliver a petition at the SDF Tachikawa base main gate. (Photograph by Yutaka Osawa, 2004)

Yutaka Osawa

Among the friends and allies who quickly sprang to the Tent Village defense, one would have an especially large impact. This was a 53-year-old member of the Tachikawa City Council named Yutaka Osawa. Osawa was a committed activist who had moved to the Tachikawa area to assist the handicapped in the 1970s, not long after graduating from college. He was first elected to the city council in 1998 on a platform of improving social services and opposing Japan's remilitarization.

Many months before the arrests, Osawa reacted to the Prime Minister's talk about sending troops to Iraq by organizing an alliance of antiwar groups in the *Santama* area[21] to agitate against the deployment. He knew Tent Village well, having joined members in antiwar protests for more than a decade. He had even placed flyers in the same mail slots at the Self Defense Force apartments many times.[22] When he received phone calls reporting that Tent Village members had been arrested, he could hardly believe his ears. Then he saw the mid-day Fuji Television report with the footage of Sachimi Takada being led from the Tent Village apartment in handcuffs. He recalls wondering, "How could this be? What could possibly justify Sachimi's arrest?"

When the shock wore off and he learned more details of the arrests, Osawa made a plan. He would alert as many people as possible of the arrests and would find some way to lead them to oppose the arrests. When his shock turned into

FIGURE 2.3 Tachikawa City Councilmember Yutaka Osawa responded to the arrests by immediately organizing a support network for the suspects. (Photograph by Toshiyuki Obora, November 2004)

anger, he thought, "We must launch a counterattack that will make the police regret what they have done."[23]

When the police took away the Tent Village computers, members lost the ability to post updates on the Tent Village website. Osawa kept a personal website that would take its place. It quickly became a tool to spread the word about the arrests and solicit support for the three suspects, the prime source for the latest information.[24] Osawa suffered many sleepless nights as he drafted posts and exchanged messages with supporters.[25] His first post appeared on the day of the arrests. Readers were greeted with a shrill title: "To Everyone Across the Country Who Opposed the Iraq Deployment! Do Not Allow the Suppression of People Who Fight the Deployment!"

After telling readers that he had "fought alongside" Tent Village members against the Iraq deployments,[26] Osawa delivered the brute facts: The Tachikawa police had launched a comprehensive attack on the Tent Village, including raids at six locations and the arrests of three members.

Regarding the January 17 flyer delivery, the councilman wrote that he knew the SDF apartments well. "Everyone distributes flyers there," he wrote, "the pizza shop, the sushi shop, the homebuilder. To single out one specific group and accuse them of 'trespass' is clearly political suppression. It must not be allowed."[27]

He called on his readers to take four steps: (1) Spread the information as widely as possible, (2) gather information on similar cases that may have occurred around Japan, (3) respond with even stronger opposition to the deployments, and finally, (4) chip in with funds to support the jailed activists. Tent Village bank account details followed.

He also noted that because the police had confiscated their computers, the group could not respond to e-mails or upload messages to its website. Telephone calls and faxes provided the best means of reaching them.

On the following day the councilman posted something new: A "joint petition" addressed to the heads of the two Tachikawa police facilities where the suspects were detained. The appeal was issued in the names of Osawa and a second councilman from the neighboring city of Kunitachi named Tomohiro Shigematsu. After repeating the text of Osawa's first message, the authors described the "sense of crisis and anger" they felt in response to the police action.

> Suppression of the Tent Village, which has engaged in activities opposing war and the activities of the Self-Defense Forces for a long time, constitutes harassment and a threat to all antiwar and peace activities by civil society and labor groups in the *Santama* area.[28]

Their petition called upon the police to release the three detainees, cease such actions against others, and return the belongings confiscated on February 27.

They invited all who opposed the Iraq deployment to join them by returning signed copies of the petition by 10 a.m. on Tuesday, March 2. The text would be read aloud at a press conference to be held at Tachikawa City Hall the following afternoon, and then the collected petitions would be submitted to the police officials.

Tent Village Declaration

A second item appeared on Osawa's website on February 28. This was a declaration from Tent Village itself. It said the arrests were an attempt to silence the people and "exposed the violent nature of a state that would deploy troops abroad." It quoted extensively from the January 17 flyer carried by the three members who now sat in jail. Like the other flyers, the January 17 edition was addressed to SDF members and their families. "Is this war correct?" it asked. "If you should kill an Iraqi person, won't you spend the rest of your life suffering from the trauma?"

The declaration reminded readers of the darkest chapter in Japan's history. "In the past, Japan silenced all voices of protest. Children were indoctrinated in the myth of a divine emperor. Japan rushed headlong into a destructive war of aggression." Then it screamed defiance.

> The government has painted its actions in bright colors while it ignores the Constitution and international law and creates a *fait accompli*. Its goal is to produce a general attitude among the people that "we have no choice

> but to support the SDF sent to Iraq." The movement to oppose the Iraq deployment confronts this great power. We vow to overcome this sophistry. We will correct the fallacies in the government's version of history and the current situation, one by one. The most important weapons in this fight are the power of words, the freedom of speech, and a path to communicate with SDF members and their families.[29]

The Tent Village declaration closed with an appeal for donations to help fund the defense of the three detainees.

Interrogation

Under Japan's code of criminal procedure, after 72 hours in custody, prosecutors must either release criminal suspects or obtain a judicial order extending the detention.[30] Given the trivial nature of the charges in the Tent Village case, one might have hoped that the prosecutors would simply release the three and move on to more serious matters.

But the arrests occurred more than a full month after the alleged trespass. They involved six SWAT teams with a total of approximately 60–80 police officers. Senior police officials had clearly decided that Tent Village was a high priority. It seemed unlikely that prosecutors would release the suspects before they extracted confessions or some other damning information.[31]

Prosecutors filed requests for extended detention on Sunday, February 29.[32] This was approved by a judge as a matter of course. The standard term of such extensions is ten days. When this expires, prosecutors are able to request one more ten-day extension before they must act, either indicting or releasing suspects. The judge also approved the prosecutors' requests that the three suspects be prohibited from meeting anyone other than their attorneys.[33] Judicial review of these requests takes place behind closed doors and defense attorneys are not present. Japan's judges rarely rule against prosecutors in criminal procedure matters like this.

Japan's police interrogations can be merciless, designed to wear down the will of suspects and force them to quickly confess to charges. Attorneys are not allowed to be present in the small, windowless interrogation rooms. Although suspects can invoke a constitutional right to remain silent, interrogations do not stop; the questioning continues, sometimes punctuated by shouts, desk-pounding, and more severe measures designed to intimidate suspects and get them to speak.[34] Few detainees are a match for experienced police interrogators under conditions like these, so attorneys almost invariably advise clients to maintain silence as their best chance to weather the assault and avoid making incriminating statements.[35]

Interrogations of the three Tent Village suspects commenced on the day after their arrests. All three declared their right to remain silent. Each one was nonetheless taken to an interrogation room from his or her cell repeatedly, typically three times each day, strapped into a hard, wooden chair and forced to endure hours of pointless questions and police harangues.[36]

All three lived on the margins of Japanese society, far from the prosperous lives of those employed by Japan's large enterprises. Toshiyuki Obora, the oldest of the three, probably came closest to full membership in Japan's middle class. He held a full-time job as a cook in a public school and was the proud owner of a condominium—called a "mansion" in Japanese—that he acquired in 2000. But his devotion to antiwar activities began when he was a college student in the late 1970s. Obora had been a member of Tent Village nearly as long as Katsuko Kato herself.

The other two suspects were quite a bit younger. Thirty-year-old Sachimi Takada, the only woman arrested, a singer and musician with local rock bands, began her career as an activist a few years before, joining various demonstrations that addressed quality-of-life issues for the less fortunate residents of Tokyo. She demonstrated against price increases at public baths, against plans to raize small, aging apartment buildings to be replaced by upscale highrises, and against other projects that would squeeze the poor.[37]

Takada had become familiar with Tent Village a few years before and first volunteered to help stage the annual autumn festival at the site of the Sunagawa Struggle in 1999. She began to work as a caregiver to the aged and disabled the year before her arrest.

The third detainee, Nobuhiro Onishi, had worked as a caregiver ever since he volunteered as a college student in the early 1990s. He decided to devote his life to this work and in 2000, formed a small company to support operations. He liked to say, "These days I walk with one foot in antiwar activities and the other in caregiving."[38] Although he made his first contact with Tent Village at a demonstration when he was a college student in 1992, it was not until two or three years before the arrest that he began to attend weekly meetings and pay dues in order to qualify as a full member.

The police interrogators used a variety of techniques to induce their detainees to talk. Of the three suspects, it seems that Takada was subjected to the harshest treatment.[39] She later published a description of life at the Tachikawa jail. According to her account, each day commenced with a wake-up call at 6:30 a.m. followed by breakfast, a brief opportunity for fresh air in an exercise space on the roof of the jail (detainees were allowed two cigarettes during this daily break), room cleanup, and then roll call. She describes a daily "changing of the guard" roll call ceremony in which a squad of police march throughout the jail, stopping at each cell to check on the detainees. A designated one-hour "letter writing time" began at 10:00 a.m. Detainees were required to submit a written request for pens and paper on the preceding day. Takada missed out because she was invariably in the interrogation room by then.

Like the other Tent Village detainees, Takada asserted a right to silence. Also like the others, this made no apparent difference, with interrogations continuing for six to eight hours each day anyway. According to Takada, questioning regarding her entry into the SDF property, slipping flyers through door slots, and other facts that might support the government's claim of trespass occupied just one portion of the interrogation periods. Police interrogators spent much of the time attacking Tent Village and declaring they would drive it out of existence. She says that they also directed a torrent of insults at Takada herself. They screamed that she was a two-faced parasite who lived off her friends. By all accounts, she was a popular figure in the *Santama* area, often playing guitar and singing with local bands. In the interrogators' shouted opinions, this was all pretense—her true motive was to live off the goodwill of others.[40]

Obora also published a report on life in detention. "The gloomy police interrogation began on the day of the arrest," he wrote.

> Morning, noon, and night, it would continue for about six to eight hours every day—about two or two and a half hours in the morning and two hours at night and there were also afternoon sessions. They were the longest.
>
> Interrogation style differed somewhat depending on the police officer.... The primary officer for me employed a very emotional style. Sometimes his voice got very loud. He played with my feelings. "Your parents are worried!" he yelled. "Even though you're prohibited from receiving visitors, if you request I can make special arrangements for you to meet them." But the content of the interrogation was really boring and repetitive, chickenshit, a waste of time. Sometimes I would start to doze off and he would pound on the desk and yell in a loud voice "Wake up!" "No sleeping!"[41]

The detainees did enjoy the benefit of a brief visit from legal counsel on the night of the arrests. After taking personal messages to be delivered to family and friends and describing their legal rights, the lawyers notified them that the prosecutors had invoked "*sekken kinshi*," meaning they were prohibited from receiving visits from anyone other than legal counsel.[42]

The judge's order of February 29 extended their detentions for ten more days and continued the prohibition of visitors. The suspects continued to maintain silence.

March 3 Press Conference

Councilman Osawa's press conference went on as scheduled on the afternoon of Wednesday, March 3. It was a hectic day at City Hall, with councilmembers and reporters fired up over an investigation into bid-rigging on public works projects, the kind of topic that often gets top billing in Japan's news media.

Yutaka Osawa himself was busy with an avalanche of responses generated by his petition to the police officials. Ordinarily his website received only a dozen or so hits per day. Suddenly it was up to several hundred.[43] Three days after he published the petition on his website, he had gathered more than 700 signatures. He spent much of Tuesday night and Wednesday morning sorting through the responses and answering questions from fellow petitioners by e-mail and telephone.

When he arrived at City Hall, he was surprised to find a group of at least 20 people gathered in the lobby, with more on the way. Although few news reporters attended the press conference, they were joined by more than 30 interested citizens in the audience. Osawa scrambled to find a room large enough to accommodate everyone.[44]

Osawa kicked off the event at 1:00 p.m. by reading the petition and describing the list of 700 petitioners. Then he introduced other speakers. They included Ken Takada, a representative of a network of antiwar groups called "World Peace Now," who described tight police restrictions on public demonstrations at train stations and on the streets and read from the group's own petition in support of the suspects. Another speaker was a former SDF member named Kenji Kataoka, who described a "hotline" where SDF members could obtain counseling about their rights, their possible roles in the Iraq deployment, and other issues.[45] This was the same hotline promoted in the Tent Village flyers.

Young Scholars Respond to the Arrests

One speaker had an especially large impact on the gathering and on developments in the days to come: Manabu Ishizaki, a 35-year-old constitutional law professor from a small private university. He was a resident of the *Santama* area himself and only a few weeks before had participated in a protest against the Iraq War, where he met some Tent Village members. A committed pacifist, he chose to study constitutional law as an undergraduate student when the Kaifu Administration dispatched minesweepers to the Persian Gulf in the aftermath of the Gulf War.[46] For Ishizaki and many other supporters of Article 9, the Kaifu action represented a major turning point in Japan's defense policy. "Until then," he told me, "We all thought of the SDF as 'exclusively for defense'; not for dispatch overseas."[47]

Ishizaki was one of a small cadre of young scholars who rose to defend the Tent Village. On the day of the police raid he received a call from a student who had seen television footage of the arrests. But since she could not explain the cause of the arrests, Ishizaki called Yutaka Osawa. Osawa told him the charge was "trespass," but he couldn't imagine Tent Village members involved in such a crime.[48]

Then Ishizaki received a call from Takato Narisawa, a graduate student at Waseda, one of Japan's elite private universities. Narisawa was among many people who received a panicked call from Katsuko Kato seeking help. He had met Kato when they both volunteered to support another activist, a middle school teacher named Kimiko Nezu, who was at the forefront of a major *cause celebre* of the time—the movement to oppose mandatory flag and anthem ceremonies at public schools.[49]

Ken'ichiro Okada, a graduate student at nearby Hitotsubashi University, also received a call for help. He had met Tent Village member Mori Inoue at

FIGURE 2.4 Manabu Ishizaki stepped forward as a spokesperson for the academic community, condemning the arrests as a violation of fundamental rights. (Photograph by Toshiyuki Obora, December 2005)

Hitotsubashi, and though he didn't join Tent Village, he participated in anti-war protests in the area. Okada would become an unofficial member of the Tent Village defense team, attending strategy sessions and researching legal questions.[50]

These young scholars, at the very outset of careers devoted to studying and teaching the grand principles of Japan's democratic Constitution that promised robust protection for freedom of speech and other fundamental rights, were suddenly confronted with a very different reality—a genuine constitutional crisis on their doorstep. Without warning, peaceful protesters they knew and had joined at demonstrations in nearby streets were thrown in jail.

What could they do? Of course, they joined the crowd that protested before the police station that night, but there had to be more.[51] Narisawa proposed drafting a declaration that made the constitutional case against police suppression of dissidents and called for the immediate release of the suspects. He set to work on the first draft and then sought input from the others. They worked quickly, e-mailing the text back and forth, until it was ready for wider distribution. Their haste was driven by the concern that while the three activists sat helpless in jail, the mainstream news media had missed the story. Narisawa would later write that he felt "a real sense of crisis, a feeling that maybe Japan's democracy had reached a turning point. I was driven by a sense of responsibility—if I didn't take action, who would?"[52]

When it was complete, they began to circulate the text among their network of constitutional scholars.[53] The proposal caught fire. Within a few days, the junior scholars had a long list of co-petitioners, including highly respected constitutional experts at Japan's most prestigious universities, including Waseda, Hitotsubashi, and others.[54]

Osawa's March 3 press conference created an excellent opportunity to release the declaration and explain the significance of a police crackdown on peace activists. Among the three young scholars, only Ishizaki held a faculty position. Narisawa's position was especially precarious because he was in the final stages of a job search and about to secure his first teaching appointment. An appearance in public to denounce the police was a very risky move in these circumstances. While the others kept their heads down, Manabu Ishizaki stepped forward to speak alone at the March 3 event.[55]

Ishizaki told the audience that this was not merely the story of three individuals punished for tweaking the noses of the authorities. Instead, he said the arrests posed the fundamental question of whether the tenuous achievements of Japan's postwar Constitution and its "guarantee" of free speech would survive. The Constitution had been under continuous attack by Japan's dominant political party, the LDP, for decades. Even as the arrests took place, LDP leaders were drafting a proposed "New Constitution" to be unveiled at the party's 50th anniversary celebration, scheduled for the autumn of 2005. Their proposal would cut back on individual rights like freedom of speech on the one hand and would increase state power on the other.[56]

But the politicians had yet to succeed in amending the liberal postwar Constitution, and there was no doubt in the young scholars' minds that the robust language of its free speech clause, which protects "all forms of expression," prohibited the Tachikawa arrests.

The declaration prepared by the young scholars presented a formally structured argument. The detainees were charged with committing a criminal trespass at the SDF apartments. Before addressing constitutional questions, they first considered Criminal Code Article 130, which defines trespass. They expressed doubt about whether it applied, explaining that the purpose of the trespass law is to protect the peaceful and exclusive use of a defined space in which residents could expect to enjoy privacy. How could anyone be charged with trespass for slipping flyers into a mail slot, they asked. The mail slot's very purpose is to enable residents to receive messages from the outside world while maintaining their privacy. The scholars argued that dropping flyers into a mail slot could not be interpreted to be a criminal trespass.

Then they explained that even if prosecutors somehow proved the elements of a criminal trespass, the activists were nonetheless protected by the overriding constitutional guarantee of free speech. The activists' obvious motivation was to engage in discussion with the residents over the SDF deployment to Iraq. According to the scholars, criminal prosecution in such a case would inevitably cause a "chilling effect" that discourages free discussion among the people on matters of national importance, an unacceptable restriction on free speech.

They concluded that "the true purpose of this action aimed at a citizens group that expresses opposition to the SDF deployment to Iraq was to restrict the free speech rights" of that group. They called for the immediate release of the suspects.[57]

Yutaka Osawa was inspired by the enthusiastic response to his call for action, including the hundreds of signed petitions and the declarations by scholars and others. But he was disappointed by the low turnout of news reporters. He counted only five, including one freelancer. Among them, he did note that one, a reporter for the *Asahi Shimbun*, Japan's second-biggest national daily, asked numerous questions.

When the press conference was done, Osawa and a group of 15 loaded into cars and taxis for a ride to the Tachikawa police headquarters. There they sought to meet the police chief. They were blocked at the entrance, but after some negotiation, four were allowed inside to deliver the petitions to one of the chief's deputies.[58]

3

ANOTHER ARREST

(March 3, 2004)

On the morning of Osawa's press conference, the state security police launched another raid in a residential district in central Tokyo. When Akio Horikoshi awoke on the morning of March 3, he found eight police officers at his door. They displayed a search warrant, so he allowed them in and they commenced a two-hour search of his small "LDK" (living, dining, kitchen) apartment. Horikoshi was a single man and he lived alone. Once the search was complete, they laid 26 documents they selected for confiscation on his kitchen table. Then they told him to pack a toothbrush and a towel and showed him an arrest warrant. As in the Tent Village case, someone had leaked word of the early morning raid, so television cameras and reporters were there to broadcast the event.[1]

Horikoshi was 50 years old. He had served as a national government employee since graduating from high school more than three decades before. He had no criminal record. Like the Tent Village suspects, Horikoshi was arrested on suspicion of illegally distributing printed materials. Unlike the Tent Village suspects, he had not climbed staircases to slip his material into individual mail slots. There were no apartment managers complaining that he disturbed the residents. He did not target the Self-Defense Force's apartments. Horikoshi had simply dropped his material at central banks of mailboxes at large apartment buildings. Although many of the basic facts from the Tent Village case were absent, in the view of Japan's state security police, Horikoshi presented a far greater danger. He was a member of the Japan Communist Party (JCP) and had been observed distributing JCP campaign literature. The Tent Village was a tiny group of peaceniks with no money or organization. The JCP, on the other hand, was a national organization with millions of members. The state security police had been keeping an eye on Akio Horikoshi. On March 3, they struck.

Horikoshi was employed by the Ministry of Health and Welfare, but throughout his career as a public servant, he had also been busy as an active member of

DOI: 10.4324/9781003193999-4

the JCP.[2] The Party was founded in 1922 and then outlawed under Japan's "Peace Preservation Law" three years later. This 1925 statute prohibited advocating any form of government that conflicted with the "*kokutai*," the system of government centered around a divine sovereign emperor. It is often cited as a central pillar in the legal system that severely limited political speech in imperial Japan. With this law in place, countless would-be revolutionaries quickly recanted under harsh treatment from the police. Nearly all members of Japan's fledgling communist party chose to recant. The party was destroyed.[3] JCP leaders who did not recant were imprisoned until General Douglas MacArthur issued an order releasing them in October 1945. But that was long ago. Japan's democratic Constitution, which took effect in May 1947, is intended to guarantee freedom of speech to everyone, including communists.

Horikoshi told me that he first became interested in politics as a high school student. He was especially concerned about the situation in Okinawa, which had been run as an American military colony since 1945.[4] Following the end of World War II, the Americans built a robust system of military bases throughout Japan, heavily weighted toward Okinawa. During the 1960s and 70s, the Okinawa bases played an especially important role in supporting American forces in Vietnam. This caught the attention of many young people like Akio Horikoshi. Okinawa was formally returned to Japanese control in 1972, but the Americans continued to have free rein in operating their bases, flying aircraft, and other military maneuvers. The postwar JCP has always opposed the presence of the U.S. military, advocated peace, and supported Article 9 of the Constitution. For Akio, this was an attractive message. He followed in the footsteps of his older brother Michio, joining a JCP youth division the year of his high school graduation.[5] He became a full member at the invitation of another Ministry employee not long after he started work.

At the Ministry of Health and Welfare, he specialized in pension insurance. Because he did not graduate from a university, he would not ascend to a senior management position, but in 1983 he was promoted to the position of advisor, charged with counseling individuals with pension claims. In this role, he was rotated around several government social insurance offices in Tokyo. He was active in the Tokyo public employees' labor union and served as a leader of the division that represented pension workers.[6]

Limiting Speech by Government Employees

The Tent Village suspects were arrested on criminal trespass charges. For Akio Horikoshi, the police had a more convenient tool. Japan's National Public Employees Law (NPEL) imposes a very strict regime that prohibits national government employees from engaging in political activities.[7] Key language in Article 102 of that Law states that "apart from exercising their right to vote," government employees "must not engage in political acts as prescribed by the National Personnel Authority (NPA)." When this law was adopted in the Occupation era, the NPA issued a long list of activities defined as prohibited political acts. The list included such matters as forming political organizations or serving as an officer, collecting funds for such groups, and "publishing, editing, or distributing" their newspapers or other publications. Violations can be prosecuted as crimes punishable by fines and imprisonment of up to three years.[8]

The application of these strict rules prohibiting political speech by government employees was challenged in a series of 1960s cases. At least three lower courts tossed out prosecutions for such acts as distributing flyers, putting up posters, and participating in political rallies, on the ground that the constitutional guarantee of free speech protected such activities.[9] But in a stunning reversal, the Supreme Court overturned the acquittals in November 1974, effectively imposing an absolute ban on political speech by government workers. This decision would come to be known as the "*Sarufutsu* Judgment," after the Hokkaido town of Sarufutsu where one of the incidents took place.

The Court held that, despite the free speech guarantee in the Constitution, prosecution of these individuals was appropriate because "the parliamentary system requires that public employees carry out policies passed into law by the Diet and that they maintain political neutrality in order to keep the trust of the people in the political impartiality of government administration."[10] In order to "keep the trust of the people," the Court upheld a complete ban on all workers subject to the NPEL for political acts listed in the NPA regulations.

Japan's leading constitutional scholars have bitterly attacked this decision as an unacceptably tight limitation on free speech. The central issue in the case was whether the defendants' specific actions had caused suspicion regarding the political neutrality of government workers. As in the case of Akio Horikoshi, there was no evidence that this was so. Rather than considering the concrete facts, however, the Supreme Court simply accepted the abstract concept that all acts listed by the NPA would be irreversibly presumed to cause doubt over the government's neutrality. Therefore, all listed acts were banned.

The eminent constitutional scholar Nobuyoshi Ashibe labeled the decision a "turning point in the history of Japan's constitutional case law."[11] Commenting on the application of the *Sarufutsu* rule in the Horikoshi case, another eminent University of Tokyo scholar, Yasuhiro Okudaira, wrote that "[f]rom the time this decision was issued until the present, it continues to be regarded among constitutional scholars as one of the Court's worst judgments."[12] Well aware of this, prosecutors had not indicted anyone for violating the prohibition on political activities since the Supreme Court's 1974 decision, a span of three decades. But the police had kept the *Sarufutsu* standard in their arsenal for possible use when the right case appeared. They decided the time had come in March 2004.

Search, Arrest, Interrogation

Senior police officials seem to have viewed Horikoshi's arrest as a golden opportunity to gather information on the JCP itself. While the team of eight officers who entered Horikoshi's apartment rummaged through his belongings, separate teams appeared at five other locations, including the JCP office located in the Chiyoda-ku district, the office of Katsuhiko Mariko, a JCP member of the Chuo-ku assembly, Mariko's home, Horikoshi's workplace, and the government office that maintained his personnel records.[13] The postwar Constitution *does* guarantee free speech for all and the JCP is a legitimate political party with elected members in the national Diet and in many local governments, but Japan's state security police continue to see the JCP as a threat to national order and they carefully keep tabs on JCP activities.[14]

Horikoshi was undoubtedly surprised by the arrest, but he was well aware of the *Sarufutsu* decision and the potential for police action. The police claimed that he had violated the law by delivering political materials on October 19 and 25 and November 3, 2003, a Sunday, a Saturday, and a national holiday, all days when his office was closed and he did not work.[15] They said he had placed political materials in mailboxes at no fewer than 126 locations.[16]

The specific dates were especially important because national elections were scheduled for Sunday, November 9, and deliveries would have to comply with the very tight restrictions that govern Japan's political campaigns.[17] The police were right on the facts. Horikoshi clearly recalled the materials he delivered and the specific dates of those deliveries. One item was an October 19 extra edition of the JCP daily newspaper, *Akahata* ("Red Flag"), memorable because it headlined an article by JCP chair Kazuo Shii titled, "The Election at Last!" together with Shii's photo. Along with the *Akahata*, Horikoshi distributed campaign flyers for Kiyokazu Muro, the JCP candidate for the national Diet in the central Tokyo Second District. He had an even stronger recollection of the Muro flyer because it featured a photo of a well-known professional boxer posing with boxing gloves.[18] Celebrities like this rarely come out in open support of JCP candidates.

Despite his diligent efforts, Horikoshi's efforts had little impact. Muro, 48 years old in 2003, finished third out of three candidates. The winner, the incumbent supported by the Democratic Party of Japan (DPJ), collected 104,477 votes. The Liberal Democratic Party (LDP) candidate finished a close second. Muro, who finished third, got only 21,334, less than 10% of all votes cast. In recent years, the LDP and DPJ candidates had alternated in taking this particular seat. The odds that Horikoshi's candidate would win were approximately zero.

After the search and the "perp walk" out to a waiting police wagon, the suspect was taken to the local police jail (Tsukijima), where he was fingerprinted and photographed. Within the hour, he was transported again, this time to the Tokyo Metropolitan Police Headquarters, a towering structure in central Tokyo that overlooks the imperial palace, across the street from the red brick Meiji-era national prosecutor's office.

After he was given lunch, the interrogation began. This was interrupted by a 2:00 p.m. visit by attorney Yūsaku Tsurumi. Defense counsel are not admitted to police interrogation rooms, but they are allowed visits with clients in detention.

Horikoshi remembered Tsurumi from a public demonstration related to environmental issues and requested police to contact him.[19] Like more than 2,000 other Japanese attorneys, Tsurumi was a member of the *Jiyū Hōsōdan* (Japan Lawyers Association for Freedom), an association of lawyers sworn to represent victims of government suppression of political activities founded in the 1920s.[20]

Attorneys ordinarily advise clients to say nothing to the police, but this case was different. Akio Horikoshi deeply believed that his actions were appropriate and protected by the Constitution. He was ready to waive his right to silence and speak freely to police investigators about his life and his work for JCP candidates in the 2003 elections. After the visit by Attorney Tsurumi, the interrogation resumed. When it was done, Horikoshi signed an affidavit prepared by the interrogators that laid out the details of his career with the JCP and his work on the 2003 election campaign. He unambiguously declared that he *did* distribute the *Akahata* and other political materials "with the intention of assisting JCP candidates in the coming election and persuading others to join the party."[21] Such activities were clearly prohibited by regulations issued under the National Public Employees Law (NPEL).[22] Moreover, he openly admitted he had regularly distributed JCP materials on Saturdays and national holidays for many years.

In most cases, the attorney's primary job after an arrest is to persuade prosecutors not to file charges, but this case was different. With the suspect's confession in hand, the prosecutors would not be deterred. There appeared to be no victims of Horikoshi's conduct and his efforts were obviously futile. The candidate he supported garnered only 10% of the vote. But the law was clear. Prosecutors filed an indictment with Tokyo District Court on Friday, March 5, charging Akio Horikoshi with violating the NPEL. With no disagreement over the facts, a trial would primarily be concerned with the validity of the NPEL restrictions on political speech.

Horikoshi received dramatically different treatment from that imposed on the Tent Village suspects. While they were locked into police jails for an indefinite period, Horikoshi was released from custody two days after his arrest. The prosecutors had what they wanted: A signed affidavit with his confession. These documents are always prepared by the interrogators; suspects simply sign their names at the end. But in this case, in the space above his signature, the suspect added one sentence of his own: "I think this arrest is an improper suppression of the Japan Communist Party by the police."

4

RECRUITING A DEFENSE TEAM

(February–March 2004)

The Japanese people subscribe to more newspapers per capita than citizens of any other large democratic country on earth.[1] The newspaper industry itself is a solid oligopoly dominated by five giant organizations that deliver tens of millions of hardcopies nationwide every day. The *Yomiuri*, a conservative paper that usually supports the government, is the largest, with approximately ten million daily subscribers in 2004. The *Yomiuri* company is well known not only for running the country's biggest newspaper but also for owning the Giants, Japan's most popular professional baseball team.

The No. 2 daily is the *Asahi*, Japan's most influential liberal newspaper. In 2004, it was delivering more than eight million copies per day. Its readers include nearly all of Japan's reporters, attorneys, politicians, and others concerned with public policy. It was an *Asahi* reporter who asked the most questions at Yutaka Osawa's press conference on March 3 and who produced a straightforward summary of the Tent Village case that appeared on an inside page of his paper's evening edition on Thursday, March 4.

Katsuko Kato and her colleagues feared their friends would languish in jail, forgotten by the world at large. Who would care about three anonymous suspects collected by the police in a distant Tokyo suburb? Aside from television reports featuring the "perp walk" when Sachimi Takada was paraded before cameras in front of the TV office on the day of her arrest and some very minor reports, the mainstream news media had ignored the case until the brief *Asahi* story of March 4. Tent Village supporters were pleased to see the March 4 report, but it did nothing to prepare them for what was to come.

The *Asahi* dropped a bombshell the following morning in the form of an editorial that severely criticized the police action against Tent Village. It began by setting out basic facts that would be repeated many times in the coming days. The suspects were well known as members of a peaceful antiwar group who

DOI: 10.4324/9781003193999-5

had operated in the open since the 1970s. They were not intrusive and made no attempt to conceal their activities. They appeared at mid-day, dropped their flyers through the mail slots, and then left. The flyers themselves identified their group and provided contact information.

In the opinion of *Asahi* editorial writers, facts like these provided no justification for a surprise police raid, arrests, and confiscation of notebooks, computers, and other material. The editorial expressed suspicion not only of the police action but also of the judges who issued the search and arrest warrants. What could they possibly be thinking?

The *Asahi* rode the tracks laid down by Yutaka Osawa and the scholars' declaration. The mailboxes also collected unsolicited material from restaurants, real estate agents, and others. Were the police planning raids on those establishments, too? "Not likely," according to the *Asahi*. "It appears that the police decided to make these arrests because the flyers expressed opposition to the SDF deployment." The editors expressed their fear that "in the face of this vigorous police action, citizens will hesitate to express their opinions or attend public gatherings." This chilling effect appeared to be precisely the result sought by the state security police.[2]

The editorial concluded with a classic call for the government to honor fundamental democratic principles.

> Mutual recognition of values that are different from one's own. The right to freely express one's opinion. These are the premises on which a democratic society is based.
>
> In particular, when we consider an issue like the deployment of the SDF to Iraq, we cannot avoid touching on the pacifist principles of the Constitution. This is a serious issue which can set the direction of Japan's future course. This is not something that can just be left to politicians and bureaucrats. It is important that people be free to express their opinions and listen to the differing opinions of others.
>
> Isn't this the kind of democratic society, complete with freedom of speech, that international society seeks to build in Iraq?[3]

Countless readers at kitchen tables, on commuter trains, and in the halls of government pondered these words. It seems unlikely that many had given much thought to a Tokyo suburb generally known as the site of some military bases. Hardly any had heard of a tiny antiwar group with the odd name "Tent Village." Later, some of the curious would actually travel to Tachikawa and ask "where are the tents?"[4]

On the evening of March 5, more than 90 people demonstrated before the Tachikawa police station to show their support for the activists in custody. Later that night, about half of them gathered to formally declare the launch of a citizens' group to support the three detainees.[5] The new organization could serve as an umbrella group for supporters of all types who were not themselves members

FIGURE 4.1 Katsuko Kato saw the 1945 Tachikawa bombing as a child. She has continued antiwar activism throughout her life. (Photograph by Toshiyuki Obora, June 2004)

of Tent Village. Osawa was the natural choice to lead the group. Henceforth, he would issue regular updates on the condition of the suspects, organize gatherings of supporters, coordinate fund raising, and publish an online newsletter, among other activities.

After the *Asahi* editorial appeared on March 5, curious reporters made the trip to Tachikawa to cover the story. The police prohibited contact with the suspects themselves, so reporters sought interviews with lawyers, Osawa and other supporters, and Tent Village members who were not in detention.

The Tent Village "organization" was perfectly horizontal. All decisions were made by consensus, so no member held any particular decision-making power or authority to direct others to act.[6] Of the three Tent Village members who remained free, Katsuko Kato was the most senior and the only one who had been involved in its 1972 founding. After the *Asahi* editorial alerted the world to the Tachikawa arrests, Kato gave numerous interviews to reporters from daily newspapers, weekly magazines, and freelance writers; she was usually identified as "representative" of Tent Village. Kato was so busy in meetings with supporters and lawyers, sending messages to the detainees and financial donors, and otherwise getting the word out about the arrests and the ordeal of her colleagues that she even decided to withdraw from her share of duties caring for her husband's 96-year-old mother.[7]

Growing Up in Tachikawa

Tachikawa was Katsuko Kato's hometown. She was born there in 1937, the second of four children.[8] Her father was a dentist recruited to serve in China during the war years. As the Americans began their intensive bombing campaign of Japan, Kato and her siblings were moved to the relative safety of the countryside in the expectation of an attack on the Tachikawa aircraft factory and other facilities. When American warplanes burned the factory and the surrounding area in 1945, Kato was far enough away to avoid injury, but near enough to see the attack. Her early childhood memories include the awful sound of the bombing and the fires of Tachikawa, seen from a distance. Soon after the war ended and Kato's family returned home, American military forces took over the Tachikawa bases.

Among the many fundamental legal and political reforms imposed by the Allied Occupation, one empowered women to vote for the first time in elections held in 1946. Kato's mother, En Suda, an especially outspoken and fearless woman, dove in head first.[9] She chose to run for a seat on the Tachikawa city council in 1951, the only woman among 72 candidates. It was a rough and tumble time. Elections were corrupted by widespread vote buying and threats of violence.

The Tachikawa election was so corrupt that 27 candidates, including Suda, filed suit to have the results declared invalid.[10] In the chaos of defeated, demolished, and starving Japan, threats of violence played a big role in getting things done. Of the 27 plaintiffs, 25 were intimidated into dropping the suit, leaving only two: Suda and a labor activist. Kato was about 14 years old at the time. The Suda family posted a large banner on the family home that declared the corrupt elections invalid, defying demands by neighbors and family members to take it down. The family was shunned. Neighbors wouldn't talk to them and they boycotted her father's dentistry. Kato even remembers that the family home was set on fire. There must have been other threats, but En Suda did not give up. Although her efforts failed in 1951, Suda ran again in 1955 and won a seat on the city council, the first woman to achieve that feat.[11]

After his return from China, Kato's father resumed his dental practice in the family building close to the south entrance of Tachikawa station. Growing up in central Tachikawa, Kato walked streets patrolled by prostitutes and blackmarket toughs. Around the station, she saw wounded war veterans and neighbors made homeless by the bombing who now relied on handouts.[12] After the Americans occupied Tachikawa air base, Kato recalls that her father often treated black American GIs. (She thinks the Americans were segregated and because black GIs appeared at the Suda dentistry first, the whites went elsewhere.)

At the peak of the Sunagawa Struggle in 1956–57, when thousands of demonstrators crowded into the area and fought battles with riot police in rice fields just walking distance from the family home, Katsuko was a freshman in college. Her mother frequently joined these demonstrations. Sometimes Katsuko did, too.

She was an original member of Tent Village more than a decade later during the Vietnam War era and became the primary force attracting new members and holding the group together thereafter. For some time after the Tent Village shack was burned by opponents in 1975, the group operated from Kato's home. Later she raised the funds to buy a small apartment that continued to serve as the Tent Village office thereafter (and where Sachimi Takada was arrested). This space is located on the fifth floor of a building near the Tachikawa SDF base, with a view over the airfield. In later years, she often said, "You cannot separate Tent Village from the Sunagawa Struggle."

The giant political demonstration that shook the political foundations of the postwar Japanese state hardest—the "*Anpo* Protests" (national security treaty protests)—took place in 1960, when the Kishi administration forced a new security treaty with the United States through the Diet. Public outrage led to protests so big that U.S. President Eisenhower canceled a visit to Japan and Prime Minister Kishi resigned to take responsibility.

For many Japanese, the most shocking and memorable incident was the death of a 22-year-old university student named Michiko Kamba, crushed by the force of a massive crowd at the south gates of the Diet building on June 15, 1960.[13] Kato was the same age as Kamba and both were fourth-year students at the University of Tokyo. Kato was in the crowd a few rows behind Kamba but managed to escape without serious injury.[14]

When the Tachikawa activists were arrested in 2004, nearly 60 years had passed since the war's end and more than 40 years since the Sunagawa Struggle and the *Anpo* Protests. Katsuko Kato was haunted by the war's death and destruction and the chaotic aftermath throughout her life. Over the decades that followed, her commitment to antiwar activism never wavered.

Now Kato suffered the agony of watching helplessly as her young colleagues endured daily police interrogations, completely cut off from friends and family. They did not lack legal representation. In fact, they received visits from local lawyers in the evening on the day of the arrests.[15] Sachimi Takada was surprised when an experienced cellmate said she'd never heard of an attorney visiting a detainee on the day of arrest. "Your case must be something special," she said.[16]

Finding Defense Counsel

Occupation-era reforms that created the constitutional guarantee of free speech, the abolition of war powers, and other innovations lauded by constitutional law professors, news organizations, and overwhelming majorities of the Japanese people also created the possibility of litigation to enforce those constitutional promises. Constitution Article 81 granted the courts judicial review, the power to decide the constitutionality of actions by the police and other agencies of government. This innovation also empowered Japan's lawyers to challenge the government in court on behalf of clients who claimed the government violated their rights.

The 1949 Practicing Lawyers Act was another critical reform that enabled lawyers to vigorously represent such clients. Under prior law, they were subject to the authority of the Minister of Justice. Lawyers who represented political dissidents, labor activists, or otherwise engaged in suspicious activity might be threatened with suspension or even disbarment by government order. The 1949 Act transferred disciplinary power to the bar associations run by the attorneys themselves. Now they were free to contest such politically sensitive matters as government donations to religious shrines, deployment of military forces abroad, and the apportionment of electoral districts, without fear of retribution from the Ministry of Justice. The Occupation-era reforms enabled lawyers to energetically represent the Tent Village defendants.

Katsuko Kato and the Tent Village were no strangers to the local legal community. The first interaction probably occurred around 1975 when opponents managed to burn down the Tent Village shack located just outside the fence of the SDF base. According to Kato, when Tent Village members returned to rebuild the shack the next day with lumber and tools, the area was already fenced off so they could not enter. They found some lawyers and filed suit seeking to regain access, without success.[17]

About two years after that event, a new law office was founded in the *Santama* area that would represent labor unions, citizen activists, and others in conflict with the government. It was called the "West Tokyo Cooperative Law Office" ("West Tokyo Office") and was located in the town of Hachioji, about a 20-minute train ride from Tachikawa.[18] The local courthouse was in Hachioji at the time, so the few lawyers in the area kept offices nearby. A key member of the West Tokyo Office was an attorney named Sadao Yamahana, who had been elected to the national Diet as a Japan Socialist Party (JSP) candidate the year before.[19] There was no doubt about the political coloration of the office. Labor unions provided the core support for the Socialists; a law office with a JSP Diet member as a senior attorney would surely represent the workers of western Tokyo. Clients also included citizen activists. As a young attorney, Yamahana had represented University of Tokyo students charged with various crimes related to their long occupation of administrative offices and other university buildings in the 1960s. Representing activists was a primary mission of the West Tokyo Office. One of the first lawyers to join told me, "we saw the activists as the front line of the battle, while we lawyers backed them up from behind the line."[20]

Japan has long been known for its paucity of private lawyers compared with other industrial democracies. Most of them congregate in the center of Tokyo and other big cities, so there were not many in the *Santama* area when Yamahana opened his office with three colleagues or even when the Tent Village arrests took place nearly 30 years later.[21]

Sadao Yamahana was not the first member of his family to run for office. The Yamahana family has been deeply involved in Japanese politics for at least three generations. When Sadao was elected in 1976, he followed in the footsteps of his father, Hideo. Hideo was one of the founders of the Japan Socialist Party, launched in 1945 when political activities were freed after the war's end. He had been a leader of a farmers' rights movement in the area before the war and was jailed for his participation in political activities banned by the infamous Peace Preservation

Law in the 1930s.[22] The Suda family had close ties with the Yamahanas. Hideo was a family friend and En Suda was Hideo's ally in the Japan Socialist Party. For a time, the Suda family home even served as the local JSP headquarters. Katsuko Kato remembers spending time with the Yamahanas and other activists as a child.[23]

By the time of the Tent Village arrests, Japan's labor unions had become mere shadows of their former selves. Mass strikes and violent confrontations with management were relics of the past. Militant unions with the mission of changing society itself as well as representing the interests of their members had largely been replaced by "enterprise unions" that tend to be dominated by company management and by growing masses of workers with no union membership at all. By the 1990s, Japan's labor movement had become so weak that the Japan Socialist Party, which had been the strongest opposition political party for four decades, collapsed. Sadao Yamahana retired during that period and although the office he founded continued to represent workers and labor unions, such work was in decline so the lawyers sought to broaden their law practice in order to survive. Despite the changing times, the West Tokyo Office did continue to serve as lawyers for the labor movement and assorted local activists, including Tent Village.

The Tent Village *Bengodan*

Three West Tokyo lawyers formed the core of the team that represented the Tent Village suspects. Due to their longstanding relationship with Tent Village, they quickly learned of the arrests. There were phone calls not only from Tent Village

FIGURE 4.2 Lead counsel Reiko Kuriyama speaks alongside her colleagues on the Tent Village defense team. (Photograph by Toshiyuki Obora, October 2004)

members but from others who had seen the perp walk on television. An attorney named Reiko Kuriyama handled the calls on the day of the arrests and rushed to the Tachikawa jails together with a colleague to check on the detainees that night.[24] She would serve as leader of the defense team (*bengodan*) that represented them thereafter. Kuriyama registered as an attorney in 1979, becoming one of only 384 female attorneys in the whole country, comprising just 3.4% of Japan's total attorney population.[25] From the West Tokyo Office, she was accompanied by Hirotatsu Kojima, five years her junior, and by Shizu Yamamoto, a young woman who had qualified as an attorney less than two years before. They were joined by two others, a resident of Tachikawa named Akio Kotō and Masatoshi Uchida, a well-known activist and prolific writer, to form the team of five that would represent the three suspects. Both Kotō and Uchida maintained offices in central Tokyo. Like the West Tokyo lawyers, Kotō volunteered at the Santama Workers Law Center (*Santama Rōdōsha Hōritsu Senta*) and worked on labor cases in the area.

Throughout their careers, Uchida and Kotō had represented political activists and other clients in conflict with the government.[26] Both men represented protesters arrested during mass demonstrations against construction of the Narita Airport in the late 1970s, not long after they had qualified to practice. In a conflict similar to the Sunagawa Struggle, thousands of students and workers joined local farmers fighting to block government's expropriation of their land. Many were injured in violent clashes and there were several deaths, among both the protesters and the police. As the number of arrests rose into the thousands, the local Chiba District Court was overwhelmed. Tokyo lawyers like Kotō and Uchida handled overflow cases assigned to Tokyo District Court.[27]

Uchida was especially well known through his many writings, including dozens of columns and essays in legal and general interest journals, as well as several full-length books. He was born in 1945 and a lengthy memoir he published in 2001 bears the ominous title *Born in the Year of Defeat*. It tells the story of a child shaken by images of conflict; he was deeply impressed by a film set on the battlefield of Sunagawa, with farmers, students, and ordinary citizens in combat with riot police who sought to convert farmland into an airfield. The book also describes his own participation in student protests and work after he qualified as a lawyer. As a student, he was a protester; as a lawyer, he represented protesters in court.

Uchida was introduced to the Tachikawa case by Takato Narisawa, the Hitotsubashi graduate student who launched the law scholars' declaration against the arrests. They had become acquainted through their participation in a study group inspired by the celebrated constitutional scholar Yasuhiro Okudaira. Uchida had no prior relationship with Tent Village and had not worked together on any cases with other members of the defense team.[28] He immediately saw that the Tent Village case concerned more than another detention of a few activists. After talking to Narisawa, he wasted no time in calling Katsuko Kato to volunteer. Impressed by his sense of the political importance of the case, Kato welcomed him to the defense team.[29]

Akio Kotō is another lawyer with a long history of representing political protesters. He qualified as an attorney in 1978, the same year as West Tokyo lawyer Tadashi Nishibatake. Katsuko Kato enlisted the two young men to represent her that year in lawsuits challenging proposed expansions of both major military bases in the *Santama* area.[30] After local residents and their allies put up such a great fight against expansion of the Tachikawa airfield, the Americans gave up on Tachikawa and concentrated their forces at Yokota instead, only ten miles away. In addition to their campaign against the SDF forces in Tachikawa, the Tent Village activists also protested the U.S. base at Yokota on a regular basis. Kato was joined as a plaintiff in the 1978 litigation by Masao Miyaoka, one of the leaders of the Sunagawa Struggle. Miyaoka and his family fought to preserve land that had been farmed by his family for 16 generations.[31] They had successfully stopped base expansion with their bodies in the 1950s and 1960s. Now they sought to stop it again, this time in court.

They filed two suits in 1978 that challenged the use of public funds to construct roads intended to serve the bases. The lawyers scrambled to find legal grounds for the suit. Their core argument—the expenditures were unlawful because the existence of the SDF at Tachikawa and the presence of the U.S. Air Force at Yokota violated Constitution Article 9—surely matched the beliefs of their demanding clients but proved useless in court. The plaintiffs and their lawyers sought to replicate a famous 1973 judgment of the Sapporo District Court that ruled the SDF unconstitutional. But the Sapporo judgment was overturned by an appellate court in 1976. As the attorneys worked on their briefs, they knew the Sapporo case was on appeal to the Supreme Court. Although the Supreme Court did not issue a final judgment upholding the dismissal until 1982, Kato's lawyers had little reason to think the final appeal of the Sapporo case—or their own constitutional challenge to the SDF—would succeed.[32]

Shizu Yamamoto joined the West Tokyo Office immediately after qualifying as an attorney in late 2002. She was attracted by the atmosphere of freedom there—senior lawyers put no particular limitation on the kinds of cases she could take.[33] The office may have been launched by a leader of the Japan Socialist Party, at that time the largest opposition political party, but by the time Yamamoto arrived, the JSP had all but disappeared. The office was no longer closely tied to any particular political party and served a wide range of clients in addition to labor union activists and others in conflict with the establishment who needed lawyers but did not want to work with a law office aligned with the Japan Communist Party.

Yamamoto was powered by an irrepressible desire to make a difference. Once she had her lawyer's license, she quickly took on numerous criminal cases involving indigent defendants. The Constitution guarantees a right to counsel, so the government pays attorneys' fees for these clients, but the allowances are minimal. In those days, the lawyers who took them were either unable to find clients able to pay or felt a strong obligation to fight for justice for those most in need.[34] When one of the senior attorneys asked if she wanted to join the team working on the arrests of the three Tent Village members, she agreed immediately.[35] She was by far the youngest member of both the West Tokyo Office and the Tent Village defense team.

As daily interrogations continued, the attorneys took turns visiting the three detainees. Of course, their primary purpose was to gather details of their clients' stories and explain the rules governing detention and what to expect in future proceedings.[36] But because the detainees were denied visits by anyone else, the attorneys also served as conduits for messages from friends and supporters and their gifts of cash, books, and other items. The attorneys passed along the detainees' mundane requests for help in stopping newspaper deliveries, checking mailboxes, and other personal items. They usually met with members of the support group before and after each visit. Support group members quickly debriefed the attorneys on their way out and took notes to serve as a record.[37]

The visits also provided an opportunity for the detainees to describe the interrogations. Attorneys learned of the verbal abuse directed at Sachimi and of various forms of intimidation. One detainee said a police officer displayed his intimate knowledge of the detainee's family and then accused him of shirking his duty to care for his ill parents. Another weathered attack on his personal lifestyle: "What's wrong with you! At your age, you live alone. Why can't you be married and raise a family?"[38] Because the attorneys were locked out of the interrogation rooms and they had no access to videotapes or other recordings, these meetings provided their only opportunity to learn about the interrogations. As for the suspects, because the court prohibited visits from anyone other than the attorneys, these brief meetings also provided the only break from the daily grind of interrogations and life in jail cells.

The court granted the prosecutors' requests for an additional ten days of detention on March 9. Throughout this period, the detainees were denied visits from anyone other than their attorneys. Unable to visit, friends and family members missed their loved ones and worried about their condition. They learned from the attorneys that the detainees endured six to eight hours of interrogation every day and despite continued harassment from police interrogators, they refused to speak. No one knew how long the detention would continue. Denied any direct communication, they relied on the attorneys to get messages in and out.

A Brief Public Appearance

Japan's criminal procedure does provide one opportunity for a public court hearing at this stage of an investigation. In order to continue a detention more than 72 hours after an arrest, prosecutors must obtain court approval. Suspects can demand a hearing to require the court to formally state the reasons for this approval.[39] The procedure is rarely used. In a typical year, around 100,000 persons are detained by police and prosecutors in Japan, but such a court hearing is requested in only a few hundred cases.[40] Most lawyers don't bother because court rules limit the time for presentations and such a hearing is unlikely to have any impact on the case. Worse, it may antagonize busy judges.

But this was not an ordinary criminal prosecution—it was a political case where the three suspects represented the interests of all Japanese who seek to protect freedom of expression. The conflict spread far beyond the walls of the courtroom. Japan's Constitution requires that court hearings be open to the public, so this would provide the first opportunity for the suspects and their supporters to see each other since the arrests. The hearing was scheduled for March 11. The lawyers told their clients to buck up and put on the best faces they could.

About 60 supporters filled the spectators' seats at the Hachioji court on March 11. Many wept as they saw their friends in shackles led into the courtroom on ropes tied around their waists.[41] They watched as a judge mechanically read the statutory grounds for detention: Flight risk and the risk that the suspects would destroy evidence if released.[42]

Defense counsel and their clients were allowed to briefly address the court. The attorneys described the lengthy interrogations and abusive treatment. They told the three-judge panel that the police not only abused their clients in custody but also questioned family members in attempts to gather personal information to be used in the interrogations. Although the suspects had maintained strict silence under interrogation, they were ready to speak up in the courtroom. The judges watched in silence as Takada repeated terms of abuse she said were screamed in her face day after day.

When the hearing drew to a close, the court confirmed that detention would continue. Voices of protest arose from the spectators to no avail. The suspects were cuffed and led by ropes tied around their waists out of the courtroom and back to their cells.

5

JAPAN'S FIRST "PRISONERS OF CONSCIENCE"

(March 2004)

After the brief court hearing on March 11, the deadline for the prosecutors' decision was just a week away. By March 19, the prosecutors would have to file an indictment or let the Tent Village suspects go. As that day approached, the nature of the high stakes became clear. If the prosecutors could be persuaded to drop the case, the three suspects would be free. On the other hand, indictment meant disaster. The suspects would remain in custody. Attorneys could file bail requests, but in Japan bail is usually denied to suspects who refuse to speak. If bail *was* granted, someone would have to raise bail money. And a trial could drag on for years. In Japan, nearly all criminal trials lead to guilty verdicts. But the lawyers would have to be paid whatever the result.

Tent Village members and their supporters scrambled desperately to find some way to persuade the prosecutors to drop the case. They handed out flyers at the Tachikawa train station and organized small protest marches to the nearby military bases and the jail.[1]

On March 15, a group of five appeared at the offices of the Tokyo Bar Association with a formal petition for assistance. In addition to help persuading prosecutors to drop the case, they also sought apologies, not only from the police for violating the rights of the detainees but also from broadcasters TBS and Fuji Television for damaging the reputations of the detainees by broadcasting the arrests and disclosing their identities. They were met at the Bar Association's offices by Uchida himself, representing the human rights committee.[2] In the near term, the Bar Association investigation would be of little value—it would take months to complete, while the prosecutors' decision was only a few days away. But the Bar's support could be valuable in the long run, especially if the case went to trial.

That night supporters held a rally at a community center in Tachikawa. The room could not hold the 150 attendees, so the crowd spilled over into the

DOI: 10.4324/9781003193999-6

hallways.[3] Seven speakers lined up to address the crowd, led by Kato. She provided background on Tent Village, the arrests, and the current status. Osawa described the petition filed with the Tachikawa police on March 3 and introduced his website as a source of updates. Then he presented law professor Manabu Ishizaki as the spokesperson for 56 legal scholars who had signed a declaration calling for the immediate release of the detainees. Ishizaki explained the law and his opinion that placing flyers in mail slots could not possibly be considered a trespass. Attorneys Kuriyama and Uchida described the current condition of the suspects, based on their repeated visits to the jail.[4]

Many in the crowd shared the fear that the Tachikawa arrests were not an isolated event, but one element of a broader police campaign to throttle dissent. Everyone knew the case of Akio Horikoshi, arrested just one week after the Tent Village members. Many also knew the story of a young man prosecuted for spraying antiwar graffiti on the wall of a toilet in a public park in Suginami. He was convicted and received the harsh sentence of 14 months' imprisonment, suspended for three years.[5] There were other recent cases of police harassment of activists.[6] From the very back of the room, a young woman raised her hand and described the harassment she and her Muslim husband suffered as they made antiwar protests outside the U.S. Embassy in central Tokyo.[7] The biggest question facing the crowd was how activists could continue antiwar protests without sharing the fate of the Tent Village activists as victims of a police crackdown. There was no clear answer. For Katsuko Kato, there was no doubt that the police action carried grave implications.

> As the Iraq deployment moved forward, we continued our regular activities in opposition, including flyer distribution, "anti-military broadcasts" and others. We ran to the Tachikawa base to continue the anti-military broadcasts, which are appeals by individual speakers directed at everyone on the base. But in wartime, a homefront is formed and sometimes spirits on the homefront are even more bellicose than on the battlefield itself. As we pursue our antiwar activities, we are well aware that we must overcome such emotions among the people.[8]

According to Kato, the police were shutting down dissent in order to impose discipline on the "homefront" and they should expect that most people would support the police. The people did not rise up to stop their country from going to war in the past. There was little reason to believe they would do so now. Kato seemed resigned to this reality. She had experienced the horrors of war as a child. Now her country was at war again and anything could happen.

Osawa told the crowd he had posted a draft letter on his website that anyone could use to register complaints with the prosecutors' office.[9] The letter summarized legal arguments for non-prosecution and ended with the threat that if the case *did* go forward, the signatories would join together to raise a national movement to oppose the prosecutors both in court and before the public. After someone read a message from the detainees, the event was closed with the declaration: "We must use all of our strength to rescue our three friends and amplify the voices against war and for peace!"[10]

In a last desperate attempt to save their friends, a group of 20 protesters gathered in front of the prosecutors' national headquarters facing Hibiya Park in central Tokyo on March 17.[11] The attorneys filed a formal request for non-indictment with the prosecutors the same day.[12]

Then just as the skies grew darkest, suddenly there was a ray of light from an unexpected source. In Japan, the state security police were accustomed to getting their way. But what if their actions were brought before the international community?

Amnesty International

With several million members worldwide, Amnesty International is one of the world's largest and most highly respected international human rights organizations. It was launched after British human rights lawyer Peter Benenson sent a letter to a newspaper in 1961. Benenson was shocked by a news story about two Portuguese students sentenced to seven years in prison for raising their glasses in a toast to freedom during the authoritarian Salazar regime, a time of severe repression in Portugal. His letter to *The Observer*, a major London newspaper, was published under the title "The Forgotten Prisoners."[13]

It told the story of the Portuguese students and launched an "Appeal for Amnesty" for political prisoners anywhere in the world. He labeled these victims of political repression "Prisoners of Conscience" and defined them as "Any person who is physically restrained (by imprisonment or otherwise) from expressing (in any form of words or symbols) an opinion which he honestly holds and which does not advocate or condone personal violence." Benenson asked readers to write their own letters showing support for the students. A few weeks later he gathered with six others, including several members of Parliament, to found a new group called "Amnesty International."[14]

A Japan chapter was launched in 1970. Membership gradually expanded. In Japan, the primary objectives of the group are to alert Japanese people to the state of human rights violations abroad, to generate letters of support for political prisoners in foreign jails, and to raise funds. By the time a graduate student named Makoto Teranaka joined in the 1990s, Amnesty was one of the largest international non-governmental organizations in the world, with millions of members and chapters in dozens of countries. The Japanese membership had grown, too. Teranaka was one of its most enthusiastic members, deeply committed to the core principles of justice and freedom. In 2000, he was appointed director of the small Tokyo office.[15]

Viewed from Amnesty's London headquarters—or from nearly anywhere else—Japan was seen as an advanced democratic country in which fundamental human rights were widely respected. Despite discriminatory treatment of women and certain minorities, Japan's general refusal to accept refugees, and certain other human rights issues, Japan has enjoyed a good reputation abroad.[16] So members of the London office were startled to receive a message from Teranaka in March 2004 that described the arrest and detention of three individuals for distributing flyers that criticized the government. When his London colleagues expressed disbelief, Teranaka provided more details. When he asked if they were aware of similar cases in other democratic countries, they did a search and then responded that there were no such arrests in western democracies—the closest example came from Israel.[17]

The Amnesty Japan chapter had never formally proposed that a detainee in Japan be designated a Prisoner of Conscience. Of course, Amnesty's Japan staff were well aware of the one-sided nature of Japan's criminal justice system and the heavily reported cases where defendants and their representatives claimed they were wrongly convicted based on false confessions,[18] but the organization itself made no formal complaints about these cases. Criminal prosecutions that do not involve threats to free speech are outside the Amnesty mandate. The Tent Village case qualified because it directly concerned criticism of government policy.

Teranaka and his Japan-based colleagues succeeded in persuading London headquarters that the three Tent Village members were detained to punish their political speech and should therefore be designated "Prisoners of Conscience." The decision was announced in a press release on March 18. It ran to about 250 words and was titled "Japan: arbitrary arrest and continued detention of peace activists is a violation of their basic rights to freedom of expression." After summarizing the facts, the release declared

> Amnesty International considers these activists to be prisoners of conscience, detained in violation of their right to freedom of expression guaranteed under Article 21 of the Japanese Constitution and Article 19 of the International Covenant on Civil and Political Rights, an international treaty to which Japan is a state party. They should be released immediately.

The Prosecutors Make Their Decision

The Amnesty declaration appeared the day before the detention period was set to expire. The morning of March 19 arrived with no news from the prosecutors. The detainees and their supporters nervously watched the clock as the hours ticked away. Then they heard that the prosecutors had called for a press conference at 5:30 p.m. More than 70 supporters gathered at Tachikawa station that evening to await the news. They prepared two separate flyers—one with the good news that the suspects had escaped indictment, the other with bad news.

As they waited, a reporter called Tent Village member Mori Inoue with the ominous message he was expecting. A senior prosecutor at a press conference declared that the delivery of the flyers at the SDF apartments was a malicious act.

According to him, no nation that sent troops into a war zone had ever tolerated activists who called upon those troops to refuse their duty. He said the government had no choice but to prosecute.

Inoue jumped on his bicycle to deliver the news to the group at Tachikawa station.[19]

The flyers and the marches and the fiery speeches—even the declaration from a famous international human rights group—were of no avail. The case would be going to trial. Now the suspects were defendants. Unlike Horikoshi, the Tachikawa defendants did not confess. They refused to speak at all, so they remained in jail. But the daily interrogations ceased. Under Japan's curious criminal procedure, once the prosecutors file indictments, they can usually keep defendants in custody, but they can no longer insist on interrogations. Now seated in a jail cell, relieved of the burden of hour after hour in the interrogation chamber, Obora said it was hard to kill time.

Commemorating the First Anniversary of the Iraq War

"World Peace Now" organized a big antiwar rally at Hibiya Park in central Tokyo on the day after the indictments. About 30,000 demonstrators gathered despite the cold and rain. A few Tent Village supporters carried the bad news from Tachikawa. They distributed flyers and sought donations for the defense. Many in the crowd would surely think that they too were potential targets and decided to give. Tent Village gathered 300,000 yen, probably the largest amount they had ever collected in a single day.[20]

The first anniversary of the thunderous "Shock and Awe" bombing of Iraq by American forces arrived the next day. The date would not go unnoticed in Japan's antiwar community. When the Americans abandoned Tachikawa, they concentrated their forces at Yokota Air Force Base, just ten miles away. On March 21, the remaining Tent Village members joined other antiwar groups in protest to demand that the United States remove its forces from Iraq. They marched from Tachikawa to Yokota Air Force Base carrying banners that called for an end to war.[21]

When the demonstration was over, a reporter from a small quarterly publication cornered Kato for a lengthy interview. After discussing the Tent Village history and the arrests, they moved on to some fundamental questions. More than three weeks had passed since her young colleagues' arrests. They remained in detention. Did Kato feel any responsibility for the incident?

She responded that her jailed comrades were all over 30 and capable of making their own decisions, but nonetheless that she did bear some responsibility. She had been criticized by experienced labor union activists who said Tent Village should have seen the crackdown coming and prepared for it.[22] She should have understood that times had changed and the current administration would not tolerate dissent.

Anyone could see the importance of speaking out about Japan's participation in the war, but what about the Tent Village methods? The world had moved on to the Internet and digital communication. Why insist on handing out paper flyers?

"'Posting' is our point of contact with SDF members," she said. "It enables us to see their living conditions to some extent and if someone stops us, we gain an important opportunity to discuss the issues with them."[23]

What about handing out paper flyers at the train station? "Sometimes one in ten people will take one; other times it may be one in a hundred," she said. "Either way, we learn what the people are thinking. This time we can see that the people really care. This kind of contact with the ordinary people—this is what's important to us."

What was the significance of the arrests?

> They have forced us to think more deeply about the situation. I have proposed that we make a flyer that explains the meaning of the arrests and the Iraq War and deliver one to every house in Tachikawa. This is a time of war. And the Iraq War is not just happening far away. It's not only the SDF members sent to Iraq who are experiencing war. Our message is that here in Japan the people are also experiencing the Iraq War.[24]

At the March 19 press conference, a prosecutor pointed out the particular risk presented by people seeking to persuade troops to abandon their duties. In fact, this is precisely the effect Kato had been seeking for at least four decades. She claimed that SDF members don't understand the reality of war. Their officers give them an incomplete picture. It was left to concerned citizens like the Tent Village members to explain the reality of war.

She cited a statement by the Prime Minister before the Diet. According to him, the people should not be involved in strange protests; instead, they should just express their gratitude to SDF members for serving the nation. Kato was incensed by such nonchalance because "Japan has experienced what this kind of attitude can lead to."[25]

6

PREPARING FOR TRIAL

(March 23–April 25, 2004)

Japan is famous for its low rate of crime. Nearly all observers ascribe the safety of Japan's streets to its "communitarian" society, with relatively stable neighborhoods and families, limited income disparities, and other positive social factors. Foreign specialists who study Japan's criminal justice system also laud the lenient approach of the police and prosecutors; they say it leads to high rates of rehabilitation and reintegration of criminal suspects into mainstream society. Government data show that police arrest only a portion of suspects they believe guilty of crime and refer an even smaller subset to prosecutors.[1] The prosecutors "suspend prosecution" (*kiso yūyo*) in many of these cases. This means they believe they have sufficient evidence to prove guilt but nonetheless withhold charges, leaving the suspect free and with a clean record.[2] The end result is that only a tiny minority of criminal suspects are fully charged and tried. David Johnson, author of the most important study of Japan's prosecutors in English, quotes a famed prosecutor and author who wrote that the aim of suspension of prosecution is "to prevent offenders from reoffending by rehabilitating and reintegrating them into society without stamping them with a branding iron."[3]

Unfortunately for the Tent Village defendants, none of this applied to them. The authorities tend to be lenient only in cases where suspects confess, show remorse for their actions, and even compensate victims. Of course, the Tent Village defendants would do none of these things. They believed their actions were lawful, and they fully intended to repeat them.

As for the government, it seemed highly unlikely that officials would show the kind of leniency cheered by foreign observers in this case. The police had carefully laid their plans for the arrests and the prosecutors backed them by obtaining the court approvals needed for daily interrogations behind closed doors. Finally, prosecutors wielded their "branding iron" on March 19 in the form of criminal indictments. These defendants would not avoid prosecution.

DOI: 10.4324/9781003193999-7

With a trial looming before them, the attorneys and leaders of the support group held a strategy session at the West Tokyo Law Office on Tuesday, March 23. They must have gone numb when they pondered the enormity of the tasks ahead. Their circumstances were dire. Nearly all criminal trials in Japan result in guilty verdicts. Even when attorneys produce a not guilty miracle, under Japan's procedure, the state can appeal. Many years might pass before a case like this is finally resolved before the Supreme Court. Someone would have to raise an enormous fund to cover the costs of the trial and appeals to follow. Those who gathered on March 23 reviewed the total expected costs: (1) bail, which might amount to millions of yen, (2) fees for lawyers and expert witnesses, (3) postage and printing costs for newsletters to supporters and other incidentals, and (4) living expenses for members who would be out of work.[4] The meeting set a goal of raising ten million yen (approximately US$ 90,000 at that time), a nearly unimaginable sum for a tiny group of activists with no more than six full-time members.

With no real organization, Osawa and the others would have to persuade the public at large to contribute. For starters, they decided to stage a mass rally to gain public pledges of support from sympathetic antiwar groups. They settled on Sunday, April 25, as the best date for a rally and march to the SDF Tachikawa base.[5]

Meanwhile, the three defendants sat in jail.

Requesting Bail

After indictments are filed, defendants are allowed to submit bail requests for the first time. Defense counsel filed on March 26. In their four-page petitions, the attorneys argued the legal foundation for the arrests was weak and cited no fewer than ten separate declarations and reports from third parties, including the law scholars' declaration, the *Asahi* editorial, and others that labeled the police action a violation of the right to free speech and called for immediate release of the suspects.[6]

Under Japan's Code of Criminal Procedure, judges must grant bail requests unless certain exceptions apply, but no one expected the March 26 request to be successful. Government prosecutors nearly always oppose the requests, citing these exceptions, and they are usually successful. For example, in 2015 bail was granted to only 25.7% of defendants detained for pending trial in district courts.[7] The most commonly cited exceptions are the risks that defendants will tamper with evidence and that they may flee. Prosecutors cited these exceptions in their opposition to release of the Tent Village defendants and defense counsel challenged them with rebuttals.

The case for a risk of flight appeared weak. As demonstrated by their long association with Tent Village, the defendants held deep commitments to their community and their cause. Running away was surely the last thing on their minds.[8]

The risk to evidence presented a more complex question. Regarding physical evidence, 40 days elapsed between the flyer delivery and the date of the suspects' arrests and the police confiscated personal computers, files, and other materials in their early morning raids, so it was hard to imagine there was anything left to tamper with. Witness testimony was likely the primary concern. Once they were released, the defendants might coordinate and modify their testimony. In Japan, there seems to be an irrebuttable presumption that all defendants would do so, and therefore, they must be detained until they have confessed or at least admitted the facts alleged by prosecutors.

The prosecutors insisted that the suspects remain in custody. They undoubtedly found the defendants' continuing silence especially infuriating. The Constitution might guarantee a right to silence, but the goal of every interrogation is to obtain a confession. Given the overwhelming advantages held by the interrogators, most ordinary people submit. Those who do not are considered incorrigible, an especially dangerous threat.

On March 31, the court ruled as expected, rejecting the bail requests.[9] The three defendants would remain in jail—and they would continue to maintain silence.

Defense counsel judged that the next opportunity for a possible release would come at the first court hearing when the defendants would have the opportunity to admit the facts alleged in the indictment. Attorney Kojima explains that "the reality of the courts' bail practice is that admission of the facts stated in the indictment is one condition for approval of bail requests."[10]

Whether the defendants should make such admissions was a major question. The pros and cons were debated at the March 23 meeting. The prosecutors had yet to disclose evidence to the defense, so some thought they might have a hard time proving the three defendants were actually the individuals responsible for the flyer deliveries.[11] The silence strategy would leave the burden to prove the facts fully on the prosecutors.[12] On the other hand, if the three suspects broke their silence in court and admitted the facts of the deliveries as alleged in the indictment, there would be no practical reason to continue their detention. The bottom line was that in order to be released from custody, the suspects would have to forfeit their constitutional rights to silence and to contest the government's version of the facts.

Even if they made the admissions, release from custody was far from a sure thing. The prosecutors would likely oppose another bail motion despite the defense admissions. If the court sided with the prosecutors, the three defendants might be stranded in detention until the prosecution finished putting on its case, perhaps many months in the future.

Organizing Support

While the attorneys drafted legal briefs and trekked to the Tachikawa jails to visit their clients, Yutaka Osawa and a small team of supporters laid the building blocks of an organization capable of raising the funds necessary for a potentially long court battle. One indispensable task was the launch of a newsletter to be sent to all supporters, the news media, and others, with regular updates on court schedules, public events, and messages from lawyers and other supporters and from Osawa himself. The newsletter would be delivered online with Osawa's website as the platform.

Osawa uploaded the first edition on April 2.[13] Readers learned that Thursday, May 6, had been selected as the tentative date for the first trial session. Of greatest urgency, the newsletter called upon all readers to submit written demands for the release of the detainees. This was the most direct way for supporters to speak to the court. On April 7, Osawa uploaded a form letter in PDF format, so anyone could download the form, sign it, and send it in. The support group would gather all petitions and submit them to the court together with the next demand for release on bail. Their goal was to gather at least 5,000 signatures.[14]

The April 2 newsletter also announced that a large rally would be held on the Hitotsubashi University campus on April 25, to be followed by a march to the Tachikawa base. Hitotsubashi is located in the city of Kunitachi, which shares a border with Tachikawa. Many Tent Village supporters lived on the Kunitachi side of the line.

In the days to come, Tent Village members and their supporters set up tables at the train station to gather signatures from passersby. They also made weekly trips to the gates of the SDF base and the nearby Tachikawa jails in their Toyota "Hi-Ace" van to trumpet their "anti-military broadcasts" and messages of encouragement to their colleagues behind bars.[15]

While the detainees struggled to kill time in the weeks that followed the indictment, the attention of the Japanese people was suddenly focused on three other Japanese detainees held in very different circumstances on the other side of the globe. On the evening of April 7, three young Japanese—two private aid workers and an independent journalist—were taken hostage in Iraq. The abductors demanded that Japan remove the Self-Defense Forces from their country, threatening to execute the three unless the evacuation commenced within three days.[16] Al-Qaeda had broadcast such executions on the Internet in the past, so the threat was especially terrifying.

The nation was transfixed as images of family members appeared on their television screens and in their newspapers pleading for the safety of their loved ones. Fortunately, the crisis did not last. The three were released unharmed on April 15, apparently due to the intervention of Iraqi religious leaders. Fear for their safety was suddenly replaced with joy for their release. But then the mood in Japan shifted dramatically. Conservative spokespeople had criticized the three for thoughtlessly creating risk by working in Iraq. Even Prime Minister Koizumi joined in, calling on them to have a greater sense of responsibility. When they arrived back home in Japan, they were greeted with a deluge of hate mail and threats of personal harm. Some members of the LDP even called for legislation restricting the people's right to travel abroad.[17] It turned out that the return home was more traumatic than the experience in captivity. Due to the strident criticism, all three former hostages were diagnosed with post-traumatic stress disorder.

Tent Village supporters were outraged at the callous attitude of the government and the right wing; many felt deep sympathy for countrymen with the courage and commitment to travel to Iraq to support the Iraqi people and provide independent reporting on the action there. In their view, it was the government's own reckless action in deploying the Self-Defense Forces that had placed the three hostages and other Japanese at risk. They shared the feelings expressed in a statement issued by a coalition of 40 Japanese NGOs that declared their "outrage and sorrow" over statements by the government and some elements of the news media.[18]

Tent Village members returned to their informal stage in front of Tachikawa station, where they denounced the government and handed out flyers explaining their view that the kidnappings were not the result of risk-taking by the hostages but instead were caused by the mistaken and unconstitutional decision to deploy the SDF. Like members of other Japanese antiwar groups, their primary focus was on the victims of war. At the time, they were especially shocked and saddened by news reports of numerous civilian casualties from the American assault on Fallujah.[19]

The contrasting fates suffered by Japanese detained in Iraq and those in Tachikawa raised serious questions. A former member of the SDF who participated in a hotline for advice regarding the rights of members of the SDF and the U.S. military expressed the feelings of many supporters when he said, "The 'self-responsibility' bashing applied to the hostages had the same quality as the suppression of Tent Village."[20] Despite the heavy emotional price the three Iraq hostages were made to pay, after four days in custody they were freed, and then they made their way home. By contrast, the three Tachikawa detainees remained in police jails many weeks after their arrests with no certainty they would be released any time soon.

The same day the hostages were released in Iraq, the three Tachikawa detainees took a step toward obtaining their own freedom. At a pre-trial conference on April 15, defense counsel notified the court that the defendants planned to admit the facts alleged in the indictments and contest only the application of the law. In the defendants' view, their distribution of the flyers did not violate any law. Eager to move forward, the court welcomed this step. The chief judge told the lawyers and prosecutors he wanted to issue a decision by October. This would be an extraordinarily fast pace for a trial like this in a Japanese court. At the April 15 conference, they scheduled four court dates for coming months.[21]

On April 20, prosecutors notified defense counsel for the first time of the evidence they would present in court. Major items included testimony from residents of the SDF apartments and documents obtained during the police raids that accompanied the arrests on February 27.[22]

Tent Village issued its own newsletter, separate from Osawa's support group, on April 21. This one would be a hard copy. Titled "Posting," it was composed of a single sheet of A-4 size paper folded over to create four pages. By now, the tentative May 6 schedule had become final. The cover of the first issue carried the schedule for the May 6 hearing, beginning with a gathering outside the courthouse at 11:45 a.m. Supporters were invited to spend the next two hours in front of the courthouse with banners, a loudspeaker, and sheaves of flyers to be handed to passersby. The actual hearing would begin at 3:00 p.m. It would be followed by an information session at a nearby union hall where the attorneys and others would review the day's events and discuss the schedule to come.

Tent Village supporters found a unique opportunity to raise the spirits of the detainees on April 23—Sachimi's birthday. She was well known in the area as a singer who performed with local bands. A cluster of a dozen or more friends appeared on the sidewalk outside the jailhouse with guitars to serenade her, singing "Happy Birthday" and some of her favorite songs. They knew she couldn't see them from her windowless cell, but the attorneys had confirmed that she would be able to hear them, as she and the other detainees had heard the noise from previous gatherings to protest the arrests.[23]

Meanwhile, as Tent Village members, Osawa, and other supporters worked to build a crowd for the rally scheduled for Sunday, April 25 in Kunitachi, they began to sense something in the air. New contacts stepped forward to say they would attend and some even volunteered to promote the event.[24] And the support group was receiving a lot of donations from people they didn't know.[25] They had rarely seen this kind of reaction in the past. Through the arrests, Tent Village seemed to have acquired much greater visibility. Now it was not merely a tiny

FIGURE 6.1 Friends serenade Sachimi Takada as she spends her birthday in the Tachikawa jail. (Photograph by Katsuko Kato, April 2004)

local antiwar group—it had become the representative for all antiwar groups throughout Japan.

Gathering in Kunitachi

While Tachikawa has long been known as a military base town, Kunitachi has a very different image. It is a college town. Since the 1920s it has been home to Hitotsubashi, one of the nation's most prestigious universities. With spacious grounds surrounding imposing neoclassical structures, this is one of Japan's most beautiful university campuses. It was laid out in the 1920s, after the Great Kanto Earthquake of 1923 had devastated much of Tokyo's core.[26]

Partly because it is a college town and partly because it originally developed as a farming village at a distance from the city center, the Kunitachi area acquired a unique identity that features a lively subculture with frequent festivals, numerous local musicians, and even counterculture coffeehouses that provide forums for antiwar activists and others to connect and hatch plans for marches and demonstrations.[27] The Tent Village rally actually fell on the same day as a regular free outdoor concert.[28] Sachimi Takata often performed at such events.

As the crowd streamed into the great lecture hall reserved for the event on the afternoon of Sunday, April 25, Osawa and the other organizers saw that their efforts had paid off. They watched as the hall filled with an audience of more than 350 persons, including representatives of 20 different citizen groups who came to make public declarations of their support for the detainees.[29]

The event opened with a greeting by Kunitachi councilman Tomohiro Shigematsu, Osawa's close friend and the co-author of the original declaration posted by Osawa on the day of the arrests. According to Shigematsu, voices were rising throughout the land to demand the release of the three defendants, held so long with no contact at all with friends and family.

Speakers included attorney Akio Kotō and Amnesty International representative Makoto Teranaka. Kotō pointed out a rather odd aspect of the case. Although the government claimed the Tent Village messengers had created a nuisance that disrupted the lives of the residents, Kotō said the complaint filed with the police was not prepared at the initiative of those residents. Instead, it was the result of an order from the SDF command. He contemptuously dismissed claims that the defendants had somehow injured the SDF building residents with their flyers.

> Claims like "the unease of the residents," "the danger of acts of terrorism," "unease created by the flyers might lead to family discord." This is just gibberish made up after the fact in an effort to justify the outrageous arrests and the prosecution.[30]

Teranaka was the primary author of the Amnesty International press release that labeled the Tent Village activists Japan's first "prisoners of conscience." By chance, he was a resident of Kunitachi, his home located only a few blocks away from the SDF apartments where the flyers had landed. Teranaka actually strolled on that very property the day of the arrests. In the days that followed, he joined other protesters who gathered outside the police station to demand that the activists be released.[31] Teranaka now told the audience what it meant to be designated a "prisoner of conscience." He compared the three Tent Village members to Burma's Aung San Suu Kyi and other political activists in places like China and North Korea who were imprisoned for expressing criticisms of their governments. In his opinion, Japan's state security police were traveling in some very bad company. Political prisoners are ordinarily found in places with authoritarian governments, not in representative democracies like Japan.[32]

Osawa told the audience the messages he received showed that people were expressing their resistance to the SDF bases and the Iraq deployment all over the country. According to him, the government was acting in fear of popular reaction to its defense policies. He said the popular resistance was a "body blow" to the Defense Agency and the Self-Defense Forces. "They cracked down in Tachikawa," he said, "to set an example for people in the rest of the country."

By Osawa's account, the government struck at Tachikawa in desperation, with the goal of creating a chilling effect against peace activists all over Japan. He called on everyone in the audience to come to the courthouse to show their support on May 6 and to open their wallets as well as their hearts by donating to the

FIGURE 6.2 Protesters parade through local streets after a rally on the Hitotsubashi University campus on March 25, 2004. (Photograph by Yutaka Osawa)

cause. He also announced the goal of raising the eye-popping sum of 10 million yen to pay for the costs of a court battle that might take years.[33]

Discussion in the university classroom closed with the reading of an appeal by the three detainees.[34] The gathering was followed by a march from Kunitachi to the SDF base in east Tachikawa adjacent to the SDF apartments. Around 300 people joined, far in excess of the expected number that was reported on the parade application filed with the police.[35] The boisterous crowd marched through quiet residential streets. The leaders had prepared a "resolution of the meeting" to be presented at the SDF base. They had expected this would be presented by a small delegation, but the big turnout made for a very different scene. The crowd pushed up against the gate entrance, and as the resolution was delivered, some shouted about the many blameless victims in Iraq, the limited constitutional role of the SDF, the poor treatment of the former hostages by government representatives, and other issues. According to Osawa, the final message for the SDF members was to "Discuss this among yourselves. If you decide to raise your voices against the deployment, we will provide full support."[36]

7

TRIAL AT HACHIOJI: THE FIRST COURT HEARING

(May 6, 2004)

"Golden Week" is one of the longest holiday periods on Japan's calendar, providing welcome relief from the workday during the most pleasant time of the year. In 2004, it ran for a full week, from Thursday, April 29, through Wednesday, May 5. Every year there is a grand migration throughout the country as hordes of city workers and their families travel to ancestral homes to gather with distant family members. For Tent Village supporters with a special interest in the law, including the 56 scholars who signed the declaration, May 3 is an especially important Golden Week holiday. This is Constitution Day, and every year there are big parades and public gatherings to celebrate the birth of Japan's democratic Constitution on May 3, 1947.

The three defendants were moved from police jail cells in Tachikawa to the Hachioji Detention Center located next to the courthouse on April 28. They had already spent two months in detention. Daily interrogations ceased after the indictments were filed on March 19, but the defendants remained in cells together with a rotating cast of other detainees until they were transferred to the detention center. Here they were held in individual units, so they had privacy for the first time since their arrests. But Onishi complained that now they were forced to listen to radio broadcasts played at high volume throughout the day and this made it difficult to concentrate and prepare his statement to the court.[1] Sachimi Takada recalled one radio announcement that was especially galling. When she heard a cheerful voice chirp out "This week is 'Constitution Week' in Tokyo! Japan's Constitution guarantees many fundamental rights to the people," she remembers thinking "they're a bunch of goddamn liars."[2]

For the three Tent Village defendants, the only effect of Constitution Day and the rest of the long holiday period was to extend their time behind bars. The first hearing in their trial was set for Thursday, May 6, the day Japan returned

DOI: 10.4324/9781003193999-8

to work. At long last, they would confront their accusers and tell their stories in open court.

May 6 Hearing (First Public Court Session)

The trial of the Tent Village activists was held in a small courthouse in the town of Hachioji, at the western edge of the Tokyo metropolitan district.[3] The court was a "branch" of Tokyo District Court, a tiny outpost of the giant Tokyo District Court downtown. The case was heard by a three-judge panel led by 54-year-old Judge Ken'ichi Hasegawa. Japan's judges are national public servants who are rotated to new postings at intervals of approximately three years. Hasegawa was assigned to Hachioji in 2003, after serving in neighboring Gunma Prefecture. He would leave Hachioji in 2007 for another assignment.[4]

The three branches of Japan's elite legal profession—judges, prosecutors, and *bengoshi* (practicing lawyers)—are clearly segmented. All serve apprenticeships in the same national legal training institute, but graduates take one of the three paths where they usually spend much or all of their careers. Members of the judiciary start as assistant judges when they are typically in their mid-to-late 20s. Criminal prosecutions like the Tent Village case are heard by three-judge panels led by a senior judge that usually include one other experienced judge and one assistant with less than five years on the bench.[5]

Due to the notoriety of the case, Judge Hasegawa reserved the largest courtroom, which provided seating for nearly 80 spectators.[6] Tent Village supporters began to assemble before the courthouse by noon and started handing out flyers to passersby and attorneys and others headed inside. Osawa was detained by city council business. When he arrived on his motorbike about an hour before the 3:00 p.m. start time, he discovered a long line of supporters waiting to draw straws to see who could gain entry. There were nearly 80 seats in the spectators' gallery, but he estimated that 120 people had already arrived. The courthouse parking lot was cordoned off to create space for the crowd.

Osawa was also surprised to see that the spectators would have to check their briefcases, cellphones, and other items with courthouse staff before entering the courtroom. He had attended several trials before but had never seen such tight security.[7]

The lottery for spectator seating and the tight security caused a delay, so by the time Osawa entered the courtroom, he found that the three defendants were already seated on a bench facing the front of the room, with their backs to the spectators. They were separated by security guards wedged in between them on the bench, apparently to prevent the defendants from speaking to each other. It was nearly impossible for them to turn to face their friends in the spectator seats behind them.[8] Like the March 11 hearing, the defendants had been led into the court on ropes tied around their waists, with shackles at their wrists and ankles.[9] The spectacle brought tears and heartfelt pain to their supporters in the gallery.

FIGURE 7.1 Spectators wait to draw straws for entry into the Hachioji Courthouse on May 6, 2004. (Photograph by Katsuko Kato)

After court was called to order and the three judges ascended the bench from a side door, Chief Judge Hasegawa began by requesting each defendant to give their name, birth date, and other identifying information.[10] Spectators cheered and applauded after they spoke, prompting the chief judge to issue a surprising warning: "Be quiet or I'll order you removed! I want to release them as soon as possible, so don't get in the way."[11] When they were done, a young prosecutor, one of two assigned to courtroom duty, rose to read the indictment aloud. Speaking in a dry, impassive tone, she cited Article 130 of the Criminal Code and said

> With the purpose of placing flyers that declared 'We Oppose the SDF Deployment to Iraq!' and similar statements, between the hours of 11 a.m. and noon on January 17 the three defendants conspired to and did trespass into a residence without just cause.[12]

When she was finished, defense counsel called for clarifications. First, could the prosecutors specify exactly where the alleged "trespass" occurred? Was it at the entry onto the grounds of the property? To the staircases? The corridors of each of the buildings? For this, the prosecutors had a simple answer: The outdoor property, the staircases, and the corridors are all connected and entry to all of these places was unlawful. Next, the attorneys said that Article 130 required the violation of someone's "legal interest." The indictment did not specify just who such victims might be and what was the nature of their legal interests. Could the government fill in the blanks?[13] The prosecutors deflected such questions with the comprehensive response that the defendants had violated the interests of both the residents and the managers of the buildings. They did not identify any of the victims by name. Regarding their legal interests, the prosecutors cited the residents' right to "peaceful daily life" (*hei'on na seikatsu*) and the property managers' "managerial rights."

The Defendants Are Allowed to Speak

Nobuhiro Onishi

After this brief swordplay among the advocates, the defendants were allowed to address the court. Japan's court procedures grant broad discretion to presiding judges, who often allow defendants in criminal trials to address the court in free-flowing "statements of opinion." Technically, these statements are not considered to be evidence and the speakers are not subject to cross-examination, but they nonetheless gain an invaluable opportunity to communicate directly with the court. The first to speak was thirty-year-old Nobuhiro Onishi.[14] He did not use his time to complain about the arrests or his treatment in detention. Instead, after making the simple admission that, yes, he did distribute flyers at the SDF buildings, Onishi launched into an erudite presentation on the Iraq War, Japan's Constitution, and the duty of the citizen in a democratic society.

> Japan's Self Defense Forces have been deployed to Iraq under the pretext of "humanitarian and reconstruction assistance." However, I believe that under international law and common morality, the Iraq War, launched at the unilateral decision of the United States, is illegal and improper and that deployment of the SDF to participate is a clear violation of Japan's Constitution. The war was started on the presumption that Iraq possesses weapons of mass destruction. However, as everyone knows, the very existence of such weapons is in doubt.

Following this introduction, Onishi led the spectators and the court through an extended discourse featuring such topics as the international law of war, relevant resolutions of the UN Security Council, and the "Bush Doctrine" by which the U.S. President asserted the power to launch "preemptive wars," and of greatest interest to the Japanese people, the response of Japan's own government to such issues.

"Japan's Self Defense Forces were first deployed overseas in the 1990s," he said. "We have always been told that there is no violation of the Constitution because they are sent abroad to contribute to peace and never to participate in acts of war." The very first SDF overseas deployment came in April 1991, when the Kaifu Administration dispatched six minesweepers to the Persian Gulf to clear mines after the Gulf War. This was followed a year later by Japan's participation in a peacekeeping operation in Cambodia and in succeeding years by several other peacekeeping operations in other corners of the world.[15] Onishi explained that the Iraq deployment was different.

> However, this time the rationale put forward is that we must send the SDF in order to fulfill our obligation as an ally of the United States. In other words, the plan is for the Iraq War to serve as the turning point when the SDF is transformed into a military that fights alongside the American military in war.

After reporting the numbers of deaths and other details from the battlefront, Onishi quoted the government's own statement on the floor of the Diet to the effect that SDF members have no legal duty to follow unlawful orders. This was the most central issue in the entire Tent Village program: Constitution Article 9 prohibits Japan's participation in war, so the legality of the Iraq deployment was unclear and SDF members have no obligation to follow illegal orders. How could SDF members reach their own conclusions on the legality of deployment orders if they are barred from receiving communications from other Japanese? Fellow citizens like Onishi stood ready to explain the realities of the Iraq War, the political goals of the American and Japanese governments, and the significance of Article 9, but they were blocked from doing so.

Then he delivered his view on the very special role of Japan's Constitution.

> After reflecting upon its own acts in wars of aggression, Japan adopted a Constitution which mandates that the country will not maintain war potential and rejects the right of belligerency … I think that the core characteristic of Japan's Constitution is … a call for continuous reflection and critical thought regarding the ideal nature of the modern state.[16]

He went on to say, "I believe it is the existence of citizens who freely express their opinions who embody this principle of critical thought … such citizens carry out the mission of the constitution in real life."

Then Onishi delivered another formulation: "In a democracy, what makes the constitution a constitution is the existence of actual citizens. Only when these citizens, including members of the SDF, can freely exchange their opinions can we say that Japan's constitution is a 'democratic constitution.'"[17]

Sachimi Takada

In contrast to Onishi's lawyerly analysis, Sachimi Takada delivered a fiery speech of rage and disbelief. She had done nothing but place flyers in mailboxes, the very same activity Tent Village members had been doing for 30 years. Then suddenly it was as if she had disappeared down a rabbit hole into an alien world she could have never imagined. In this world, she was not a musician surrounded by a circle of beaming friends—suddenly she was a criminal, a prisoner forced to endure screaming interrogators, hour after hour, day after day. Before the arrest, she knew nothing of Japan's police or their methods. Why would they attack her? She's just a singer and caregiver who chose to express her opinion about the war. What threat could she possibly be to anyone?

Takada reminded the court that Tachikawa is a military base town. In her opinion, local residents in such a place bear a special duty. "Delivering flyers to the mailboxes of SDF members is a regular form of expression for many individuals and groups," she said.

> SDF members and their families tend to be overwhelmed by powerful military ideology. On the other hand, we express the voices of the local community and the viewpoints of antiwar activists so that when SDF members and their families confront questions involving the Constitution and individual rights, they have some resources to help them think for themselves and decide how to act.

Then she reported the gruesome details of her detention, including a sampling of the insults screamed in her face while she was strapped into a chair in the windowless interrogation room. According to her, the three weeks of interrogation had not served the legitimate government objective of gathering information relevant to the case; instead, the true purpose was to humiliate her and threaten the destruction of Tent Village.

She rebutted the government's justifications for her continued detention. "They say there is a 'risk of escape.' *Escape?* That would mean abandoning our work. Unthinkable!" She similarly dismissed the government's claim that the defendants might destroy evidence. "How could we possibly 'destroy evidence' months after the deliveries, following searches of our homes and the interrogations?" she cried.

Finally, she recounted the conditions of life in Tachikawa, side-by-side with a military base. "People constantly talk about the danger overhead and the terrible noise of the jets. And there is always the ghost of the 'Sunagawa Struggle,' which could rise up at any time with a new demand for base expansion."[18]

When she was done, she turned to face the crowd of spectators. Many were waving and smiling and some applauded in a spontaneous gesture of love for a friend in distress. As she slowly walked from the witness stand to her seat at the defendants' bench, she imagined she was gazing upon a field of flowers.[19]

Toshiyuki Obora

The final defendant to speak, Toshiyuki Obora, had been a member of Tent Village for nearly as long as Katsuko Kato herself. For the police SWAT team, he was the biggest prize. Obora did not waste time. He immediately launched into an attack on the entire process, including the arrests and the very broad searches and seizures that encompassed locations and the confiscation of materials that had nothing to do with the flyer deliveries. He was especially incensed by the denial of visitors throughout his long detention.

> Recently it seems as if the courts are approving unlimited visitor prohibitions even in cases where it isn't really necessary. In our case, not only was the prohibition unnecessary, but when it was briefly removed after our indictments, the prosecutors quickly filed an opposition and it was put in place again. For them to cite our silence as the reason for their opposition is completely unfair. The Constitution and the Code of Criminal Procedure recognize the right to remain silent as an ordinary right of the accused. We did nothing more than exercise this right to protect ourselves.[20]

"Takada-san already described the conditions during the interrogations," he said, "I was also the victim of mistreatment." He repeated much of the story told by Sachimi Takada and then added that he was forced to endure not only the screams of the interrogators but also desk pounding and physical abuse when they used the table in the interrogation room as a battering ram against his body while he was strapped into a chair and could not move.

> They made all kinds of threats and insults as they tried to make me surrender, yelling things like "You'll be fired from your job!" "We can launch raids on your family's home and on your workplace!" "We can re-arrest you!" Clearly, they were inflicting this emotional torment on me in order to force me to recant.[21]

For recant, he used the word "*tenkō*," a loaded historical term that refers to the mass renunciations of Japan Communist Party members caused by the extreme tactics of the "Special Higher Police" (*tokkō keisatsu*) during the 1920s and 1930s.[22]

Obora also treated the court and the spectators to a brief version of the Tachikawa story, beginning with the postwar confiscation of land by the U.S. military, the Sunagawa Struggle, and the birth of Tent Village itself in the 1970s. He described the Tent Village's mission of reaching out to individual members of the SDF and the longstanding practice of "posting."

"From the 1970s through the early '80s," he said

> Tent Village published a newspaper for distribution to SDF members. We handed out copies in front of the base, sent them by direct mail and slipped copies through mail slots at individual apartments. We used individual mail slots rather than central banks of mail boxes in order to be sure the SDF members would read them.[23]

Such activities are obviously protected by the right to free speech, he said. He stressed the role of free speech in a democracy and how the failure to protect free speech in the past had led to the rise of Nazism and Japanese militarism. He also explained that the right to free speech implies a right to receive information. It was the members of the SDF themselves who were victims of the police crackdown and other efforts to block information from reaching them. Then he shared an anecdote from his time in jail.

> During my interrogation, an officer taunted me by saying, "You know, this case is important for both sides. Wouldn't it be interesting to see whether flyer deliveries at SDF residences are going up or down?" Clearly, the crackdown on Tent Village had the effect of a warning to antiwar and peace activists all over the country. The interrogator's statement indicated his expectation that antiwar flyer distributions would decrease.
>
> When local residents telephoned the Tachikawa Police Station to complain about the crackdown and asked why there was a different response for antiwar flyers and other kinds of flyers, the police responded that "antiwar flyers might result in a decline in SDF morale and other problems." Statements like this show that the crackdown had a political purpose.[24]

Obora finished by describing conditions in Iraq and how the SDF deployment had damaged Japan's image in the Middle East. He criticized Koizumi's decision to blindly follow the Americans into a war that caused nothing but harm to the Iraqi people and he spoke of the need for more Japanese people to speak out against it. The people must not give the government a pass: "We must reassess the meaning of the war and the damage caused by the deployment of the SDF, beginning with the failure to uncover the weapons of mass destruction that provided the original pretext for the launch of war."[25]

The three defendants finished before 4:00 p.m. and then yielded the stage to the professionals, who had listened patiently to their passionate speeches decrying the outrageous interrogations and the illegality of the Iraq War. We can only wonder whether the judges were moved by the defendants' strident words and shocking images. Judges with long experience on the criminal bench had surely heard such passionate speeches before. But the defendants in this case were not common criminals, nor were they violent radicals. Whatever the judges' true reactions, as stoic professionals they could betray no sign of sympathy. As for the prosecutors, they were themselves the representatives of Japan's notorious "hostage justice" system, the very institution that had inflicted such pain and humiliation on the defendants. For them, the speeches were simply irrelevant. The defendants were charged with violating Article 130 of Japan's criminal code and it said nothing about illegal wars or the rights of suspects in detention.

"Just Cause"

Defense counsel moved the discussion from the personal experiences and emotions of the defendants back to the law. It was clear to everyone that the centerpiece for any defense would be Article 21 of the Constitution, which protects "freedom of assembly and association as well as speech, press and all other forms of expression." In order to succeed they would have to carve a clear pathway from the abstract words of the Constitution to the human story of the tiny group driven to reach out to individual SDF members.

Advocates are trained to present multiple theories that lead to their desired conclusion, enabling judges to select the one they like best. When she addressed the bench regarding the central role of Article 21, Lead Counsel Reiko Kuriyama suggested several different routes to a not guilty verdict. One stressed the importance of flyer deliveries to people like her clients.

> In modern society, where means of communication like television, newspaper and others are monopolized by large pools of capital, handing out flyers is one of the few means available to ordinary citizens that enables them to communicate their thoughts and beliefs, their knowledge and their experiences, to others.[26]

If the court ruled against them, her clients might have no means at all to exercise their constitutional rights.

Citing the *Asahi Shimbun* article of March 5, she pointed out the inevitable chilling effect of the police action on others who might wish to distribute flyers door-to-door, but feared they would become subject to the same treatment as Tent Village. "This kind of prosecution will have an extremely powerful effect on all citizens who may seek to express themselves in the future."[27] Clearly, if the court ruled in favor of the government, the damage to free speech in Japan would not be limited to Tachikawa.

Then she flipped the focus of free speech protection from speaker to listener, asserting that the Constitution protects both. "Suppression of the acts of the defendants deprives the SDF members of the opportunity to come into contact with other opinions and therefore also violates their 'right to know.'"[28]

But the most fundamental issue was the requirement of Criminal Code Article 130 that visitors only become criminal trespassers if they lack a "just cause" to enter the property. For this most important issue, her response was emphatic:

> They did not enter the property without a 'just cause' like thieves. They did so in order to distribute flyers expressing opposition to the SDF deployment, an act of free speech guaranteed by the Constitution.[29]

Kuriyama then moved from the defense of her clients to an attack on the prosecution. She reminded the court that in every case the Code of Criminal Procedure requires prosecutors to consider the characters of suspects and the seriousness and circumstances of a crime when deciding whether to indict. Those factors, she said, compelled the dismissal of the charges. Her clients' actions did not amount to a crime and even if they did the injury was so trivial that the case did not warrant prosecution.[30] Their behavior was in sharp contrast to that of the police. The

FIGURE 7.2 Attorney Reiko Kuriyama visited the defendants on the night of their arrests and then served as lead counsel in their trial and the appeals that followed. (Photograph by Toshiyuki Obora, November 2004)

very first article of the Code of Criminal Procedure mandates that prosecutors protect fundamental individual rights and public welfare. No lawful prosecution could be predicated on the surprise police raid and the "prisoner of conscience" detention that followed.

In summary, she declared

> Even though the injury was slight and such cases were long overlooked, the government not only employed the coercive measures of search, arrest, and detention, but went on to file indictments, forcing the defendants to defend themselves in this court. The purpose of this prosecution can only be to suppress certain acts of expression and to suppress and put a stop to the activities of the defendants' group and is therefore an abuse of discretion and void.[31]

This attack on the legality of the prosecution was a long shot indeed. Japanese courts have only rarely mustered the strength to invalidate a prosecution as an abuse of discretion. The best-known example occurred nearly three decades before in the infamous Minamata case when the Fukuoka High Court ruled the prosecution of the leader of protests by the victims of mercury poisoning invalid. In reaching its conclusion, the court cited the authorities' failure to address the injury to thousands due to mercury poisoning for more than a decade and the failure to bring charges against company officials responsible for the mass injury.[32]

Reiko Kuriyama's clients' hopes for acquittal surely rested on the hallowed right of free speech, but in her final words she actually sought to reach even higher ground. This case involved more than the defendants' exercise of their rights, she said. It also concerned their fulfillment of a duty.

> The defendants continued to raise their voices ... seeking to correct the errors of the government in deploying the SDF to Iraq in violation of Constitution Article 9 and the Iraq Special Measures Law. In this way, they sought to fulfill their duties as citizens ... to protect the Constitution.

Kuriyama cited Constitution Article 12 which declares that "freedoms and rights guaranteed to the people by this Constitution shall be maintained by the constant endeavor of the people."

Bail Granted

The hearing ended at 4:30 p.m. As the three defendants and their guards stood up to leave, suddenly the spectators' gallery broke out in a spirited rendition of "Happy Birthday, Toshi." Defendant Obora celebrated his 47th that day. After they left the courtroom, many spectators gathered in the alley between the courthouse and the detention center, shouting and waving to their friends as they were led across the open space outside and back to their cells.[33]

With the hearing finished, the lawyers and prosecutors met with the judges in chambers to discuss the bail request filed on April 30.[34] Supporters had managed to gather more than 4,000 signatures to an appeal demanding the defendants' release and this was appended to the bail request.[35] At the supporters' meeting held later that day, the attorneys said it appeared the judges would look favorably on their request. Regarding the trial itself, the judges had expressed an interest in examining the site of the flyer deliveries. This was an unusual step, a clear indication that the court had taken a strong interest in the case.[36]

The attorneys received a phone call from the court clerk at 5:00 p.m. Friday evening with joyful news: Judge Hasegawa and his colleagues had approved bail for all three defendants. The bail amount was set at 1.5 million yen each (about US$ 13,500 in 2004); this was a considerable sum, but less than they expected.[37]

Surely, the defendants' admissions of the basic facts in court the day before had made the difference. But it was still too soon to celebrate. As expected, the prosecutors filed an immediate appeal of the bail order. This meant the Tent Village defendants would remain in detention for at least a few more days while the Tokyo High Court reviewed the appeal.

A small group of Tent Village supporters rode the train downtown to demonstrate before the central Tokyo courthouse on Monday morning. They unfurled their large banner and handed out 500 flyers to passersby that demanded the immediate release of their friends. When they were done, several rode the courthouse elevator to the 15th floor where they read their petition aloud to a Tokyo High Court clerk.[38] Late that afternoon, attorneys Uchida and Kotō argued the case for release before a High Court panel.[39]

FIGURE 7.3 The defendants and some supporters celebrate their release from jail on May 11, 2004. (Photograph by Katsuko Kato)

As this took place, back in Tachikawa the remaining Tent Village members led a small group of demonstrators in their regular monthly demonstration against the C-1 military cargo planes that operated from the Tachikawa SDF base.[40]

The High Court denied the prosecutors' appeal of the bail order the following day. Now it was really time to celebrate. Sachimi Takada was the first defendant released. She walked out of the detention center at 6:00 p.m. wearing the same clothes she'd worn on the day of the arrests. Obora and Onishi followed about 20 minutes later. They were greeted by seven or eight supporters with smiles and tears of joy.[41]

The Tent Village defendants were free after spending 75 days in jail. Their ordeal behind bars had come to an end. But their trial—and their lives after the long detention—had just begun.

8

AN UNDERCOVER INVESTIGATION

(July 20, 2004)

The first hearing in the trial of Akio Horikoshi was held at Tokyo District Court on Tuesday, July 20, a brutally hot summer afternoon. Temperatures rose to nearly 100 degrees while more than 130 people lined up outside the courthouse in the noonday sun to draw straws for one of the 86 seats allotted to courtroom spectators. On the street in front of the courthouse entrance, Horikoshi and a band of supporters handed out flyers to passersby while they stood by a van with a loudspeaker emblazoned with the declaration that the police were seeking to crush free speech. Attorneys and other spokespeople took turns at the microphone to decry the police action and deliver previews of arguments to be made in court.[1]

After spectators, advocates and the defendant himself settled into the courtroom, the hearing was called to order and three judges ascended the bench. Akio Horikoshi formally identified himself to the court and then it was time for prosecutors to read the indictment. They asserted that Horikoshi had violated Articles 102 and 110 of the National Public Employees Law by distributing political messages "with the goal of supporting the Japan Communist Party" in national elections held on November 9, 2003. The allegation was as expected, along with the potentially onerous penalty: Up to three years in prison and a maximum fine of 100,000 yen.

Courtroom spectators would surely be surprised by other details read out by the prosecutor. The indictment identified three dates: October 19 and 23 and November 3, and specific times and places where prosecutors claimed that Horikoshi had illegally delivered JCP materials. For example, on November 3, the indictment read, "from approximately 10:06 to 10:18 a.m." the defendant distributed political materials at "Harumi Garden Court # 506, 1–7-1 Harumi, Chuo-ku, and 56 other locations." Harumi Garden Court is a high-rise condominium development where a messenger can quickly reach many residences by

DOI: 10.4324/9781003193999-9

dropping materials in mailboxes at a common bank at the building entrance. (Unlike the Tent Village defendants, Horikoshi did not deliver at individual apartments.) Similar details were provided for the other dates.[2]

When defense counsel first saw the indictment, they were amazed at its specificity. Their client *had* confessed to delivering political materials, but this did not explain the precision in dates and times. The police could not have gotten such details from Akio Horikoshi himself. He didn't remember things like that and didn't keep a record. How could the police be so sure that their client appeared at a specific place between "10:06 to 10:18 a.m."?

With the defendant's confession in hand, we might assume the court would decide that all factual disputes had been resolved and discussion could move on to defense challenges to the constitutionality of the police action. But Japan's law of criminal procedure requires prosecutors to present evidence that proves all elements of a crime even in cases like this where a defendant has admitted the facts.[3] What evidence did they have to prove that Horikoshi had appeared at Harumi Garden Court between 10:06 and 10:18 a.m. on November 1, 2003? Horikoshi's physical appearance was that of an ordinary middle-aged man who would blend into any Tokyo crowd. He was just one of many messengers who delivered commercial flyers, newspapers, and other materials in the course of a day. And the police had received no complaints from residents, as in the Tent Village case.

The mystery was solved during a series of pretrial conferences held prior to the July 20 court hearing when prosecutors revealed nine police investigation reports they intended to present as evidence in the upcoming trial. Each report was prepared by officers who had observed the defendant as he made his rounds. The authors were ready to testify that they had themselves seen the defendant make the deliveries.

FIGURE 8.1 Akio Horikoshi speaks before supporters following his first court hearing on July 20, 2004. (Photograph courtesy of *Shimbun Akahata*)

But defense counsel responded that disclosure of these reports selected by the prosecutors was not enough. They repeatedly demanded to see *all* evidence in the prosecutors' hands relevant to the trial. Above all, the nine reports did not answer their most important question: What caused the police to begin their investigation in the first place? What had put them on the trail of Akio Horikoshi?

A Change to the Rules

Disclosure of evidence held by police and prosecutors has long been a source of controversy in Japan. Lawyers in the United States and other jurisdictions expect prosecutors to disclose all relevant evidence in the pretrial "discovery" process to enable the defense to prepare for trial. But this has not been the case in Japan, where the longstanding rule has been that prosecutors are not required to disclose anything other than items they plan to present at trial.[4] In a matter-of-fact fashion, experts say that prosecutors often withhold evidence. As explained by one expert:

> In general, the police and prosecutors have a mass of evidence at their fingertips, but they do not disclose evidence detrimental to their case. Because of this, defendants and attorneys are placed in a highly disadvantageous position in preparing the defense.[5]

Some experts link this problem to the stories of false convictions periodically reported in the press. In extreme cases, defendants convicted in such cases have spent decades in prison before retrials led to their release.[6] Commenting on a series of such cases, one American expert wrote, "all of these miscarriages resulted, at least in part, from prosecutors' failures to disclose potentially exonerating evidence to the defense."[7]

The early 2000s were a time of change for Japan's judicial system. From 1999 through 2001, a 13-member blue-ribbon panel called the "Judicial System Reform Council" examined all aspects of Japan's judicial system in order to define "the role of Japanese administration of justice in the 21st Century."[8] The Council's final report called for a long list of reforms, including some concerned with criminal procedure.

Among the recommendations, the panel proposed a revamped pretrial conference that would more effectively "sort out the contested issues and fix a clear plan for the proceedings in advance of the first trial date." Panel members were especially concerned about charges that prosecutors withheld evidence from defense counsel; their report declared that "rules regarding the timing and scope of the disclosure of evidence should be clearly set forth by law" and that the issue should be dealt with by a new pretrial conference procedure.[9]

On May 21, 2004, just two months before the first hearing in the trial of Akio Horikoshi, the Diet responded by passing revisions to the Code of Criminal

Procedure. One new rule concerning pretrial conferences unambiguously directs courts to order the disclosure of evidence in appropriate cases.[10]

But the ink had barely dried on the reform bill and the new law was not scheduled to take effect until the autumn of 2005. Lawyers and judges had only just begun to study its application. As prosecutors and defense counsel sat down with Judge Yūjirō Nakatani to plan the coming trial, they were bound by the old law that empowered prosecutors to control the evidence to be disclosed. But the attorneys were adamant. They demanded to see the prosecutors' entire file. Most importantly, they sought to learn how the police had singled out their client for surveillance.

In the end, their persistence carried the day. At a closed-door pretrial conference, Judge Nakatani resolved the conflict by proposing that "we follow the spirit of the new rules." Prosecutors protested vigorously, but the judge was unmoved.[11]

The payoff came at the July 20 hearing when it was time for a formal ruling. Prosecutors offered to present as evidence the nine investigators' reports that directly supported the allegations in the indictment. Defense counsel responded by demanding disclosure of all evidence in the government's possession. The judge ordered a compromise. While denying the defense's request for disclosure of everything, he did order disclosure of videos, video reports, and other items related to the nine items offered by prosecutors together with any evidence that might support the defense's claim that the commencement of the investigation and the investigation itself were unlawful. Under this umbrella, Nakatani ordered the disclosure of 29 items.[12]

Although the order covered only a portion of the evidence (one defense lawyer would write that it covered only one-tenth of the prosecutors' cache of evidence),[13] Judge Nakatani had broken through a solid wall that protected secret evidence—and the attorneys would be shocked by what they found. The judge's order was even reported in the national press, an uncommon occurrence for such a technical matter.[14]

Judge Nakatani's order would have a big impact on the case.

Opening Statements by the Defense

With the court's order entered into the record, the hearing moved on to statements from the defense, beginning with a brief message from the defendant himself. He began with the simple declaration that "I am being prosecuted for exercising the ordinary rights of a citizen. This prosecution violates the Constitution and the prosecutors should immediately withdraw the indictment." He also provided a few details from his personal history, emphasizing that his sincere efforts as a public servant had been formally recognized by not one, but two Ministers of Health and Welfare, one with a statement celebrating his 20 years of good service and the second celebrating 30 years. He also reminded the court of the importance of citizen participation in elections in a democratic country. How ironic that his own work to support his chosen candidate led to his arrest.

Then he shared a rather ominous anecdote from his brief time in detention. A prosecutor had told him that he had been "under surveillance for a long time." In the defendant's opinion, this meant that "the government spied on me and violated my privacy." Finally, he came to the inevitable conclusion that his arrest and prosecution were executed "for a political purpose."[15]

The Horikoshi prosecution was a grave matter for the Japan Communist Party, which relies heavily on volunteer distribution of its daily newspaper and other materials. We don't know how many government employees support the JCP or become volunteers like Horikoshi, but Japan's national government employed well over a half million people in 2004, so the number could be considerable.[16] The Horikoshi case might have also had broader significance for the freedom of political speech in general. If the police could arrest him on such a trivial matter, they could find grounds to treat other dissidents the same way. As indicated by the search of multiple offices related to the JCP and the perp walk, the case was a big deal for the government, too. This was more than a standard attack on a political opponent. Aside from any longstanding grudge the police might hold against the JCP, the party's firm stance in support of the antiwar clause of the Constitution, and more seriously, against the constitutionality of the SDF itself, put it at sharp odds with the political establishment. This conflict took on especially great significance when the Koizumi administration deployed SDF contingents to Iraq.

Befitting the importance of a major case, the *Jiyū Hōsōdan* mustered a mass *bengodan* of 28 attorneys working from 13 different offices in the Tokyo area. The lead counsel was Kazuhiko Ishizaki, a senior attorney with more than three decades of experience. The invaluable role of administrative chief was filled by Kenji Kato, more than a decade his junior. At the time, Kato held a senior position in the *Jiyū Hōsōdan*. This was undoubtedly the most important political case that arose on his watch.

After the defendant finished his brief remarks, five members of the defense team delivered a three-hour opening statement relay-style intended to show the prosecution was unlawful and should be dismissed by the court.[17] They started with a very basic question: What is the primary characteristic of this case? The central fact is that the defendant placed political flyers and a political newspaper into mailboxes on his day off. "As an act, this is the simplest of acts, one that anybody can do."

> In Japan today, whether it concerns support for specific political candidates or parties or is part of a campaign to increase the number of child care centers, for countless purposes countless people distribute flyers. For most people, the distribution of flyers is the first and the simplest form of expression.[18]

Everyone agrees that such acts are protected by Article 21 of Japan's Constitution.

"The special characteristic of this case is that acts that do not constitute a crime if performed by ordinary citizens are suddenly transformed into crimes if they are performed by national government employees."[19] Most crimes are immediately apparent—auto theft, sale of illegal drugs, crimes of violence. Any witness would recognize that a crime is in progress. But what about the mailbox delivery of flyers and newspapers? Because this is such an ordinary, everyday act, no one who observed it would think they are witnessing a crime.

Therefore, it is not possible to conclude that the delivery of flyers is a crime merely by observing the act. The police need something more. They need to know that the actor is a government employee. How can they know this? According to defense counsel, the only way they could know that Akio Horikoshi was a government official was by conducting an investigation. Such an investigation of an otherwise law-abiding citizen is an obvious violation of that subject's right to privacy.

After establishing this fundamental point, defense counsel reminded the court that there had been no prosecutions for violating the ban on political activity by government workers since the heavily criticized Supreme Court judgment in the *Sarufutsu* case, 33 years earlier. Why not? Was it because no government employees had engaged in political activities in all that time? Certainly not, according to defense counsel. "Political activities of national government employees range widely, from high-ranking officials who gather votes across the country to others who favor political parties that support labor unions."[20] But there had been no prosecutions for more than three decades.

One reason for the lack of cases, they asserted, was the overwhelming consensus that the Supreme Court's decision in the *Sarufutsu* case was simply wrong. Another reason is that five years *after* that judgment, the Diet ratified an international human rights treaty which creates broad protection for free speech.[21] Defense counsel asserted that the *Sarufutsu* judgment was effectively overruled by the treaty.

They found yet another reason for the lack of prosecution in the history of the statute itself. The National Public Employees Law, along with regulations that designate a long list of proscribed political acts, was a legacy of the early postwar era, created at the direction of the Allied Occupation authorities when they sought to clamp down on political activities. According to defense counsel, due to the unchallengeable authority of Occupation officials, this law "was pushed through the Diet without significant debate." Such an absolute prohibition on political activities remaining from such a radically different time is a preposterous limitation "far from the common beliefs of the people."

In summary, they argued that although the law remained on the books, the prohibition on political activities was invalid, so prosecution raised very serious questions.

One long section of their argument was devoted to a close analysis of the police reports presented as evidence by the prosecution. Each report gave a specific place and time and identified the items that Horikoshi was said to be delivering. The earliest reports were dated October 19. The prosecution disclosed three separate reports for that date, each prepared by a different police team. One indicates that surveillance at Horikoshi's apartment began at 8:30 a.m. with a police team in place prepared to record the suspect's "illegal acts." When he came out, the surveillance team followed and began to video record his movements.

But defense counsel stressed that the reports said nothing to explain why the police chose this time and place and Horikoshi as their target.[22] Obviously, the police had identified him in advance. In fact, they had already gathered much personal detail. Of critical importance, their reports indicated he was a national government employee who worked at the Meguro Social Insurance Office. For some reason, they also had sufficient confidence that he would commit illegal acts that they detailed multiple surveillance teams with video equipment, including at least one team at his home at the start of the day. This was a big operation that had surely been approved at a senior level.

Defense counsel concluded that the investigation of their client was unlawful:

> From these facts, it is clear that the state security police acquired a huge volume of confidential information concerning the defendant and they organized this information and probably created and preserved an individual file on him. Then they used the personal information they gathered to the maximum extent for the arrest and prosecution we see in this case.[23]

Collecting such personal information about an ordinary citizen without good cause is an obvious violation of the privacy rights guaranteed by Article 13 of the Constitution. For the defense, the fine reports by diligent police officers presented as evidence that Horikoshi violated the ban on political activities also proved the gross violation of the privacy rights of an ordinary citizen.[24]

The defense statement was exhaustive, not limited to attacks on the surveillance and arrest of their client. Among other complaints, counsel argued that the prosecution was a political act directed at a specific political party and therefore violated the Constitution's non-discrimination clause (Article 14). The political nature of the operation was shown not only by Horikoshi's surveillance but also by the early morning police raids at six different locations on the morning of his arrests, including the JCP Chiyoda-ku office and the office and home of Katsuhiko Mariko, a JCP member of the Chuo-ku Assembly. Counsel pointed to the police raids and the "confiscation of membership records, computer hard drives and other material from the Chiyoda-ku offices of the JCP," which they said were completely unrelated to the Horikoshi case. They also cited the perp walk, with television news cameras in place to report Horikoshi's arrest, as evidence of the political nature of the action. According to defense counsel, this was an opportunity for the police to curry favor with their sponsors in the government and the business world who also viewed the JCP as an enemy.

Counsel concluded that this was not ordinary police work. The police did not act with the intention of uncovering their client's actions in order to bring him to justice. Instead, this was a surveillance operation whose real purpose was to gather information on the JCP. The arrest of Akio Horikoshi simply provided the pretext for a dawn raid and the confiscation of a large volume of JCP information. The entire operation was an extension of police surveillance of the JCP.

Such an operation would only be conducted by a special arm of the police known as the "state security police," charged with defending the state against potential political crimes. At this point, defense counsel lectured the court on the history and organization of the state security police, including their report on an infamous case where they had been caught tapping the phones of senior JCP officials.[25]

Although the Tent Village and Horikoshi cases both concerned the prosecution of individuals for alleged crimes related to distributing political flyers, there were many differences. The alleged crimes were different. The suspects' responses were different. While the Tent Village suspects maintained a rock wall of silence in the face of police questioning, Akio Horikoshi immediately confessed and was quickly released. Then there was the question of support. The Tent Village suspects were members of a tiny local citizens group who scrambled to gather an ad hoc group of supporters. By contrast, Horikoshi was a member of a national organization with millions of followers. For him, there would never be a shortage of people to attend court hearings or public rallies.[26] And even if the mainstream news media looked the other way, trial progress would be reported in detail in the JCP newspaper, the *Akahata* ("Red Flag"), which printed several million copies daily. Of greatest importance, Akio Horikoshi would be represented by attorneys from the *Jiyū Hōsōdan*, a national network of 2,000 members with roots going back to the prewar era.

In the Tent Village case, Judge Hasegawa declared at the very outset that he wanted to move at a fast pace and deliver an early judgment. There was no such prospect in the trial of Akio Horikoshi. His trial represented a major conflict between the JCP and the state security police. There were many witnesses to be called and many legal arguments to address. The case would go on for years.

9

TRIAL AT HACHIOJI: THE GOVERNMENT CASE

(June–July 2004)

The second court hearing in the trial of the Tent Village defendants did not take place until nearly a month had passed since their release from custody. This was not unusual. Japan's criminal trials ordinarily proceed through multiple sessions separated by a month or more. This enables attorneys, prosecutors, and judges to handle many cases simultaneously, doing their best to allocate sufficient time to prepare for court sessions in each case. Because Japan's system does not rely on American-style citizen juries empaneled from start to finish, there is no particular need for concentrated trials that continue from one day to the next.[1] In fact, back in April chief judge Hasegawa notified the advocates that he wanted a *fast* trial, with the goal of delivering a judgment by October. In cases where defendants contest their charges, Japan's staggered hearing approach tends to produce lengthy trials. If Hasegawa succeeded, he might have broken the speed record for a case like this.

In every criminal case, the government bears the burden to prove guilt. In the Tent Village case, the prosecutors were required to prove all the elements required by Article 130 of Japan's criminal code, which punishes "A person who, without just cause (*seitō na riyū*), trespasses into a residence of another person or into the premises, building or vessel guarded by another person, or who refuses to leave such a place." Thus, the prosecutors would have to prove that (1) the defendants "trespassed" into a personal residence or a "guarded space" and (2) they had no "just cause." If they succeeded, the penalty could be severe, including imprisonment for up to three years.[2]

At the May 6 hearing prosecutors asserted that the repeated visits of the Tent Village messengers had disrupted the "peaceful daily life" of the residents. Although these words do not appear in Article 130, a key Supreme Court precedent had held that even when individuals enter a private space without an invitation, if there is no harm to "peaceful daily life," there is no crime under Article

DOI: 10.4324/9781003193999-10

130.[3] The prosecutors also asserted the defendants had violated the "managerial rights" of building managers. The distinction between the respective rights of residents and managers would later take on great significance.

Whether Self-Defense Force residents or managers had actually suffered harm was a question of fact unlikely to be resolved by documentary evidence alone. Any trier of fact would want to hear the direct testimony of live witnesses who could support these claims. The government selected three witnesses for this role.[4] Of the three, two served as managers of the apartment buildings and the third was the resident who had confronted defendant Toshiyuki Obora at his building on the afternoon of January 17. Under Judge Hasegawa's expedited schedule, they would testify on June 3, June 17, and July 8.

June 3 Hearing (Second Public Court Session)

Tachikawa is home to operations of both the Ground SDF and the Air SDF, and members of both branches resided in the buildings targeted by Tent Village. The first witness was a GSDF officer ("GSDF Officer A") who appeared on June 3. He managed four buildings (Buildings 5–8) and his testimony was critical because his actions laid the foundation for the arrests of the three activists two months later. In response to prosecutors' questions on direct examination, he testified that after the third Tent Village flyer appeared in mail slots on December 13, he consulted with his superior officer and then took a course of action designed to stop the flyers. His plan involved three separate measures. First, he posted warnings against uninvited visitors at the entrances to his buildings and other locations on the property. Second, he made a complaint to the police. Finally, he distributed a memorandum to all residents instructing them to immediately contact the police and SDF management if they observed any "anti-SDF flyers" or persons distributing such flyers.[5]

GSDF Officer A was himself a resident and he testified that the flyers were a terrible nuisance and that he felt a "sense of anxiety and danger" due to the flyers. When a prosecutor asked about the significance of the flyers, he responded that "if the court does not punish the defendants, this would affect not only the Tachikawa residents, but SDF residents all over Japan."[6] This suggestion that there was more at stake than tranquility in Tachikawa was matched by comments from a prosecutor published in the *Mainichi Shimbun* that evening who said, "We also had the goal of preventing crimes by other groups that may engage in illegal activity."[7] His words seemed to confirm that the chilling effect generated by arrests and detentions on trivial charges like distributing flyers was not an accident but was actually the intended result of the Tachikawa arrests. The defendants and their supporters would refer to this comment at every opportunity.

GSDF Officer A had made two complaints to the police, one on December 22, triggered by the Tent Village flyer of December 13, and the other on January 23, following the January 17 flyer. Attorney Akio Kotō began his cross-examination by asking about the January complaint. "Did you contact the Tachikawa police *before* filing the complaint on January 23?" he asked. The witness responded that he did. "Did someone from the police come to see you before January 23?" he asked. When the witness admitted this was also true, Kotō responded by asking whether the police had instructed him to file the complaint. When he admitted this, several audible gasps arose from the spectators. A key issue before the court was what had motivated this man to file a formal report with the police. The court just learned that it was suggested by the police themselves.[8]

Having established police involvement in the January complaint, Attorney Kotō moved to the first complaint, filed on December 22. Did the police request this one as well? The witness admitted that they did. Kotō pressed on. "Did a police officer write the complaint for you?" This was also true. Kotō finally elicited the admission that the complaint had been typed on a police office word processor and presented to the witness so that all he had to do was sign.[9] Thus, Kotō neatly planted the suggestion that perhaps it was the police rather than the SDF residents who were most disturbed by the flyers.

Now defense counsel Uchida took over the cross-examination and shifted the focus to another important issue. "It's your understanding," he said, "that anti-Self Defense Force flyers injure the 'peaceful daily life' of the residents, correct?" After the witness agreed, Uchida asked whether flyers from pizza shops and other local businesses that frequently appeared in residents' mail slots also caused such injury. The witness said they were a nuisance, but they did not disturb the residents like the anti-SDF flyers did.

At this point, the youngest of the three judges, 30-year-old Judge Wakana Suzuki, intervened. As a building manager, GSDF Officer A would naturally have contact with many residents and was therefore in a good position to learn how they were affected by the flyers. His testimony could help the court determine whether the catalyst for the witness's complaint came from the residents or from the police. Judge Suzuki posed a critical question: Had the witness ever received complaints about the Tent Village flyers from residents? When the witness replied that he did, the Judge proceeded with the natural follow-up: What were the details of these complaints? Inexplicably, the witness lost the thread, saying that he did not remember any details.[10] Due to his faulty memory, the prosecutors missed a good opportunity to persuade the court that the flyers posed a serious problem.

Next, Attorney Uchida approached the witness to show him a copy of one of the warnings he had posted around the property and asked him to point out the specific prohibitions violated by the Tent Village messengers. When he did, Uchida read out the selected text. "'Entry by any unauthorized person onto the property, any solicitations including handing out or otherwise distributing flyers, and any other act which causes a nuisance' correct?" The witness confirmed that these were the key words. "If so," the defense counsel asked, "doesn't the same prohibition apply to pizza flyers?" Of course it did, but the witness confirmed that he had never filed a police complaint against the pizza man or others who had stuffed their flyers into the mail slots.

FIGURE 9.1 Defense counsel addressed Tent Village supporters after each hearing. Here Attorney Akio Kotō comments on the trial developments after the second hearing on June 3, 2004. (Photograph by Toshiyuki Obora)

The defense had established a clear record on a crucial point. Among the many unauthorized messengers who climbed the stairs of the SDF apartments, the witness complained only about Tent Village. Moreover, he was acting under police direction when he did so. Constitutional scholars might call this "selective enforcement of the law." In this case, the police directed their action solely at critics of the government.

And what did the witness know about these dissidents? Before he was done, Uchida also elicited the admission that the witness knew of the existence of Tent Village because of their marches and demonstrations and the flyers they handed out and that he had never heard that Tent Village engaged in violence.[11]

June 17 Hearing (Third Public Court Session)

The second witness for the prosecution was an ASDF officer ("ASDF Officer B") who served as the manager of another group of SDF apartment buildings, numbered 1–4. He was not a resident of the Tachikawa complex, so he didn't learn of the December 13 flyer until a few days later when his superior told him of a resident's complaint. In direct testimony at the third trial hearing on June 17, he said that he followed the same procedure as the preceding witness, placing warnings against trespassing at his buildings, notifying residents to contact him or the police if they saw any suspicious visitors with anti-SDF flyers, and finally contacting the police himself on December 22, the same day as the preceding witness. He also applied his signature and personal seal to a complaint form prepared by the police. He filed a similar complaint about a month later, in response to the January flyer. Again, the complaint was prepared by the police.[12]

Regarding the content of the flyer, in cross-examination Attorney Uchida asked what part of the January flyer the witness found to be "anti-SDF." The witness responded that it criticized SDF activities, including the deployment to Iraq. When Uchida asked whether he knew that there were differences of opinion in the country regarding the Iraq deployment and many people opposed it, the witness responded that, whether or not opinion is divided, it's up to the Diet to decide. At this point, Judge Hasegawa cut in. "Are you aware that the Iraq deployment was debated in the Diet and that some members are opposed?" he asked. The witness quietly acknowledged that he did. Uchida pressed on by showing the witness evidence of widespread opposition to the deployment, including news reports of public opinion polls and quotations from former SDF officers who expressed opposition, thereby showing that by expressing its opposition to the deployment, the Tent Village was not espousing a radical or even unusual opinion.[13] In fact, Tent Village views fit within the mainstream.

The flyers clearly identified Tent Village as the author and provided the address and phone number. Uchida asked ASDF Officer B why he didn't call Tent Village directly to complain. "The warnings I posted had no effect," he said. "I didn't think a telephone call would make any difference either." Then he

FIGURE 9.2 Attorney Masatoshi Uchida had no contact with Tent Village prior to the arrests. He quickly impressed members with his grasp of the broad political significance of the case. (Photograph by Toshiyuki Obora, October 2004)

added a slightly sinister twist. "And I was afraid they might take a bit of something I said and publicize it."[14]

Why was there no call? The Tent Village phone number was featured prominently on the flyers; in fact, the very purpose of the flyers was to solicit phone calls and create opportunities to discuss the Iraq deployment with SDF personnel. Unfortunately, ASDF Officer B was not the best person to explain why no one made the call. From his standpoint, calling the police for help or advice might have seemed like a reasonable course of action. Uchida's question would be better addressed to the police official who authorized the early morning raids and the arrests. Why didn't the *police* telephone—or visit—the Tent Village office to discuss the flyer deliveries? The police could have instructed the Tent Village messengers to stop. They could have explained their view of the law and threatened the messengers with arrest if they didn't stop. But the police did not contact the Tent Village. Instead, they requested the SDF officers to sign formal complaints. Then, rather than directly acting on those complaints, the police appended them to requests for the judicial warrants that empowered them to search the homes of Tent Village members and haul three of them off to jail.

But there were no police officials called to the witness stand, so the best defense counsel could do was to pose these questions to the ASDF officer.

Antiwar Rally in Shibuya

As witnesses testified in Hachioji, others were protesting Japan's participation in the Iraq War on the streets. A July 4 antiwar rally organized by a network of antiwar groups called "World Peace Now" provoked an especially aggressive police response, including three arrests. The rally was timed to occur one week prior to the House of Councilors elections, with speakers calling on the crowd to vote for candidates who opposed the war. According to a report by Japan's national bar association, approximately 2,000 riot police surrounded about 1,200 marchers when they departed on a scheduled parade on public streets and police taunting led to confrontations and arrests. The police response stoked the anger of leaders of the antiwar movement. Ken Takada, a key World Peace Now organizer, complained bitterly about the mistreatment of Shibuya protesters at a press conference held at national Diet offices on July 13. The highlight of his presentation was a five-minute video that showed police kicking protesters and dragging a handcuffed and shirtless man on the pavement.[15] As he spoke, three protesters arrested at the event remained in police detention. They would be released 11 days after the arrests and not charged with any crimes.

July 8 Hearing (Fourth Public Court Session)

The third and final prosecution witness, ASDF Officer C, appeared in court on Thursday, July 8. Unlike the others, he was not a building manager, but a resident who occupied an apartment on the fourth and highest floor of his building.

In direct testimony, he confirmed that he had received Tent Village flyers on five occasions and, feeling some unease about their message, reported them to his superior. And he had done more. It was ASDF Officer C who confronted defendant Obora as he was delivering the flyers on Saturday, January 17. When he heard the flap of his mail slot as the Tent Village flyer came through, he quickly went out onto the landing and, peering down, saw Obora distributing a flyer on a floor below and Sachimi Takada waiting with a bicycle at the side of the building. Following instructions, the witness quickly called the police hotline to let them know the antiwar protesters were back. Then he went down the stairs and caught up with Obora on the ground floor of the building. Pointing to a message board, he said that distributing flyers was prohibited at the building and engaged in the brief conversation that ended with Obora's departure.[16]

The witness seemed well prepared for his testimony. Why did he feel unease at the flyers? He found the message that SDF members might "kill people in Iraq" especially disturbing because there were families with small children in the apartments and parents would be hard-pressed to explain such a message to them. And unlike the first witness, who told the court that he was aware of Tent Village activities and didn't think the group was dangerous, ASDF Officer C said he knew nothing about Tent Village or what they were about. In response to a prosecutor's question about his fears, he said there was no telling when the situation "might escalate and lead to white powder" coming through the mail slots.[17] This reference to anthrax or some other lethal poison was the most startling testimony delivered by the prosecution. Residents relied on building managers to provide security by posting warnings and taking other measures to keep dangers from their doors. For him, the uninvited visitors posed a potentially serious threat.

After a short break, Attorney Kojima started cross-examination for the defense. Regarding other messengers who had appeared at his door, the witness said that he received a religious flyer a few Sundays ago and that he told the messenger to stop. He didn't think it necessary to call the police or otherwise complain about the religious flyer. Despite this unexpected visitor, the witness suggested that the warnings posted around the property were having some effect because the amount of materials coming through his mail slot had declined. As for his mailbox at the central bank on the ground floor, the witness said he just rolled up the items he found there and dropped them in the trash without reading them. When Kojima asked him what he thought of the arrests, he said this was a matter for the courts and that he had no particular opinion.[18]

The final government witness delivered a strong message and then easily deflected the cross-examination. Like SDF personnel, Japan's judges reside in housing provided by the state. Maybe as they returned home that night they would think about the security around their own apartments and wonder if someone might come by with a sprinkling of "white powder."

Less than a decade had passed since the horrifying spread of deadly sarin gas at mid-day in subway trains running beneath central Tokyo. Thirteen people were killed that day in the attack by members of a doomsday cult and more than 5,000 sickened. Images of masses of commuters streaming from subway exits and bodies on stretchers carried to hastily assembled emergency vehicles were etched in the minds of all Tokyoites. Although the police had long since arrested most of the leaders, a few escaped and as of July 2004, were still at large. Their photos remained posted at police boxes around the city. And all Japanese were jolted by a stark reminder of the horrifying event when Tokyo District Court ordered the cult leader to be put to death. By an odd coincidence, the court announced the order on February 27, the same day as the Tent Village arrests.[19]

The July 8 hearing was the final court session before Tokyo descended into the trough of the hot and humid summer. Three days later, Japanese voters went to the polls to elect candidates to the House of Councilors, the "upper house" of the Diet. Despite the unpopularity of the Iraq deployment, Prime Minister Koizumi's LDP lost just two seats and his ruling coalition maintained control of the chamber. Opposition parties attacked the ruling coalition for the Iraq deployment and for Koizumi's reported promise to U.S. President George W. Bush to keep Japan's Self-Defense Forces in Iraq as part of a U.N.-sponsored multinational peacekeeping force. For most voters, however, the top issue was not the distant Iraq War, but a pocketbook issue of more immediate concern: Reform of the national pension system.[20]

Expanding Government Surveillance

The Tent Village case attracted new attention the following week with the publication of the August issue of the popular legal journal *Hōgaku Seminar* ("Legal Studies Seminar"). Manabu Ishizaki, co-author of the scholars' declaration that appeared immediately after the arrests, served as chair of a mini-symposium that featured three articles on the Tent Village and Horikoshi cases. Why pair two cases of arrests based on very different statutes? Aside from the fact that both concerned the delivery of political flyers to residential addresses, Ishizaki explained that he was especially concerned about police tactics. In both cases, arrests were made not at the scene but were based on warrants issued long after the alleged violations, and in both cases police SWAT teams made dawn raids and confiscated personal computers and other materials. Such tactics, especially the searches and seizures, went far beyond the requirements for two cases that concerned rather trivial threats to public safety.

Ishizaki suggested that the aggressive police action was but one manifestation of a broader trend. He cited the recent adoption of local "safety of daily life" ordinances (*seikatsu anzen jōrei*) that sought to enlist the cooperation of citizens in fighting crime in their neighborhoods. For observers like Ishizaki such campaigns, incited by sensational crime reporting in the news and public relations efforts by the police, needlessly promoted public hysteria.[21] He also cited the installation of countless surveillance cameras by public and private bodies as evidence of great anxiety across the land. In the early 2000s, many legal scholars and other writers echoed these sentiments. They said Japan was moving in the direction of a society that featured less freedom and greater police power. This startling turn was initiated by conservative political leaders who discarded longstanding taboos to pass 1999 legislation that expanded government surveillance power. That year the Diet formally authorized police wiretapping for the first time and adopted Japan's first citizen numbering system, long feared as a tool that government agents might use to monitor people they don't like.[22]

The specter of even more surveillance tools appeared on the horizon. In response to widespread fear over the theft and improper use of individual information in the hands of government agencies and commercial organizations, the Koizumi Administration proposed legislation to improve information security. But an initial draft bill leaked to the press would grant government investigators so much power that it incited an uproar at bar associations, news organizations, and among public intellectuals. The most shocking proposal would empower government agents to enter newsrooms to check whether reporters followed the rules. An April 2002 statement of the Japan Newspaper Publishers and Editors Association summarized the opponents' position: The proposals would "pave the way for government intervention in the freedom of speech guaranteed by the Constitution."[23]

But the government initiative was stopped in its tracks by a scandal that clearly showed what was at stake. In a rare move toward improving government transparency, the Diet passed a national information disclosure law that took effect in April 2001. Just a year later, however, on May 28, 2002, the front page of the *Mainichi Shimbun* carried the stunning news that officials in the Defense Agency and all three branches of the Self-Defense Forces investigated individuals who had exercised the new right to seek documents in their files. A law intended to enable citizens to monitor the government had been converted into a government surveillance tool. The blowback from this revelation was so severe that opposition political parties boycotted Diet proceedings and the government was forced to abandon its information protection program and settle for a sharply downsized law a year later.[24]

Clearly, the Tent Village and Horikoshi arrests had not occurred in a vacuum. The contentious environment was shaped not only by the constitutional dispute over deploying troops to a war zone but also by the government's campaign to expand police surveillance powers. In Ishizaki's opinion, the country was already blanketed by a plethora of rules that had shrunk the "public space" for political speech. He also expressed fear over what the arrests meant for the future. The Tent Village and Horikoshi cases showed the police acting against individuals who delivered their messages door-to-door. The professor foresaw that surveillance cameras everywhere would train their lenses on people like them and label them "suspicious characters."[25]

Finally, he pointed to the prosecutor's declaration to *Mainichi* reporters that the targets of the Tent Village arrests were not limited to Tachikawa but extended to "preventing crimes by other groups." The arrests and long detentions of harmless peace activists suggested the country was at a turning point.[26]

The law journal collection appeared just as defense counsel and prosecutors worked on final arguments that would soon be made in court. The articles would be seen not only by the thousands of readers of the popular journal but also by advocates in the Tent Village case. Perhaps they would even be read by the three judges with power to determine the fate of the Tent Village defendants.[27]

10

TRIAL AT HACHIOJI: DEFENSE WITNESSES

(September 2004)

There were no Tent Village trial sessions in August, but Judge Hasegawa and his colleagues had something else in mind. Their appetite for the facts was not satisfied by the arguments of lawyers or even the testimony of live witnesses. They also wanted to inspect the actual site of the flyer deliveries.[1] By placing themselves at the "scene of the crime," they might be able to get a real sense of the threat posed by intruders with antiwar flyers and the fears of the residents.

On August 16, another extremely hot day in Tokyo, a crowd of about 25 people, including the judges and their clerks, the prosecutors and defense counsel, and the defendants themselves, trekked to the SDF apartment buildings on the eastern edge of Tachikawa, near the city's border with Kunitachi.[2] There the judges examined the walkways and the warnings posted at building entrances and the defendants climbed the stairs of the buildings and made a pantomime of their actual flyer deliveries.

After the on-site inspection, the trial went into a hiatus of another three weeks. When the trial resumed on September 9, two months had passed since the last courtroom session.

September 9 Hearing (Fifth Public Court Session)

On September 9 counsel began their formal presentation of the defense with a 26-page opening statement. The main points struck familiar themes: With the country divided over the legality of the SDF deployment, the Tent Village messages were within the mainstream of political discussion in Japan; Tent Village members and others had been distributing flyers in this way for decades; a guilty verdict would not only penalize Tent Village and send a chilling effect throughout the country but would also block SDF members and their families from receiving meaningful political communications.

DOI: 10.4324/9781003193999-11

Finally, the September 9 statement reached its inevitable conclusion that the police action had nothing to do with protecting the "peaceful daily lives" of the residents. Instead, it was clearly political suppression intended to silence antiwar groups in the face of the unprecedented SDF deployment to an active war zone.[3]

The judges were quite familiar with such theoretical arguments, but they remained hungry for facts. In their search for the facts, the judges had signaled their desire to learn more about the history and activities of the odd little group called "Tent Village."[4] The defendants must have made a strong impression. For years, they had shown a resolute determination to deliver their political message through flyers, public demonstrations, and other means. Under arrest, they had demonstrated the strength to maintain silence while enduring many weeks of abusive police interrogation. Finally, when at last they had the chance, they delivered spirited and high-minded defenses of their actions in court. They had nine lives. The judges sought to uncover the source of this tenacity. Commitment like this suggested possible membership in an extreme organization like a religious cult, a radical fringe group, or maybe the Communist Party.

But the defendants did not repeat the slogans of communists or radicals—they spoke the words of democracy and peace, the central tenets of Japan's Constitution. Anyone searching for a mysterious or nefarious motive behind Tent Village activism would be sorely disappointed by the Tent Village story of a few activists whose antiwar agenda was rooted in the desperate struggle of local residents who fought to protect their homes from expropriation by the overwhelming force of a distant government. For decades the Tent Village had operated in the open and its agenda was clear. There was no evidence that members advocated violence.

The court wanted to hear the defendants tell their stories in their own words, so each of the defendants prepared to appear on the witness stand to testify, subject to questions from the bench and cross-examination by the prosecutors.[5] But before the defendants addressed the court themselves, their counsel requested court approval to call three other witnesses: A celebrated constitutional scholar, a retired LDP politician, and Yutaka Osawa. The prosecutors objected to all three. Ordinarily, courts will approve the testimony only of individuals with some direct knowledge of the events at issue or, in some cases, experts in technical matters. On this standard, none of the witnesses qualified. Among them, only Osawa could be considered a possible witness to the facts, but even he was not directly involved in making or delivering the flyers and he was not even a formal member of Tent Village. Despite their lack of direct knowledge of the events, the court approved all three.[6]

Professor Okudaira's Testimony

The first to testify was Yasuhiro Okudaira, Japan's most celebrated expert on the right to freedom of speech. Okudaira was born in Hakodate on the northern island of Hokkaido in 1929 and entered the University of Tokyo as a freshman in 1950, seven years before Katsuko Kato. He was in the first wave of Japanese scholars to begin their studies under Japan's postwar Constitution. As a student and then a young scholar in the 1950s, he grappled with the fundamentals of the 1947 "Peace Constitution" that accomplished a revolution, replacing a legal system based on the will of a divine monarch with a radically different system founded on popular sovereignty. Dissatisfied with senior scholars' efforts to reconcile lifetimes of study under the old system with Japan's new constitutional democracy, he applied to study in the United States. In the 1950s, Japan was fighting its way out of the poverty left by the utter devastation of the war years; opportunities to study abroad were scarce. Among other challenges, access to foreign currency was limited. But Okudaira's application was accepted and he began studies at the University of Pennsylvania Law School in the fall of 1959, the first Japanese to study there after the war.[7] He returned to Japan two years later and in the decades to follow compiled a record of research and writing that earned him the exalted status of one of Japan's most prolific and respected constitutional scholars.[8]

There is no doubt that Okudaira held deep sympathy for the plight of the Tent Village defendants and others in the antiwar movement. This sympathy was rooted in his own commitment to peace and his fear of unlimited government power.[9] Like Kato Katsuko and others of their generation, Okudaira's gruesome war memories were deeply imprinted. In a memoir, he recalled that in his student days

> There was one problem that never left my mind. With a single slip of red paper, the state could draft people into military service and send them off to war. Their death in battle would be a source of glory. What was this "state"? What was the source of its power? When I was a child, men that I knew were taken away with a single slip of red paper. And I saw that when they died in battle, only their bones returned home. Yes, the state held immense power.[10]

He was driven to study the Constitution because "Constitutions were made to restrain this power. Little by little, I learned that something called fundamental human rights served to restrain the state."

Okudaira quickly accepted Narisawa's request to sign on to the scholars' declaration back in March and then took on much greater responsibility when he agreed to testify on their behalf in court. Defense counsel who met with him at a mountain resort in late August found that he had been thinking deeply about the case and planned to make a strong statement in court. Of course, the purpose of his testimony was to bolster defense claims for protection under the free speech provision of the Constitution.

FIGURE 10.1 University of Tokyo Emeritus Professor Yasuhiro Okudaira, Japan's most celebrated expert in the law of free speech, testified on behalf of the Tent Village defendants. (Photograph by Toshiyuki Obora, April 2005)

Attorney Shizu Yamamoto, the most junior member of the defense team, conducted his examination. She began by posing a series of questions calculated to lead the court step-by-step through a constitutional analysis: Did he think that free speech enjoys a "preferred position" under Japan's Constitution? If so, how would that affect the court's analysis and decision regarding constitutional protection for the defendants' actions? How should a court balance free speech protection against the right of the residents to enjoy peaceful daily lives? What was the significance of blocking the SDF members' access to Tent Village messages? What effect did he think the prosecution might have on other citizen groups? There were other basic questions like these.

The old scholar patiently responded to these questions with explanations that had become orthodoxy in Japan in the early 21st century and in most constitutional democracies of the world: Yes, the right to free speech was really important and it lies at the foundation of democratic society. The notion of a "preferred position" means that the government can limit speech only in the most extreme cases. Courts should certainly consider the rights of people in their homes to be free of nuisances, but they must also consider the rights to communicate and to receive communications.

Notes from courtroom spectators do not record the reactions of the three judges, but one suspects that they nodded off from time to time during this stretch of the testimony. The witness was simply reciting generalities that could be found in any textbook on constitutional law in Japan.

After this went on for half an hour or so, Attorney Yamamoto changed direction by asking whether arrests followed by detentions as long as

75 days and prosecutions "might have an effect on the right to free speech, not only on the defendants, but on the people in general?"

"I think so," he responded

> because you see trespass is a prime example of a matter for the general criminal law. If applying such general laws to cases like this becomes routine, it means not only that punishing such acts becomes routine, but also that police action, with interrogations and then indictments, with very broad investigations, or as you point out, extremely long detentions, could follow.

Regarding the political effect of such a regime, he said, "If the law is managed in a way with a very strong political coloration … it would not only be the detention of certain people, it would have a huge effect on others around them."[11]

If this became the new normal in Japan, Okudaira feared that such aggressive application of criminal law would *not* be limited to allegations of trespass. He explained that

> All kinds of matters could lead to crackdowns and arrests. There could be arrests followed by investigations that cast a broad net around suspects. In other words, forgive me for expanding the scope of the discussion, but I have done much study of the Peace Preservation Law. This would be just like cases prosecuted under the Peace Preservation Law in the prewar period.

The dreaded words "Peace Preservation Law" sent a shockwave through the courtroom. First adopted in 1925 and later revised to mandate even tighter restrictions including the death penalty, the law made it a crime to hold beliefs incompatible with the *kokutai*, the doctrine that Japan is a unique society led by a divine monarch.[12] It empowered the authoritarian police of the prewar and wartime eras to arrest and imprison political dissidents. It was an ideal tool for an authoritarian government to silence its critics.

The judges and lawyers he faced in the courtroom in September 2004 had grown up in postwar Japan. They had been taught that the door to the country's past as a police state had been firmly closed by the 1947 Constitution and other laws adopted to protect the people from the abuse of police power. Now their witness suggested that door might open. Professor Okudaira was not only the nation's best-known expert on the law of free speech; he had also researched and written a definitive history of this repressive law at the heart of that dark chapter in Japan's modern history.[13] The judges and lawyers were well aware of the standing of the celebrated scholar who spoke these words. In a sense, they were all his students.

Attorney Yamamoto requested the witness to explain what he meant when he said cases processed under Japan's current laws could be "just like" the Peace Preservation Law.

> I mean a process where individuals were arrested, prosecuted, found guilty, and imprisoned. The decision to prosecute was a secondary matter. The accepted practice was one of searching for reasons to arrest and for reasons to place individuals in detention while swirling them round and round through the system .... People think that those were the days of the Meiji Constitution and we don't have that anymore. And I also believe that it would be no simple matter to return to the past.

"In my understanding of modern Japan," he continued

> to pass special criminal statutes like the Peace Preservation Law, the Peace Preservation Police Law and others would be extremely difficult. We would have to consider their relationship to the Constitution and it would take great political power. Therefore, today the police must act under the ordinary criminal law. The ordinary criminal law exists in order to protect social order for ordinary citizens. This system to protect the social order could be turned around to manufacture criminal acts. In the future it is very possible that these developments could be controlled in a way to suit the state security police. Look at the present case. It clearly shows that just because we haven't seen these things yet, doesn't mean we won't see them in the future.

Was the old scholar spinning some sensational science fiction plot inspired by a writer like Orwell or Huxley? Was it really possible that Japan's police could easily disregard the protections so carefully laid out in the Constitution in order to "manufacture criminal acts"?

"Some might say that I'm a very old man and so I imagine these groundless fears," he said. "But for a constitutional scholar, this is a serious matter. It is our job to think about the steps to take in order to prevent such fears from becoming reality."

The witness had quietly converted the discussion of an abstract concept like free speech into the very concrete topic of abuse of police power.

Then Attorney Yamamoto picked up the theme of "other" provisions of the general criminal law and suggested that Okudaira's prophesy of similar political use of other provisions of the general criminal law had already come to pass.

"I'd like to ask about some specific cases," she said.

> For example, someone got into an argument in front of the U.S. Embassy and was then charged with the crime of assault. This was followed by a police search of that person's home. In another case, an employee of the

> Health Ministry distributed political flyers near his home on his day off and was arrested for violating the National Public Employees Law.

What did the scholar think about cases like these?

> These days they can't crack down on political acts with specific political motivations based on special criminal statutes, so they use things like the crime of assault or Article 14(7) of the National Public Employees Law. These are general statutes. They use these general rules for indictments and after arrests there are lengthy detentions. They can confiscate computers and gather information on a very large number of people . ... Even though there is no Peace Preservation Law, a new, modern *something* can arise that could be very similar.[14]

With this, the direct testimony came to an end. There was a brief cross-examination by the prosecution in which Okudaira confirmed that he did not directly participate in any of the events and was not a witness to the facts of the case.

Like his explication of the constitutional status of free speech, Okudaira's declaration of his fears was not unusual. Similar fears resided in the breast of nearly every scholar who had chosen the path of constitutional studies. Back in March when a couple of young scholars were inspired to draft a declaration condemning the Tent Village arrests, they gathered the signatures of 56 more senior colleagues within a few days. To one degree or another, they all shared the same fear and sense of crisis. After all, the revolutionary declarations of the 1947 Constitution were just words. The grave danger that would arise if the authorities chose not to follow those words could be seen most clearly by comparing them against the reality of what had come before. Due to his personal history and memories of the war years, Okudaira's fears had very deep roots.

An Unlikely Ally

The professor was followed by a man who was unquestionably the most surprising witness to appear in the Tent Village trial. Noboru Minowa was a retired LDP politician and one-time Cabinet member. Born and raised on the northern island of Hokkaido, he had been elected to the national Diet eight times and served for 23 years before retiring in 1990. Minowa was a respected expert on national security issues and was appointed to the second highest position in the Defense Agency by Prime Minister Kakuei Tanaka in October 1972.[15]

In a sense, Minowa was a witness to the facts of this case. He had never actually met any members of the Tent Village or even seen their flyers until shown them by defense counsel, but he had played a tangential but important role in triggering the formation of the group. It was Minowa himself who had traveled to Tachikawa in November 1972 to inform the mayor and other officials that the land occupied by the American military would not be returned to civilian use; instead, it would become the home of a Self-Defense Forces base and other government buildings.[16] It was this decision that led to the creation of the Tent Village, dedicated to monitoring and protesting the operations of Japan's Self-Defense Forces in their town.

Now, more than 30 years later, Minowa was 80 years old. Frail and mobile only with the aid of a cane or wheelchair, he returned to Tachikawa to testify in support of three members of the tiny group that had opposed the Self-Defense Forces ever since he welcomed their deployment to Tachikawa in 1972.

After reading the old man's personal history into the court record, Attorney Uchida referred to a recent newspaper article. "According to this column in the August 10 edition of the *Asahi*, you filed suit in Hokkaido in January of this year seeking a judgment that declares the SDF Iraq deployment unconstitutional. Is that correct?"

The witness confirmed that it was true and in the exchange that followed described his attempts to contact the Prime Minister and other former colleagues in the Diet in order to tell them to stop the Iraq deployment because it violated the Constitution. When they ignored him, he decided that filing suit was the only way he could get their attention.

Noboru Minowa was the last person anyone would expect to challenge Japan's defense policy or testify on behalf of antiwar activists. Throughout his career, he was known as a national defense hawk who repeatedly called for increased funding for the Self-Defense Forces. Resolute support from political leaders like him enabled Japan to develop one of the most sophisticated militaries in the world, despite the unstinting language of Article 9. To show his patriotic fervor, Minowa insisted on prominently displaying Japan's national flag whenever his photo was taken. But he was absolutely certain in his conviction that the Iraq deployment was unconstitutional. A passage in his complaint set out his position:

FIGURE 10.2 Noboru Minowa was the most surprising witness to testify for the Tent Village defendants. He addressed supporters alongside Attorney Masatoshi Uchida on September 9, 2004. (Photograph by Katsuko Kato)

> For decades, the government has consistently espoused the "exclusively self-defense" constitutional interpretation regarding the Self-Defense Forces, that strength at the minimum level necessary for Japan's self-defense is constitutional. Based on this position, for the SDF to go to the territory of a foreign country and use force there even though there is no act of aggression by that country against Japan, is completely unthinkable. Accordingly, the deployment … is a clear violation of Constitution Article 9.[17]

A court challenge against the government on a matter of national defense was no small matter, especially for a man who had spent his entire career defending the SDF. When Uchida asked whether Minowa had found much support for his action, he told the court that 109 attorneys, fully one-quarter of all attorneys registered in Hokkaido, volunteered to represent him, that he had received countless phone calls and messages in support, and that he was much sought after as a public speaker. The old man had appeared at some 20 venues around the country so far, wheelchair and all, to talk about the Iraq deployment, the Constitution, and why he had filed suit.

Prosecutors had opposed Minowa's testimony on the ground that it was not relevant to charges of trespass, but Judge Hasegawa allowed the testimony to go forward. It would surely bolster defense claims that there was nothing particularly unusual about the messages carried to the homes of the SDF members in Tachikawa. Those messages matched the beliefs of a man who had outranked them all during his time as the number two official in Japan's Defense Agency.

Attorney Uchida sought historical context for Minowa's lawsuit and the present conflict over the Iraq deployment. "Based on your long experience," he asked, "when you consider the Iraq deployment, what are the important issues?" Here Minowa provided some history.

> Exactly thirty years ago a Hokkaido court ruled the SDF unconstitutional in a case known as the 'Naganuma case.' I was just getting started as a Diet member at the time. The government responded to the Naganuma judgment by declaring that the SDF was constitutional because of three conditions. … The first was that the SDF is exclusively defensive, its only role is to protect Japan from attack. Therefore, the SDF would not go abroad as Japan's military had in the past in the Manchurian Incident, the China Incident, and the Greater East Asian War.
>
> The next condition was that it would not be involved in "collective self-defense" and the third was that Japan would abide by the "three non-nuclear principles.[18]

Because of these conditions, throughout his career Minowa had supported the SDF as a constitutional force despite the strong language of Constitution Article 9. In his view, the Iraq deployment clearly violated the first condition and therefore the Constitution itself. Minowa told the court that the situation reminded him of Japan's war years.

> The twenty-year period that followed my birth were years of war, war, war. Except for Okinawa at the very end, all of these wars were fought abroad. These were wars without purpose, truly wars without meaning. In those days, people who opposed the wars were swept up by the Special Higher Police (*tokkō keisatsu*), thrown in jail, and silenced. (For jail, Minowa used the slang term *buta bako*, literally "pigs' box.") Now we have popular sovereignty, don't we? So if there are people who are opposed to the Iraq deployment, it's quite natural that there be voices in opposition rising from among the people.
>
> Now when I look back on those years of war, war, war, I am filled with regret. If the voices of the people had been raised on high, if there had been popular sovereignty, there would have been no war. I deeply regret that we fought such meaningless wars.[19]

After taking a deep breath, Uchida moved on to other topics. The government's witnesses had asserted that the Tent Village flyers had caused great uneasiness among the residents of the apartment buildings. Minowa responded that it was quite natural that SDF members would feel this way. Uchida asked, "You don't mean they would feel unease at the flyers, you mean they would feel unease because of the unlawful Iraq deployment. Is that right?" "Yes," he responded. "It's quite natural that the SDF would feel uneasy and their family members, too. What's wrong with that? I think they *should* feel uneasy (about what they're being asked to do)" "Good information, information that's uncomfortable to hear, the more information the better," he said. Uchida followed with "You think they should participate in all kinds of discussions." The answer was "Yes, I think so."

Minowa was followed by the surprise appearance of Toshihiro Yamauchi, a professor of law at a private university in Kyoto. Yamauchi had submitted a statement accompanied by a batch of flyers he had received in his mailbox at his apartment near the university campus. The flyers were solicitations from the Japan Self-Defense Forces, seeking new applicants. He was not scheduled to appear as a witness, but when prosecutors objected to the defense counsel's request to submit Yamauchi's statement, the lawyers sought immediate approval for his testimony. At that moment, Yamauchi happened to be seated in the spectators' gallery because he had come up from Kyoto to observe Okudaira's testimony. Over prosecutors' objections, the court allowed him to testify regarding the SDF flyers in his mailbox.[20] Uchida told me that in his decades of law practice, he had never seen an unscheduled witness approved in this manner.[21] Judge Hasegawa had delivered another surprise.

11

TRIAL AT HACHIOJI: FINAL TESTIMONY AND CLOSING ARGUMENTS

(September–November 2004)

September 30 Hearing (Sixth Public Court Session)

The last witnesses to testify in the Tent Village trial appeared in court on the afternoon of Thursday, September 30. The first to speak was Yutaka Osawa, the Tachikawa City Council member who had worked so hard to bring the story of the Tent Village defendants before the public. Osawa grew up in Kyushu and first arrived in Tachikawa in 1977 while in his late twenties. He soon became involved in public interest advocacy, especially efforts to assist the disabled.[1]

Responding to questions from lead counsel Reiko Kuriyama, Osawa told of his evolution as an antiwar activist. Like Manabu Ishizaki, his interest was triggered by debate over Japan's potential involvement in the Gulf War and the UN peacekeeping deployments that followed. In 1989, he joined in forming the "Tachikawa Citizens Group Opposing Overseas Deployments" to serve as a platform for local antiwar and antibase activism. Tent Village members were naturally attracted to this group and Osawa coordinated with them from time to time thereafter, though he did not become a formal member of Tent Village. In 1992, he launched a newsletter called "STOP Overseas Deployments" and began delivering it himself at the Self-Defense Force (SDF) apartments in 1997.[2] He continued these deliveries for two years, at a pace of one newsletter every other month or so. Like the Tent Village messengers, he dropped his material directly through mail slots at individual apartments because he feared that items deposited at central mail banks would be discarded. He never imagined that such actions could lead to arrest.

Osawa was elected to the city council in 1998 while he continued his newsletter and other antiwar activities. The newsletter carried his phone number and he said that he looked upon calls he received as opportunities for conversations with residents. He stopped deliveries to residents who complained.[3]

DOI: 10.4324/9781003193999-12

When questioning turned to events that followed the arrests, he told the court of his calls for support of the defendants and the extraordinary response. He took on the responsibility to lead the defendants' support group because he believed the Tent Village outreach to SDF members was an important example of "maintaining open lines for discussion among people with differing opinions," an "essential element of a democratic system."[4]

Osawa concluded his testimony with a reprise of the passionate call for democracy he had been making since he first learned of the arrests at the end of February.

> Many people see this arrest and prosecution as an attack on their own activities. Is the delivery of flyers something that justifies arrest, 75 days in detention, and prosecution? Such prosecution is the suppression of democracy. It must not be allowed![5]

Yutaka Osawa was the last of the four outside defense witnesses approved by the court, so when he was done only the defendants were left to testify.

Testimony by the Defendants

Toshiyuki Obora had appeared at the end of the September 9 session, after Professor Okudaira and the other outside defense witnesses. On direct examination, Reiko Kuriyama led him through his account of the Tent Village history, its catalog of protest activities, sources of funding, and other administrative aspects. The judges were wrestling with the question whether Tent Village members were potentially violent extremists or just ordinary citizens with a strong political agenda. Judge Suzuki specifically requested more factual background, preferably in the defendants' own words.[6] Obora's recitation of basic facts was calculated to satisfy the judges' queries. Before he was finished, they would place their own questions regarding basic facts of the events of January 17. One question stood out—would the defendants have continued flyer deliveries if they had received a written complaint from the residents? Obora said they might have stopped.[7]

On direct examination he also repeated his statement that prosecutors had hinted at a broader agenda when they taunted him in detention with this question: "Wouldn't it be interesting to see if the number of flyers to the SDF went up or down following your arrest?"[8]

During cross-examination, the prosecutors sought to paint a different picture of the fundamental nature of Tent Village. In their version, the defendants were not quite as innocent as they claimed. A prosecutor questioned Obora concerning his 1983 arrest under the minor offenses act and his 2003 confrontation with police before the SDF base main gate during the base festival, an annual event when local residents and other visitors are allowed onto the base to inspect the helicopters and other SDF equipment. He was not arrested on the latter occasion, but the confrontation helped the government present the image of a troublemaker.

Defendant Nobuhiro Onishi took his turn on the witness stand on September 30. In response to questions from Attorney Kojima, Onishi told the court of his first contact with Tent Village at a demonstration against Air Self-Defense Force (ASDF) cargo flights at Tachikawa airfield and how he admired the group's focus on the local community. Regarding his flyer deliveries at the SDF apartments, Onishi said this was an earnest attempt to reach out to Self-Defense Force members who might be sent to battlefields abroad. As for his confrontation with the airman on January 17, Onishi said he got the impression that the airman complained only because he was ordered to do so by superiors, not because he was actually disturbed by the Tent Village flyers. At the end of direct testimony, Onishi suggested hypocrisy in the SDF policy regarding door-to-door flyer deliveries. Like Professor Yamauchi, he said that Kunitachi City Council member Tomohiro Shigematsu had also received recruiting flyers from the Self-Defense Forces at his residence in the autumn of 2003 and then again in March, while Professor Ishizaki received such flyers at his home in April.[9]

As in the cross-examination of Obora, a prosecutor attacked the witness's credibility. The first questions were relatively uncontroversial. Why did he disregard the numerous warnings against trespassing posted around the SDF apartments? Didn't he think they should have asked permission of the building managers before delivering the flyers? After this went on for some time, Judge Hasegawa directed the prosecutor to move on. But now she took a more

FIGURE 11.1 Nobuhiro Onishi addresses passersby outside the Hachioji Courthouse. (Photograph by Toshiyuki Obora, September 2004)

aggressive line. Was the witness a member of a group "that wears black helmets"? Then she stepped onto even more sensitive ground. Was the witness "opposed to the emperor system?" This caught the ire of Chief Judge Hasegawa who suddenly intervened. "Whatever beliefs the defendant may hold have nothing to do with this trial," he said. "In this court, we judge people's actions and not their beliefs." This remonstrance was followed by a sharp sidebar discussion between judge and prosecutor. Observers wrote that this was the most contentious exchange of the entire trial.[10]

Sachimi Takada was the last defendant to testify and the only one who had not been directly challenged at the SDF apartments. She had observed Obora's confrontation and discussed it with the others, but didn't think there was a serious problem. If the residents had genuine complaints about the flyers, she said, they would have called the Tent Village office. But no such calls were received. Her testimony also provided another opportunity to tell the court about the rough treatment she endured during detention. She said the interrogation was nothing other than an attempt to force her to commit "*tenkō*."[11]

On cross-examination, a prosecutor made sure the court was aware that the February arrest was not Sachimi's first encounter with the police. She brought up Sachimi's participation in demonstrations opposing construction of a museum to honor the Showa emperor (*Showa Tennō Kinenkan*) the year before and how she was removed by the police, though not arrested.[12]

This was the last evidentiary presentation to the court, leaving only final arguments which were scheduled for Thursday, November 4. Judge Hasegawa closed the September 30 session with an extraordinary statement. "I expedited

FIGURE 11.2 Sachimi Takada addresses passersby at the entrance to Tachikawa Station. (Photograph by Katsuko Kato, May 2004)

FIGURE 11.3 Attorney Hirotatsu Kojima addresses a gathering of Tent Village supporters on October 30, 2004. (Photograph by Yutaka Osawa)

the proceedings," he said, "because I thought that the nature of the case required a swift judgment. Thank you for your cooperation. The court will do its best in writing the judgment." Attorney Uchida later remarked that in his 30 years of legal practice he had never heard a judge express his thanks like this.[13]

Supporters organized one of their biggest rallies on Saturday, October 30, at a labor hall in Kokubunji, with 130 in attendance. The keynote speaker was Professor Hiroshi Sasanuma, a constitutional law specialist from Shizuoka University who was a signatory to the March declaration of law professors. He fired up the crowd with his message that government officials, including SDF members, have a duty to listen to the voices of dissent. He warned that without dissent, democratic states fail. There was a lot at stake in this case, he said: "The antiwar flyer trial is a fight for the survival of democracy."[14]

November 4 Hearing (Seventh Public Court Session) Closing Arguments

Closing arguments were set for November 4, but just as this date approached, the prosecutors made a surprise move. On October 29, they suddenly petitioned the court to allow the testimony of another witness, a state security police detective who was prepared to testify on a rather sinister topic. The detective would tell the court that Tent Village members had frequently collaborated with a remnant wing of the "*chūkaku-ha*" faction of the *zengakuren*, a violent radical group that wreaked havoc in the 1960s and 1970s, and that *chūkaku-ha* had issued a declaration claiming responsibility for an explosion at the Tachikawa SDF base.[15]

Defense counsel opposed the request for lack of relevance and the court quickly rejected it. But the prosecutors did not give up, filing a formal opposition to the court's action. So the November 4 session opened not with final arguments, but with the dispute over the proposed witness. After hearing argument, the court rejected the witness once again. Chief Judge Hasegawa expressly declared that the evidentiary stage of the trial was over and again stressed his desire for a fast end to the trial. "Because this case affects the exercise of the important right to free speech," he said, "we must act expeditiously."[16]

The prosecutors were left with one more task before commencing their closing argument. They had gathered 33 written statements from residents in which they described their anxieties and fears inspired by the Tent Village flyers. Some called for strict punishment of the defendants. Like the more than 8,000 petitions submitted to the court by Tent Village supporters on October 14, these statements did not formally qualify as evidence to be evaluated by the court in deciding judgment, but they did provide an opportunity for the residents to speak their minds.

The Government's Closing Argument

The government's closing argument made a point-by-point rebuttal of defense claims and presented a powerful case for prosecution of the Tent Village messengers. There was no dispute between defense and prosecution on the basic facts of the case. Examining those same facts, however, they reached opposite conclusions. Did the facts describe an innocent delivery of political messages—or a crime? The government argument was divided into several major sections.

Prosecutorial Discretion

The prosecutors began with their response to the most extreme attack made by their opponents: the decision to prosecute itself was an "abuse of discretion" and should therefore be dismissed. Japan's prosecutors hold the sole authority to bring criminal charges to court and to dismiss cases with no charges at all. The scope of their discretion is extremely broad. Citing Supreme Court precedent, they described a very high bar for attacks on this discretion: "even if it is possible for an abuse of discretion to render a prosecution invalid, this is limited to cases where the commencement of prosecution itself is a crime." The best-known example of such a case occurred in a prosecution that arose out of the infamous mercury poisoning of residents in the fishing village of Minamata in the 1950s. There, an appellate court found the government's decision to prosecute a leader of a victims' group rather than those responsible for the toxic release that caused injury and death to be unlawful.[17] Even defense counsel would have to agree that the circumstances of the Minamata case were radically different from the Tachikawa arrests.

In their next step, defense counsel argued that even if the prosecutors did not unlawfully abuse their discretion, they nonetheless showed terrible judgment by bringing this case to court. Article 248 of the Criminal Procedure Code guides prosecutors in the exercise of their great power, mandating that they consider the "character, age, and circumstances of the wrongdoer, gravity of the offense, and circumstances or situation after the offense" when deciding whether to institute prosecution.[18] In their closing argument, the prosecutors cited three specific factors that weighed heavily in their decision to act.

First, they reminded the court that the Tent Village messengers' visits on January 17 were not a one-time affair. Instead, the flyer deliveries on that date were just one step in a much broader plan "repeated in an organized and calculated manner." Second, they stressed the residents' strong desire to be free of such intrusions: "The victims do not want the kind of intrusions seen in this case repeated. They submitted complaints to the police and called the police emergency number to report the incident." Finally, the prosecutors noted that "The defendants have not indicated that they would not repeat their actions or otherwise expressed remorse." This is a very important factor in nearly all criminal cases in Japan. Those who say Japan's criminal justice system is a great success always point to the rehabilitation of those accused of crime. But rehabilitation cannot begin until wrongdoers confess and express remorse for their actions. By this standard, the Tent Village defendants were especially dangerous. They not only refused to confess, they also loudly accused the government itself of wrongdoing.[19]

In the same section of their brief, the prosecutors also addressed defense charges that the government's motivation was to suppress the political speech of the defendants. They began by reciting some basic facts. The investigation began in response to calls to the police emergency line (110) and to written complaints filed by residents. Alleged perpetrators were apprehended by the police. From that point, the prosecutors simply followed standard procedure, filing indictments based on consideration of all the facts and circumstances revealed by the investigation. Their conclusion was obvious: the government was *not* motivated by the desire to suppress the defendants' activities.

Did the Defendants Violate Criminal Code Article 130?

Next, the prosecutors moved on to application of Criminal Code Article 130, the rule that lay at the heart of the case. They divided their analysis into six sections.

(1) Did the Defendants "Trespass" into the SDF Property?

Article 130 sets out two separate definitions of illegal trespass. One concerns "trespassing" into a "residence" (*jūkyo*). The other applies to entries to "premises" (*teitaku*), a broader concept than residence. The law forbids entry to premises only when they are "under the guard of a person."

The prosecutors addressed the residence rule first. Here they ran directly into a fundamental conflict. Backed by established precedent, the defense claimed that only those entries into residences that disrupt "peaceful daily life" meet the requirement of "trespassing" set by Article 130. They claimed the Tent Village messengers caused no such disruption and therefore did not violate Article 130.

But there appeared to be precedent on both sides of the issue. Citing a 1983 Supreme Court judgment, the prosecutors responded that the law requires only that entries be "contrary to the will" of residents or property managers, whether or not there is disruption. They reminded the court of the managers' actions in posting warnings around the property and filing complaints with the police. This left no question regarding the managers' opposition to the flyer deliveries. As for the residents, the prosecutors cited their calls to the police emergency line and their reports to superiors along with the in-person challenges to Onishi and Obora on January 17. For the prosecutors, residents' opposition to the flyers was also clear.

As for the definition of "residence" in multifamily housing, they found a precedent that expanded its scope to include staircases, corridors, pathways, and even roofs.[20] By this standard, the defendants had trespassed into the residences long before they reached the doors of individual apartments.

(2) Were the Premises "Guarded" as Required by Article 130?

Even if the court rejected the broad definition of residence, the prosecutors argued that "premises" encompassed not only staircases, corridors, and pathways, but also the surrounding grounds enclosed within the chain link fence at the outer edge of the property. The fence did have openings for the entry of residents on foot, bicycle, or in their cars, but there was no confusion regarding the boundary between the SDF property and the public rights of way outside.[21]

The Tent Village intrusions were against the will of the property managers. This left the question whether the premises are "guarded." Here the prosecutors described the system in place to protect the property and residents. They told the court the apartments were nearly full and that, as residents moved about the property, they were "under observation" (*kanshika*), that managers had posted the aforementioned warnings, and that they made three inspection tours of the property every day. For efficient communication between managers and residents, certain residents were designated as contacts with managers and it was their duty to distribute messages and instructions regarding safety and upkeep of the premises. Although there were no formal guard posts at the perimeter, the prosecutors described a rational organization designed to monitor conditions throughout the property. They argued that these measures fulfilled the statutory requirement that the premises were guarded.

(3) Did the Defendants Have a "Just Cause" to Enter the Property?

In order to secure a conviction, Article 130 clearly required that prosecutors show not only that the defendants entered the property, but that they had no "just cause" to do so. This was a central question. Does the delivery of a political message constitute such a just cause?

Tent Village supporters had homed in on this issue from the very beginning. Within a few days of the arrests, 56 scholars signed a declaration that stressed not only the appropriateness, but the vital importance of free communication among citizens. As for the propriety of door-to-door flyer deliveries, they said the very purpose of door mail slots is to enable residents to receive messages from the outside with no loss of privacy. They saw the mail slot as an invitation to receive material like the Tent Village flyers. At the first court hearing on May 6, Lead Counsel Reiko Kuriyama delivered an uncompromising summary: "They did not enter the property without a 'just cause' like thieves. They did so in order to distribute flyers expressing opposition to the SDF deployment, an act of free speech guaranteed by the Constitution."

But according to the prosecutors, the requirement that entrants have no just cause merely states the obvious and the phrase has no function other than repeating that the law prohibits unlawful entry.[22] They explained that the purpose of Article 130 is to protect the individual interests of the residents and managers of the property and it empowers them to exclude others from entering residential space, the "center of daily life." No matter how great the importance of the right of free expression, according to the prosecutors, it does not create a just cause to enter a residence or related premises without the approval of the people who live there.[23] The prosecutors did not fail to mention that the defendants were free to distribute their flyers outside the boundaries of the SDF apartment premises and that through their regular protest marches, "anti-military broadcasts," and other activities, Tent Village members vigorously exercised their right to free speech in many ways.

(4) Did the Defendants Act with Intent?

Prosecutors must show a "mental element" that indicates a defendant acted with intent or gross negligence in every criminal trial. Here, defense counsel argued that because the Tent Village defendants believed their actions were protected by the Constitution, they had no consciousness of violating the law and therefore the necessary mental element was lacking. Tent Village members and other activists, including witness Yutaka Osawa, an elected member of the city council, had gone door-to-door at the SDF apartments for many years, but until February 2004, had never had a problem. The defendants and their supporters repeatedly declared they could not imagine that their well-established activities violated the law.

But the prosecutors stressed that the defendants were well aware that they acted against the will of the residents and the managers. Anyone could see that the ideas espoused in Tent Village flyers were diametrically opposed to those of individuals who volunteered to serve their country in the Self-Defense Forces. Any doubt on this score was extinguished by the warning signs and even confrontations with residents who demanded that they leave the property.

Under the prosecution's theory, no entry contrary to the will of the residents or managers is lawful. The defendants were well aware that their entry contravened the will of the residents and managers and therefore their acts were not lacking in intent.

(5) Did the Defendants Violate a "Legally Protected Interest"?

Defense counsel argued that the defendants' entry to the property did not cause the violation of any "legally protected interest" and even if there was such a violation, the injury was so slight that it does not justify prosecution. The prosecutors vigorously attacked this claim. They began by describing the Tent Village as an organization that calls for the dissolution of the SDF. For the members of such a group to enter the SDF residences under any circumstances, "the only place where SDF members can relax, away from their duties," SDF members would surely feel great discomfort and anxiety. The Tent Village flyers were not generic messages, but were addressed directly to residents, with such salutations as "Dear SDF Members" and "Dear SDF Family Members" followed by messages titled "SDF members must not kill or be killed," "Reject deployment to Iraq!" and "'Support for rebuilding' is really support for theft." By comparing the work of the SDF with such crimes as killing and theft, these messages obviously caused great discomfort and anxiety to those who received them and the law surely protects the residents from such suffering. The legal interests violated by the defendants were certainly not abstract, but very real. According to the prosecutors, it is absurd to suggest that the defendants' actions did not violate any legal interest.

Next, the prosecutors addressed the defense claim that even if there was a violation of a legal interest, the injury was so slight that it should not be subject to a criminal penalty. The prosecutors said that here the defense appeared to rely on the so-called doctrine of "punishable illegality" (*kabatsuteki ihōsei*), which asserts that minor violations should not be subject to punishment. According to the prosecutors, if such an approach was adopted it would result in legal standards that are vague and unclear and court decisions would become subjective and arbitrary. For this reason, they said there were no recent judgments that applied this theory to support not guilty verdicts. Judgments based on such uncertain standards would threaten the stability of the rule of law.

In the present case, the injury to the SDF residents was especially painful because of the unprecedented deployment into Iraq and the national debate over the role of Japan's SDF. In their effort to protect the residents from the pain caused by the Tent Village flyers, the managers had posted warnings around the property and had taken other actions, which they had never done before.

Although the defendants did not actually enter into the residents' apartments, their actions were aggressive. They disregarded the posted warnings and walked through the property directly to individual doorways. The intrusions and the emotional suffering of the residents cannot be described as trivial.[24]

(6) "Accepted in Society"

Putting aside the strict terms of statutory law, defense counsel argued that door-to-door delivery of political flyers, commercial flyers, and other material is broadly accepted in Japanese society. But prosecutors pointed to the many signs at Japanese homes that read "No Solicitations" to show there is much opposition. The warnings posted at the SDF apartments prohibited *all* entries by unapproved messengers, political, commercial, or otherwise. Regarding the residents' failure to complain about commercial flyers, the nuisance level of such material is so low that the residents simply put up with them.

The prosecutors concluded this section by declaring that delivery of any flyers or other material contrary to the wishes of residents violates not only the rights of those residents but also violates social standards.

Demand for Punishment (Kyūkei)

Prosecutors' final arguments are accompanied by requests for punishment, which include a statement of the grounds that support the severity of the sentence requested. In this case, they identified seven separate grounds including, of course, the lack of remorse and the likelihood of repetition. As punishment, they demanded that the three defendants each be imprisoned for six months.

Final Statements by the Defense

Now that the government had made its final demand, it was the defense's turn. The attorneys submitted a lengthy brief and addressed the court. In their final plea to the court, defense counsel submitted a comprehensive retelling of the saga, beginning with the birth of Tent Village as a liaison among local antiwar groups in December 1972, when they learned that Japan's own SDF would be moving into the military base evacuated by the Americans, and continuing all the way through the 2004 arrests. They described the illegality of the war launched by U.S. President Bush, denied sanction by the United Nations, and condemned around the world. They summarized Prime Minister Koizumi's confusing assertions that the SDF Iran contingent would be present only in "non-combat areas" (*hisentō chiiki*) and accused him of employing the "magic of words" (*kotoba no tejina*) to justify his obvious violation of the constraints of Constitution Article 9.[25]

Finally, the court allowed each of the defendants to make their own closing statements.[26] Although they sometimes repeated the kinds of comments made by lawyers, during the time set aside for "opinion statements" on November 4, the three defendants were free to put aside narrow rules of law and instead tell the court of their personal experiences and feelings during the ordeal of the past ten months. A few themes were repeated by each of the three defendants: the general shock that anyone would be jailed over such a trivial matter, the anger at prosecutors' attempts to smear them as terrorists, and most central to police action itself, the arrests were just one element of a larger government program to intimidate anyone who would consider protesting the Iraq deployment.

Nobuhiro Onishi spoke first. "On February 20 of this year," he said, "I was suddenly arrested on a charge of trespass for delivering flyers at the SDF apartments. After 75 days in detention, on May 11 I was released on bail." He then very politely expressed his thanks to the many people who made financial contributions, signed petitions, or otherwise supported the defendants. He also made the ominous point that many people told him that because of the police action against the Tent Village, they feared they too might become the victims of similar treatment.

Onishi told the court that after his release he was invited to speak at a number of public gatherings. At an event held in August, he shared a speakers' dais with Junpei Yasuda, the freelance journalist who was one of the three hostages taken captive in Iraq in April. Yasuda, who had feared for his life as a prisoner in a distant war, expressed his shock that back home in peaceful Japan someone could be jailed for 75 days for nothing more than distributing flyers.[27] Onishi also read excerpts from messages he received from people around the country. One after another condemned the arrests and expressed their fear that freedom was slipping away: "This is the kind of repression seen in wartime." "This is what happens in a country that can go to war." "The arrests are especially shocking in a country with a 'Peace Constitution.'" "When I learned of this, I wondered when it was that Japan had reached such a state. I thought the country has begun to prepare for war." "In this country there is freedom for low-brow television programs and gossip columns," he read, but apparently no freedom for political speech.[28]

As he thought about the case over the preceding months, Onishi developed a theory for the government's decision to devote such great resources to the prosecution of three harmless protesters. The February 27 arrests occurred during the initial stages of the unpopular Iraq deployment and "the SDF leadership and the state security police thought they could shut down the possibility that rising uncertainty and suspicion among SDF members and their family members could lead them to join the antiwar movement."

Citing ten separate incidents where individuals involved in antiwar demonstrations or similar activities were recently arrested, he told the court that the TV arrests were part of a much larger government program of intimidation. With a Madisonian flourish, he expressed his fears for the future of democratic government in Japan:

> A society in which there is no free speech becomes a society in which people must make decisions and act solely on the basis of information provided by the state. If so, when the state's policies are wrong no one will step forward to speak against them.[29]

Onishi followed this declaration with a meticulous review of the trial, commenting on the testimony of each witness. Then, he restated his theme that open discussion among citizens is the foundation for law in a democratic society. Citizens include SDF members and Onishi was convinced that some of them read his flyers. "Please don't take away our only means to communicate with SDF members," he asked. Finally, he called upon the judges to have courage because he knows it's not easy for them to stand up to the police and the government.[30]

Sachimi Takada spoke next. Her overall theme concerned the relationship between the SDF and the communities around them. She told the court that she continued to live in the Tent Village apartment after her release, so she was in a good position to see the many messages of support flowing in from the community.[31]

She said that she didn't know that Tachikawa was home to a military base before she moved there and didn't actually notice the military presence until one day she was startled by the terrifying sound of low-flying aircraft. She compared her experience to that of the Okinawan people who must put up with a much larger military presence. Then, she placed herself in the position of Iraqis desperate to survive in a country torn by war. Whatever Japan's prime minister might say about the limited mission of Japan's Self-Defense Forces, surely the Iraqi people themselves would see them as nothing other than another military force joining the war. She concluded her remarks by stressing the importance of allowing people to communicate with SDF members directly to let them know the impact they have on others. As for Tent Village members and others like them, the only practical opportunity they have to deliver such a message is through flyers like the ones she delivered in Tachikawa. Like Onishi, she concluded with a plea to the judges to allow this to continue.

Toshiyuki Obora spoke last. He began by describing the particular cruelty of the ban on visitors he suffered in jail. As a cook working at a public middle school, he was the only defendant to serve as an employee in a large organization. His sudden disappearance for more than ten weeks with no warning and no ability to communicate with managers or fellow workers was a serious problem. Most Japanese workers in these circumstances would be fired. Fortunately, Obora was a member of a strong labor union that fought vigorously on his behalf. The union succeeded in preserving his job, but even so regulations required him to take mandatory leave for the duration of the trial and his compensation was cut by more than half.

Then he attacked the legitimacy of the prosecution. According to Obora, in order to provide some reasonable ground for the arrests, the government sought to show that the apartment residents had been injured by the messengers. But this effort failed because there was no injury. So the prosecutors shifted their focus and sought to smear the reputations of the Tent Village members in the eyes of the court. Thus, when the government's third witness appeared, he described his fear that the situation would escalate and lead to "white powder" coming through his mail slot. Obora said this alleged fear was completely groundless.[32]

When they cross-examined the defendants, the prosecutors repeatedly attacked their reputations. For example, when Obora testified, the prosecutor brought up his confrontation with police when he protested at an Air SDF festival in Tachikawa, even though there was no arrest. Then, when Onishi testified, the prosecutor raised the possibility of Tent Village ties with unidentified "black helmet groups." When she asked whether Onishi was opposed to the emperor system, Judge Hasegawa intervened to stop the questioning.

For Obora, the government's attempts to claim some injury to the residents and paint Tent Village as a threat to their safety was a sham. It was abundantly clear to him that "what the prosecutors have really placed on trial is the specific philosophy of opposing war."[33]

Obora said the Tent Village trial was really about the Iraq War and Japan's participation. He told the court that even before considering the role of the SDF, it was important to keep in mind the genesis of the "war of aggression" launched by U.S. President George W. Bush, based on false claims that the Iraqis possessed "weapons of mass destruction." He then moved on to tell the court of relentless pressure from American leaders not only to join the war, but even to revise Japan's Constitution to enable the country to go to war more easily. The Americans shamelessly dangled their support for Japan's candidacy to the U.N. Security Council as a carrot to lead Japan to revise the no-war provision.

For Obora, the goal of the police crackdown was clear: to isolate and ultimately eliminate the antiwar movement.

12

JUDGMENT DAY

(December 16, 2004)

On the morning of December 14, the *Asahi* published a guide to the upcoming court judgment that occupied about a quarter of a newspaper page.[1] It told a story of strong police intervention, beginning with testimony of the government's own witnesses who admitted it was not the building residents but actually the police who prepared the complaints that led to the arrests. The article pointed to the controlling role of the state security police, which surely accounted for the intensive searches of the defendants' homes and other locations. It also quoted statements from the two primary defense witnesses, Professor Okudaira and retired Liberal Democratic Party (LDP) politician Noboru Minowa, both to the effect that it is inappropriate for apartment building managers or other third parties to cut residents off from communications like the Tent Village flyers. According to these respected elders, it should be the residents themselves who decide whether to give the flyers careful thought or toss them in the trash.

The *Asahi* report also cited Chief Judge Hasegawa's rejection of the prosecutors' 11th hour attempt to insert evidence suggesting that Tent Village was in contact with extremists, quoting his powerful declarations that "this court does not judge thought" and "this case involves an important interpretation of the right to free expression that could have a big effect on the flyer deliveries of others." To further underscore the significance of the constitutional issues, the report carried a sidebar interview with constitutional scholar Shōjirō Sakaguchi. His opening words could have been lifted directly from Professor Okudaira's court testimony: "Because the Constitution prohibits laws that crack down on political speech as in the prewar era, there is strong suspicion that the crime of trespass has been used (instead) to limit certain kinds of speech." He mentioned the Horikoshi case as another example of this pattern. In his opinion, the claim that the Tent Village flyers caused greater disruption than mundane commercial flyers was obviously true, but that's why they must be protected: "It is because

DOI: 10.4324/9781003193999-13

such statements are powerful that they are indispensable to a democratic society and must be accorded preferential treatment." In any event, the decision whether to accept or reject such messages must be made by individual residents rather than apartment managers. The interview closed with a warning: "My fear is the notion that 'flyers are a nuisance and should be stopped' will become fixed in the popular consciousness and this will lead to restrictions on free expression."[2]

The account appeared alongside a montage that captured the essence of the Tent Village campaign in three images. Juxtaposed with a copy of the first flyer titled "Let's think together and raise our voices against the Iraq deployment," readers found photos of a Self-Defense Force platoon in helmets and battle gear marching in formation and a smaller photo of the three defendants seated at a table. With this report in hand, *Asahi* readers were prepared to judge the significance of the pending court judgment.

As judgment day drew near, the pressure on the defendants sharply increased. If the verdict was guilty, the defendants would be tagged for life. For Toshiyuki Obora, the risk was especially severe. A guilty verdict could mean permanent loss of his public-school employment. Despite the passionate words of constitutional experts and other supporters, it's hard for a defendant in a criminal trial in Japan to be optimistic. Even the most ardent supporters of free speech are well aware that not guilty judgments are exceedingly rare. Japan's district courts issued judgments concerning more than 80,000 defendants in 2004. Only 89 of those defendants were found not guilty.[3] As for this particular case, the Tent Village member Mori Inoue wrote, "There were various predictions of the trial's outcome among our friends and acquaintances. Overall, those with relatively little experience in civil protest tended to be optimistic; the more anyone had experienced suppression, the more pessimistic they became."[4]

Whatever the outcome of the trial, the defendants could be proud of the attention they had brought to the Iraq deployment. According to a *Mainichi* public opinion poll, the share of the Japanese public who opposed the deployment had expanded over the course of the trial from 54% in December 2003 to 62% percent in December 2004.[5]

Judgment Day

The people of Tokyo often enjoy clear blue skies in early winter. December 16, 2004, a sunny day with temperatures that reached 17 degrees, was no exception. As they had throughout the trial, a crowd of Tent Village supporters gathered before the courthouse well before the 1:30 p.m. hearing to hand out flyers that demanded a not guilty verdict. People gradually formed a line to draw straws for the limited number of seats. Well over a hundred gathered, but the largest courtroom held just 80 spectator seats. They would be quickly filled while another 70 or so interested observers waited outside.[6] In cases that attract significant public attention, supporters customarily prepare a large banner that declares their reaction to the verdict, with designated members assigned to dash through the courtroom doors the moment the judgment is announced to display their reaction to news photographers and the world. Because they didn't know how the court would rule, Tent Village supporters prepared two banners: one that read "We Won! Not Guilty!" and another that read "We Don't Accept the Unfair Judgment!"[7]

After the defendants, the spectators, and the others filled the room, a bailiff called the court to order and the three judges filed in and took their seats behind the bench. Then, Judge Hasegawa looked out at the courtroom and announced, "Due to the nature of this case, I will leave the verdict to the end."

There was a general stir throughout the spectators' seats as people considered what this might mean. In nearly all cases, the presiding judge reads the verdict at the outset and the court proceeding is over in minutes. According to one reporter, "The verdict is usually announced at the end only in especially important cases like those involving the death penalty. This is extremely rare for a case that involves only a trivial crime."[8]

Judge Hasegawa not only delayed the verdict till the end of his presentation, he also spent about an hour reading key portions of the judgment aloud.[9] Courtroom tension gradually rose as the judge revealed the direction of his analysis, with listeners locked in, searching for hints to the outcome.

After a brief summary of the facts, Hasegawa presented the court's legal analysis, beginning with the defense charge that the prosecution was actually a political act with the goal of suppressing the Tent Village antiwar agenda and therefore the indictment was unlawful and should be dismissed. Hasegawa echoed words from the prosecutors' final argument when he noted the extremely broad discretion enjoyed by Japan's prosecutors in their charging decisions. "Even in cases where prosecutors have exceeded the lawful bounds of discretion in filing an indictment," he said, "this does not immediately render such an indictment invalid." He repeated the commonly stated rule that the courts should act only in extreme cases where prosecutors themselves have committed a crime. The prosecutors were off the hook.

Defense counsel had made much of the fact that the police singled out the Tent Village while ignoring flyers from local pizza shops, real estate offices, and other commercial operations. Judge Hasegawa acknowledged this: "many commercial advertisements and other materials are inserted into both the central mailboxes and the newspaper slots in the front doors of individual apartments just like the Tent Village flyers," he said, "and even though the individuals who distribute such materials are outsiders who intrude onto the property without permission in the same manner as the defendants, they are not prosecuted." He concluded that "it cannot be denied that one dimension of these prosecutions is a focus on the content of the flyers."

If the court also agreed that the prosecutors acted in order to shut down criticism of the government's Iraq policy, the defense charge of government misconduct had a chance of success. But the court identified another motive for their action: "more than a few SDF members and their families" were disturbed by the content of the flyers and saw the visits of the defendants as a nuisance. "If we focus on such matters as the feelings of the residents, we cannot definitely conclude that the indictments in this case were filed solely for the purposes claimed by the defense." In other words, the residents' complaints provided a sufficient lawful cause for the government to act and therefore the focus on Tent Village did not render the prosecution unlawful.

Judge Hasegawa also considered whether the government had broken the law by illegally securing evidence. Sachimi Takada's repeated descriptions of abuse by interrogators had left a mark. But here the defendants' iron resolve worked against them. "Even if we assume that illegalities occurred during the investigation stage as asserted by the defense, we cannot find that the indictments are based on illegally obtained evidence." Because the defendants had remained silent, the interrogators' work had yielded nothing.

The court's conclusion was clear. The prosecutors had not exceeded the bounds of discretion so severely that their action amounted to a crime; therefore, the court would not dismiss the indictment.

Next, Judge Hasegawa moved on to the primary focus of the trial—Article 130 of the Criminal Code. First, he considered the significance of the defendants' use of pathways and staircases to reach the doorways of individual apartments. He quickly simplified the problem. The lot surrounding the apartment buildings and the stairways that connected the apartments with the "outside world" were "indispensable to the daily lives of the residents" and therefore deemed to be an integral part of the "residence." There was no need to discuss the statute's distinction between residence and broader premises at all.

Did the Tent Village messengers "trespass" into this residence? Defense counsel had asserted that there was no trespass unless there was some disruption of the daily lives of the residents. The court had a different view: Trespass at the SDF apartments "means entry that is contrary to the will of the residents or managers." The very act of such entry constituted disruption to daily lives.

According to Judge Hasegawa, the regular visits of "the postmen, deliverymen, meter readers from the electricity and gas companies," and some others was accepted by the residents, but other uninvited visitors violated the will of the residents and were therefore trespassing. Of course, this included the defendants. The judge took pains to emphasize that this was true whether or not the defendants had seen the warning signs directing them to keep out.

With each step in his analysis, Judge Hasegawa seemed to deliver another blow to the defense case. As he spoke, clouds of gloom descended on the defendants and their supporters. They turned darkest when the judge announced his devastating conclusion: "The defendants' entry to the property fulfills the constituent elements of the crime of trespass." At this point, some spectators may have been tempted to head for the exit.[10] But the judge was not finished.

According to Judge Hasegawa, there are some cases where *even though the government proves all the elements of a crime*, nonetheless

> in consideration of the propriety of the motivations that led to the act, the substance of the defendants' behavior and other circumstances including the

> extent of resulting injury … there are cases where *the extent of the illegality is not sufficient to apply a criminal penalty, and therefore may not amount to a crime.*

"Not amount to a crime?" Courtroom spectators must have questioned their own ears. Did the judge just say that there are times when a crime is not a crime? The lawyers would be wide-eyed in anticipation of what might come next.

After stating this confusing principle, the court entered into an analysis of the defendants' motivations, behavior, and the results of their actions. Regarding motivation, the court had no doubt: "Defendants entered the Tachikawa Apartment Complex in order to directly communicate the views of Tent Village concerning the dispatch of Self-Defense Forces to Iraq." Here, Judge Hasegawa expressed skepticism concerning the prosecutors' attempts to link the Tent Village to known extremist groups: "Tent Village does not coerce individuals to join or to remain in the group or compel the payment of fees" or otherwise display the characteristics of a suspicious organization, he said. In wording that was especially important to all Tent Village members and their supporters, he said that Tent Village is just "one citizens group" (*ichi shimin dantai*) made up of people who share the same beliefs. They were definitely not terrorists.

Regarding conduct, the court emphasized that the defendants had maintained the highest standards of behavior during their presence at the property. They spoke with no one and did not ring doorbells or otherwise seek to directly draw the attention of residents; they simply placed single-page flyers into the mail slots of individual apartments. As for the results of the defendants' actions, the court considered the messages carried by the flyers and found that the manner of expression was restrained and the content was not significantly different from what building residents would see when they read the morning newspaper. The court found that although the flyers contained statements of opposition to government policy, they did not carry either criticism of the SDF members themselves or threats of violence to anyone. Further, the court found that any injury to the rights of the residents was trivial, beneath the threshold of injury necessary to support prosecution. Anyone who didn't like the flyers could easily dispose of them along with other junk mail.

In Judge Hasegawa's summary,

> it can be said that the defendants' motives in entering the Tachikawa Apartment Complex were proper and it cannot be said that their behavior exceeded the bounds of propriety. Any invasion of legal interests of residents and property managers was extremely slight.

Under these circumstances, could the police raids and the prosecution of "one citizens' group" be justified? At long last, the court addressed the constitutional guarantee of free speech:

> the defendants' act of distributing flyers was an example of political expression protected by Article 21(1) of the Constitution which, as a

> pillar of democratic society, holds a preferred position when compared to the distribution of commercial flyers protected by Article 22(1) of the Constitution.[11] When viewed in comparison to the treatment of distribution of commercial flyers at the Tachikawa Apartment Complex, which was not subject to any imposition of criminal liability, the sudden prosecution of the defendants without any formal prior notice of opposition or warning by the Defense Agency, the Self-Defense Forces, or the police, even though the same kinds of acts had long continued without complaint, cannot be said to escape suspicion when viewed in light of Article 21(1).

Now the court reached its conclusion.

> "In light of the circumstances indicated above, when considered in the context of the Constitution as a whole, we cannot find the degree of criminality sufficient to impose criminal penalties against the acts of the defendants in entering the Tachikawa Apartment Complex.[12]
>
> "Therefore, as a result, there is no proof of a crime in any of the claims in the indictment and we judge the defendants not guilty."

The courtroom burst into cheers and applause. Judge Hasegawa's calls to order went unheeded.[13] As the spectators spilled out into the open area before the courthouse door, many embraced and laughed and cried with joy.[14]

FIGURE 12.1 Supporters gathered outside the Hachioji Courthouse to celebrate the rare not guilty verdict on December 16, 2004. (Photograph by Yutaka Osawa)

Reactions to the Judgment

The defendants and their lawyers held a press conference in a crowded room at a labor hall nearby. One observer estimated there were 30 reporters in attendance, a far cry from the tiny group that came to Osawa's first press conference in the spring.[15] When asked for his reaction, Defendant Onishi gushed "The verdict was left to the very end—it was thrilling! When I heard the judge say our flyer delivery is a 'pillar of democracy,' it struck me to the core." Obora said

> I was really surprised that we received so much support from around the country, including financial donations. This kind of support showed that the "suppression" we suffered was really terrible. Somehow, we had to bounce back. With the support from people around the country, we were able to fight our way through.[16]

Whereas lead counsel Reiko Kuriyama and others lauded the court for its respect for the constitutional right to free speech, for attorney Akio Kotō, the court had really just exercised common sense: "Whether or not there was a crime sufficient to warrant a criminal penalty, was a matter of obvious common sense," he said. "The court almost completely accepted our argument that there was no way the defendants would consider their actions a crime."

FIGURE 12.2 The three defendants are flanked by their five attorneys at the post-judgment press conference on December 16, 2004. (Photograph by Yutaka Osawa)

FIGURE 12.3 Tent Village supporters march in Hachioji on the night of the not guilty verdict. (Photograph by Yutaka Osawa, December 2004)

That night a crowd of 130 marched through the streets of Hachioji. When they passed by the prosecutors' office, they blasted away with bullhorns to proclaim the innocence of the three defendants and chastise the government for misconduct.[17]

Jubilation over the not guilty verdict was not limited to the courtroom supporters and friends who marched in Hachioji. Peace activists and free speech advocates all over Japan shared the joy. According to Mori Inoue, Tent Village received congratulatory phone calls and telegrams from around the country, some with financial contributions. Also, on the financial front, he noted that the court returned the bail money, which was applied to pay off loans from supporters.[18]

The judgment was frontpage news the next day. Major newspapers carried comments from constitutional scholars who supported the decision and touted the court's veneration of the right to free speech. The *Mainichi* quoted one who called the judgment epoch-making and complimented the court for ignoring the background noise to clearly state that "this case is about the effort to shut down political discourse."[19] Another pointed out that the judgment would be especially important to civil society organizations. To get the civil society viewpoint, the *Mainichi* interviewed Makoto Teranaka, principal drafter of the Amnesty International press release that labeled the defendants Japan's first "Prisoners of Conscience." Teranaka had no doubt that the Constitution protected the defendants. As for the government's actions, he said, "It was the attempt to punish the defendants because of the contents of the flyers that is wrong. The prosecutors should not abuse their power. They should sincerely accept the judgment of the court."[20]

The *Asahi* quoted Nagoya University Professor Kōji Aikyō to say,

> As you read the court's opinion it becomes apparent that around the time of the deployment, the police and the SDF collaborated to target "anti-deployment" flyers. The fact that the Iraq deployment led to this kind of suppression should be long remembered.

Professor Yūji Shiratori, a criminal procedure expert at Hokkaido University, did not pull any punches. "The prosecutors should hang their heads for bringing this 'trespass' case to trial. Something very big was lost in the process of the investigation. This kind of investigation and prosecution must not be repeated."[21]

Of course, there was another view. Newspapers carried brief comments from the police, the prosecutors, and the Self-Defense Forces. According to a spokesperson for the Tachikawa police, "The investigation was conducted properly under the law, with arrests, detentions, and other actions taken under warrants issued by the court." The Hachioji prosecutors' office released a statement that expressed disappointment at the verdict and said that any further action would be decided in consultation with superiors. That left the SDF, the primary representative of victims of the alleged trespass:

> Although the residents individually expressed their feelings that this was a nuisance, the court said that any violation of their rights was slight. We must accept this as one judgment. We must think about the best means to prevent crimes and other problems just like an ordinary apartment complex where anyone is able to enter onto the grounds.[22]

In their search for a more expansive comment from the government side, *Tokyo Shimbun* reporters found retired prosecutor Takeshi Tsuchimoto, then serving as a professor of criminal procedure at one of the new law schools that opened in 2004. For Tsuchimoto, the acquittal was a mistake. Regarding the court's criticism of the police failure to contact Tent Village before making the arrests, Tsuchimoto bluntly declared that "Article 130 of the Criminal Code does not call for such prior notice. I could understand if the court had just reduced the sentence. By acquitting the defendants, the court went too far."[23]

The former prosecutor's comment was triggered by language in the judgment in which the court quietly lectured the police on basic procedures. The court's view of hardball police tactics appears near the end: "It is possible the police could have stopped the entry to the SDF apartments and the flyer deliveries by making a formal complaint to Tent Village." If the residents and managers had communicated their strong opposition to the visits but Tent Village persisted anyway, or if the flyers carried threats of violence or other objectionable content, only then in the court's view was it time for arrests. Sachimi Takada and other Tent Village members had said essentially the same thing.

Defense counsel were cheered by many statements Judge Hasegawa made that day, including his admonition regarding the police raid. But they had hoped the court would specifically find that their clients had a "just cause" to visit the SDF apartments and therefore rule there was no violation of Criminal Code 130. In the words of lead counsel Kuriyama, "they did not enter the property without just cause like thieves." Instead, they made "an act of free speech guaranteed by the Constitution." Although the court's judgment fully agreed with Kuriyama in substance, nonetheless, it was not the "just cause" judgment that anyone could understand. Instead, the court's peculiar ruling—the defendants' actions lacked a "degree of criminality sufficient to impose criminal penalties"—raised more questions than it answered.

Faced with the same case, American courts would be expected to rule that the arrest and prosecution constitute state action that restricts free speech and would then apply the well-established "strict scrutiny" standard to determine whether the state action was constitutional. Japan's courts sometimes refer to strict scrutiny standards (*genkaku na kijun*) but the approach is not well established in Japanese law. The Hachioji court's comment on state action was stunningly restrained and indirect: The "sudden prosecution … cannot be said to escape suspicion." The court's implied "suspicion" was that the police had targeted the Tent Village and made no warning because they wanted highly publicized arrests that would have a chilling effect on other antiwar activists.

December 16 was a day for celebration, but defense counsel knew their work was not finished. Under Japan's law of criminal procedure, prosecutors can appeal the rare acquittals issued by Japan's courts. And they usually do. As they pondered the court's complex reasoning, defense counsel scratched their heads and wondered how they could defend this judgment if the prosecutors chose to appeal.[24]

The immediate task was to find some way to persuade the prosecutors to forego an appeal and let the verdict stand. On December 18, Yutaka Osawa posted a call to action titled "Let's Stop the Appeal!" After declaring that the lawyers had achieved a "historic judgment" that exposed the "terrible investigation and prosecution" and thanking everyone for their support, he delivered the news that their work was not finished. In order to preserve the "Hasegawa Judgment," he called upon supporters to lobby the prosecutors and the press. His message included the phone numbers and addresses for the prosecutors' offices in Hachioji and downtown Tokyo. Regarding the news media, he wrote:

> This time, all the news organizations have written about it very well. I really think this is a decision that will go down in history … I hope that more and more people will write articles and draw attention to the awfulness of the police investigation, the unreasonableness of the prosecutors, and the way the courts allow easy arrests.[25]

That same day, a group of 20 supporters gathered before the Tokyo prosecutors' headquarters in Kasumigaseki to demand that they stand down and allow the not guilty verdict to survive.[26] Supporters launched other small demonstrations in succeeding days.

Meanwhile, Manabu Ishizaki organized another legal scholars' declaration, this time to express support for the District Court judgment. The statement was issued under the names of three leaders on December 16. By December 20, it had attracted 96 signatures.[27]

Then everyone waited. If the prosecutors were to appeal, they would have to do so within 14 days of the District Court judgment.[28]

13

IT'S NOT OVER

(December 2004–Summer 2005)

Arrest in the "Low City"

December 23 is the birthday of now-retired Emperor Akihito. In 2004, it was celebrated as a national holiday, for most Japanese, a day of rest and recreation. Around 2 p.m. that day, a 57-year-old Buddhist monk named Yōsei Arakawa performed a regular monthly chore. Following his usual path, he carried stacks of printed material to slip into the mail slots of his neighbors. That day his package included reports on issues before the Tokyo metropolitan and local ward assemblies, a questionnaire to provide residents' input to local representatives, and a return envelope.[1] Most of this material was produced by the Japan Communist Party (JCP). The Tokyo assembly report discussed such matters as medical costs for infants and small children, nursing care insurance, and the welfare budget. There are government funds to print material like this, but only a limited amount for postage, so hand deliveries help to get the word out.

Arakawa distributed this material in the Katsushika district of Tokyo in an area commonly known as the "*shitamachi*," literally the "low city," located along the Sumida and Arakawa rivers that flow into the northern end of Tokyo Bay. Whereas Tachikawa is located about 20 miles to the west of the Tokyo city center, the *shitamachi* forms the eastern edge of the city. This was the merchants' and tradesmen's quarter during the Tokugawa era. Today, it is mostly a densely crowded working-class area that ranks among Tokyo's lowest districts in per capita annual income.[2] This is fertile ground for the Japan Communist Party.

As he made his rounds, Arakawa dropped his material into mail slots at the front doors of single-family homes and at apartments and condominiums.[3] Among the older buildings, there were many without "auto-lock" doors that required a key to enter building corridors, so along with representatives of local real estate agents, pizza shops, and other merchants, he walked down corridors

DOI: 10.4324/9781003193999-14

and gently slipped his packets into the mail slots in or alongside doors of the residents.

But this day was different. He stepped into the elevator and rode to the top of a seven-story building and then began to work his way down. When he got to the third floor, he suddenly heard someone demand in a rough voice that he stop.

In response to the man's complaint, Arakawa naturally told him that if it was a nuisance, he would stop deliveries at his door. But the man was not satisfied. He told the monk to go down to the first floor and wait, then he pulled out his cell phone and placed a call to the police emergency line (110) and demanded that police be sent to the building. Arakawa says that he overheard him using code words like "PC" for patrol car and other odd police lingo, as if the man was or had been a police officer himself.[4] In Tokyo, 110 calls are received by a central call center. Operators log the calls and contact appropriate police stations to follow up. In this case, the operator noted that the call appeared to concern delivery of political materials by a JCP member and pushed a special button to indicate that the call was of great importance.[5]

Soon, two officers from the local police station came running. They were joined by more officers in a couple of squad cars. After questioning the monk about the incident, the police asked him to accompany them to the station. In a cooperative spirit, Arakawa agreed and joined them in a squad car. At the police station, several police officers took turns questioning him. As time wore on, he grew tired and announced that he had to get back home. Home? they asked. You can't go home. You're under arrest.[6] It was approximately 5 p.m. The police had questioned him for nearly three hours without notifying him he was under arrest, that he had the right to remain silent, or that he had the right to contact a lawyer.[7]

By chance, Arakawa was acquainted with a lawyer, so he asked the police to call him.[8] This lawyer was also a Buddhist monk like himself. The monk-lawyer was able to get to the police station that evening to meet his friend-and-suddenly client, but when he left, Arakawa remained in jail.[9] Yōsei Arakawa must have felt lost and confused when he found himself spending the night in a jail cell in the local police station.

The lawyer who visited Arakawa on the night of his arrest contacted the "Japan Relief Network" (*kyūenkai*) the following day to seek help. The *kyūenkai* is a nationwide organization founded in the 1930s devoted to assisting individuals under arrest, especially those arrested during public demonstrations or other political activities.[10] *Kyūenkai* is not a law firm and does not provide legal assistance itself; it serves as a clearinghouse that works closely with the *Jiyū Hōsōdan*, a national lawyers network also committed to defending victims of political suppression. A *kyūenkai* staff member called the Tokyo Tōbu Law Office, a small firm of about 15 lawyers affiliated with the *Jiyū Hōsōdan*. Their offices are on the sixth floor of a small office building located across the street from the busy Kinshichō train station in the *shitamachi* district.

FIGURE 13.1 Buddhist priest Yōsei Arakawa was arrested on December 23, 2004, on a charge of trespass when he distributed Japan Communist Party material in the Katsushika district of Tokyo. Here, he addresses supporters after judgment by the Tokyo High Court. (Photograph by the author, December 2007)

When three lawyers from the Tōbu office arrived at the police station on Friday the 24th, they found a small line of protesters parading on the sidewalk in front of the station.[11] Residents had been alerted to the monk's arrest that morning by a single-page insert to *Akahata* produced by the local JCP office. The "breaking news" announcement reported that "A-san," a 57-year-old local man had been arrested for distributing flyers at a condo building.

Two of the three lawyers were very young; one had qualified to practice just that year. This was his second case. The young lawyers found the arrest incredible and thought the monk would be quickly released. It fell to Kōichi Omori, 20 years their senior, to explain the nature of arrest and detention in Japan. Although this would appear to be a trivial matter to any ordinary person, he said, it's possible the police had some hidden agenda. They could keep the priest behind bars for a long time if they wished. The lawyers could see that Arakawa, a man who devoted his life to serving his community and had never been accused of doing wrong, was deeply shaken by this news. He had never entered a jail cell before and now a lawyer was telling him he might be there for a long time. He would be further shocked to learn that all visitors other than lawyers were prohibited.[12]

As they were meeting with Arakawa, a police team arrived at his home to conduct a search. His wife was out so their 20-year-old son answered the door. He was studying in Kyoto at the time and had just returned home for a family visit during the New Year holiday. Shocked by the appearance of the police, he said his parents were not at home so they should come back at another time. Some of the officers must have had a good chuckle at this. They brandished a search warrant and burst through the door.[13]

In the immediate aftermath of the arrest, the lawyers' first task was to gain their client's release from detention. They went to work immediately, visiting the prosecutors' office and the courthouse the following day. They filed a formal demand on Sunday, December 26, in which they declared that their client had an appropriate reason to visit the condominium building, that he had nothing to hide, and there was no reason to detain him or file charges. They received no response other than a court order that extended their client's detention for ten days. The order cited the risk that he might destroy evidence, especially by contacting others. The attorneys' formal opposition to this order was swiftly rejected.[14] They also demanded a public hearing on the reasons for detention. There was little hope that it would lead to Arakawa's release, but at least his friends and family would be able to see him in open court.

The arrest and detention of the monk were puzzling enough, but what could possibly justify the judge's order for extended detention? In the opinion of Minoru Nishida, a lawyer who represented Arakawa, the only explanation was political and it was linked to Tent Village. He explained that the state security police deeply wanted to get a guilty verdict in Tachikawa. The Prime Minister had just ordered deployment of the Self-Defense Forces to Iraq, so the political stakes could not have been higher. The police appeared to be on high alert for cases like this. If not for the Iraq deployment and the Tent Village arrests, it seems unlikely that anyone would have bothered Yōsei Arakawa.

The prosecutors might have wished the police had allowed Arakawa to go on his way, but now that he was in custody, the pressure would be intense.[15] The prosecutors had lost at the Hachioji court. Now the Katsushika case offered the opportunity to turn this around. If antiwar activists who delivered flyers door-to-door were reassured by the Hachioji not guilty verdict, they would have to think again.

The Tent Village defendants and their lawyers knew nothing of developments on the far side of Tokyo as they searched for some means to forestall an appeal in their own case. On the morning of December 23, just a few hours before Arakawa's arrest, a delegation of four members of the Tent Village team including two attorneys visited the Tachikawa Police Station to deliver a formal complaint against the police actions. But the police representative refused to accept it and instead referred them to the statement reported in newspapers to the effect that the police had simply followed the law when apprehending their clients.[16]

The following day, Yōsei Arakawa's first full day in jail, the Tent Village defendants received the bad news that the prosecutors had filed an appeal. Now, the Tent Village team would have to defend their not guilty verdict in Tokyo High Court.

This decision was not unexpected, but it must have been a shock nonetheless. The three defendants and their attorneys had been allowed to bask in the warmth of the not guilty verdict for only a week and a day before the hammer came down. Once they delivered the news to their clients, there was not much for the attorneys to do. The next chapter in the legal battle would not commence until the prosecutors filed a brief setting out their grounds for appeal. Then, the attorneys would mobilize to deliver a formal response.

Meanwhile, Yōsei Arakawa remained in jail. When Yutaka Osawa learned of the Arakawa arrest, he posted a poignant comment on his website. The arrest was made right on the heels of the not guilty verdict in Tachikawa, which declared that "freedom of expression is a pillar of democracy and must be heavily protected." By arresting Arakawa, he wrote, the police "ignore the not guilty verdict and instead seek to expand the suppression of free speech. This must be seen as not merely an attack on the Japan Communist Party, but also an attack on democracy and free society."[17]

When the ten-day detention period expired, a judge approved the prosecutors' request for ten more days on the ground that Arakawa might destroy evidence. Then, on January 11, Arakawa received even worse news. The prosecutors indicted him that day for violating Article 130 of the Criminal Code, the same charge filed against the Tent Village defendants ten months before. Now, he too would be brought to trial. A guilty verdict would label him a criminal. Arakawa was not released until three days after the indictment, so he ended up spending 23 days in jail.[18] The timing of the detention was especially bad because it prevented him from performing traditional year-end rites for his followers.

The Tent Village Campaign Continues

Although there was little Tent Village defense counsel could do until they received the government's formal statement of appeal, the support group could not rest. They would have to keep their spirits up and find ways to gather the resources necessary to fight the appeal. Yutaka Osawa and other supporters met in January to plan their next steps. Their first question was when the appellate proceeding would start, but the attorneys said only that they should not expect any court hearings before summer.[19] They settled on a series of tasks to be accomplished by then, including (1) organizing an event on February 27, the one-year anniversary of the arrests; (2) publishing a complete account of the story from the arrests through the December 16 judgment; and (3) gathering at least 10,000 signatures on petitions calling for a final judgment of not guilty.[20]

The first task was completed on time with an event held at a public hall in Tachikawa on February 27 to commemorate the anniversary of the arrests.

Osawa reported that 120 persons gathered, many from outside the *Santama* area, even though the schedule clashed with other antiwar rallies. A duo from the local rock group "Kokubunji Experience" performed, helping to create a celebratory mood. The formal session began with a screening of the Fuji Television news clip from the arrest, showing closeups of Sachimi Takada in her long dreadlocks and in handcuffs as she was led to a police vehicle.

This was followed by a speech by Hitotsubashi University philosophy professor Satoshi Ukai, who provided some political context for the Tent Village arrests. According to Ukai, Japan had begun a rapid rightward shift over the past year in the direction of prewar ideals. He called for an aggressive fight in the appellate courts that would not be limited to defending the democratic Constitution, but would also seek to secure peace.[21]

The speakers introduced two books that reported the Tent Village story and the broader fight against Japan's participation in the Iraq War. One was an insider's account by Mitsuru Munakata, a young freelance writer and close ally and friend of the Tent Village. Munakata attended all court hearings and was able to take notes and write his own record of the trial. He wrote his book in an engaging novelistic style with a good deal of local color based on his intimate knowledge of the Tent Village members and their work. In an effort to protect the privacy of the main actors, he gave them all assumed names.

The second book was written by Toshihiro Yoshida, an award-winning author of several non-fiction works. Yoshida's book, titled "*Refusing to Cooperate in War*" (*Sensō Kyōryoku Kyōhi)*, details the efforts of several antiwar groups that protested Japan's participation in the Iraq War. The chapter on the Tent Village case begins with a comparison of the Tent Village flyers with Self-Defense Force recruitment flyers delivered door-to-door in the same manner. His treatment addressed the story from many angles, including the ubiquitous nature of junk mail, the startling admission of a local prosecutor that the government was after a chilling effect, a summary of the statement of the 56 scholars and other legal theory, and more. He even covered the trial and showed how the testimony of the government's own witnesses supported the defense theory that the arrests were a product of collusion between the state security police and SDF officers. Overall, Yoshida painted a picture in which it was obvious that the Tachikawa arrests were one element of a larger government program to silence dissent. Yoshida's book appeared under the imprint of a major liberal publisher in a popular paperback format that was available in bookstores throughout Japan.[22]

Yoshida chaired the panel discussion. Speakers included Munakata, Obora, and Kanako Burukitch, a young woman who protested the Iraq War in front of the U.S. Embassy in Tokyo. She told the audience that

> I went to the American Embassy to tell them to stop the war because I wanted to say it in person, because I wanted to hear it in person. But after I spoke into a loudspeaker, the police questioned me on suspicion of assault and my house was raided.

She told the audience she was fighting for free speech. "What would happen if there were no more flyers, voices, newspapers, graffiti?" she asked. Then she provided her answer: "We would have a dictatorship."[23]

The rally ended with the adoption of a resolution in support of victims of political repression. This was followed by a march through Tachikawa, with stops at the police station and SDF base along the way. When he first emerged from the building, Osawa was startled to see a cluster of about 40 plainclothes police, some with cameras out, intimidating the marchers by snapping their photos as they walked by.[24]

Judge Hasegawa had pushed the trial along at a fast pace because he thought the verdict would have influence throughout Japan. As far as the state security police were concerned, however, the effect seemed to be the opposite of what the judge intended. Rather than respecting the court's not guilty verdict, the state security police appeared to be ratcheting up the pressure on the Tachikawa activists instead.

The second item on the support group's to-do list was publishing a complete account of the Tent Village story. Keen to document their experience, Yutaka Osawa and Tent Village members and supporters worked at a breakneck pace. They produced a 260-page paperback that collected articles by ten authors, two "roundtable discussions" (a common format in Japanese publications), and many primary documents. The book was released on May 2, the day before the "Constitution Day" holiday.[25]

The introduction was written by Hitotsubashi professor Ukai and the closing comments were by Osawa, the indefatigable leader of the Tent Village support group. Supplementary documents included a sample Tent Village flyer, the February 29 detention order approved by a local judge, a diagram of the SDF apartment complex, the texts of public declarations by supporting groups, and more.[26] Kato wrote the first substantive chapter, "What is Tent Village?" which provides a quick overview of the group's history. As a whole, the book serves as an invaluable reference for students of the era.

The not guilty verdict brought unprecedented attention to Tent Village. Suddenly, the defendants and their supporters were invited to make public comments and to write about their experiences. According to a commemorative pamphlet, "There were even requests from the kinds of groups we had never had contact with, including events to support refugees, a gathering to oppose changes to the education law, and journalists' symposia." The defendants felt that their image had changed. They were no longer known as "criminals" (*hannin-tachi*), as they had been in the more extreme accounts.[27] Now, if they could win in the appellate court, they would preserve this status.

The Government's Appeal

As the Tent Village supporters continued their campaign, the prosecutors labored on their "Statement of Reasons for Appeal," a formal document setting out arguments for reversing the Hachioji judgment. Defense counsel would find no surprises in the 19-page document prosecutors filed on May 30. Although they had lost at District Court, the prosecutors' primary goal was actually to persuade the Tokyo High Court that Judge Hasegawa and his colleagues were *correct* in a critical section of their ruling. The prosecutors fully endorsed the District Court's conclusion that the defendants' acts violated Criminal Code Article 130 and they copied the court's words as if they were their own. The first three pages of the document are filled with quotations from the District Court judgment, especially findings of fact. Thus, the defendants entered the SDF property "without permission" and their actions were therefore "contrary to the will of the property managers and the residents and constitute 'trespass'" required by Article 130. Further, the District Court held that whether or not the defendants were aware of the signs that prohibited outsiders from entering the property was irrelevant. Their actions fulfilled all the requirements of Article 130.

With that bird in hand, they launched into a vigorous attack on the District Court's notion that "the extent of criminality was not sufficient to apply a criminal penalty." The prosecutors expressed their shock that, despite finding that the defendants had violated Article 130, the District Court had somehow conjured a power "superior to law" (*chōhōteki*) in order to find them not guilty.[28]

In the prosecutors' opinion, the District Court's approach would undermine the very foundation of Japan's legal structure. The purpose of the criminal code is to "clarify what is a crime and what is not a crime and thereby to achieve the objectives of protecting legal interests and maintaining the legal order while protecting the rights of the people." In order to maintain the legal order, they argued, fundamental rules of law such as the criminal code must be strictly interpreted. The District Court failed by introducing a set of vague standards: the "legitimacy of motivation," the "propriety of behavior," and the "degree of injury resulting from their acts" and then relying on them to conclude that the "degree of illegality" was insufficient to justify a criminal penalty.

In the prosecutors' summation, "Introducing such extremely vague standards not provided in the law … would allow arbitrary judgments instead of the strict interpretations required, invite loosening of the criminal law structure, and damage the stability of the law." They followed this by addressing each of these vague standards in turn and explaining how the District Court had erred in their application of each one.

The prosecutors turned away any suggestion that they sought to punish the defendants for their political beliefs; they claimed to be solely concerned with the threat posed by the defendants' acts. Although political expression must be protected in a democratic society, they said, "No person has the right to enter into the residence of another as they please without permission in order to express political opinions."

Regarding the defendants' reliance on Constitution Article 21, the prosecutors repeated an expression that appears frequently in Japan's judicial opinions: free speech rights are "not without limits." Then, they cited two key judgments from the Supreme Court that featured these precise words when rejecting the free speech claims of others prosecuted for minor offenses.

In the first case, decided in 1970, two defendants were found guilty of placing 84 political posters on telephone poles without permission. They were sentenced to ten days in jail under the Minor Offenses Act.[29] The Supreme Court upheld the convictions, despite the constitutional guarantee of free speech. In the Court's view, criminal prosecution of such actions is "necessary and reasonable" in order to protect property and managerial rights of telephone companies and thereby to protect the public welfare.

In the second case, decided in 1984, the Supreme Court similarly upheld convictions for unlawful political speech, citing the need to protect the public welfare. The defendants were arrested for distributing flyers to passersby at a major station on a private train line without the approval of station personnel. According to the reported facts, they both handed out political flyers and spoke through a loudspeaker, continuing to do so for 20 minutes after station personnel requested them to stop.[30] The defendants were charged with trespassing under Criminal Code 130 and a separate provision of a law regulating the operation of train lines.

Although Japan does not follow the common law rule of *stare decisis* that requires lower courts to follow the precedents of senior courts, Supreme Court judgments carry great weight. The prosecutors selected two that clearly indicated the Court's attitude toward the balance between property rights and freedom of expression. They knew that defense counsel would search in vain for equivalent precedent to support their cause.[31]

In their final flourish, the prosecutors called on the court to protect the SDF residences "which should receive a high level of protection as the foundation of daily life." The document ends with its demand that the Tokyo High Court overturn the District Court judgment and impose a verdict of guilty.

While the support group was waiting for appellate proceedings to begin, they planned a nationwide tour led by Kato and Obora designed to build and maintain support for the three defendants. The tour served not only as an opportunity to explain the Hachioji judgment and report on preparations for the appeal, but also to express thanks to activists around the country who had supported the Tent Village defendants with their words of encouragement and their cash. The tour formally launched with visits to Sendai and Morioka in the Tohoku area at the end of June and the final event was held in Matsumoto in September. Kato, Obora, and their colleagues rallied antiwar activists at more than a dozen gatherings around the country. Some were organized by local chapters of Amnesty International. Each visit was unique. Some events were held in college classrooms and others at festivals or other gatherings. The number of attendees ran from only ten or so to nearly one hundred. When they visited Nagoya, they made sure to visit the Air Self-Defense Force (ASDF) base at Komaki, which served as a primary departure point for SDF forces headed to the Iraq war theater. There they presented a formal petition to base personnel as was their custom back in Tachikawa.[32]

14

COURT JUDGMENTS IN 2005 AND 2006

The Extreme Surveillance of Akio Horikoshi

The arrests of the civil servant Akio Horikoshi and the Tent Village defendants were separated by just one week, but the two cases followed very different trajectories. The first court hearing in the Tent Village trial took place on May 6. The government called just three witnesses and the court issued a judgment on December 16. The Horikoshi trial was a different story. The first hearing did not take place until July 20 and the government ultimately called 13 witnesses to make its case. The trial court would not issue a verdict until after the Tokyo High Court had already ruled on the Tent Village appeal. The 13 witnesses against Horikoshi were all police officers who had observed him as he made his rounds. Prosecutors called these witnesses to prove that Akio Horikoshi violated the law by distributing political literature. Defense counsel had a different interpretation: the intense surveillance showed a gross violation of personal privacy.

Mainstream news organizations paid little attention to the tedious testimony spread out over the long months of the Horikoshi trial, but a team of four undergraduate college students attended the trial beginning with the eighth court hearing on April 22, 2005. They diligently compiled reports for each hearing and then published an account in a popular monthly legal journal in March 2006. It begins in dramatic style.

> The defendant and the investigators must clearly recall that cold mid-winter day. On March 3, 2004, the defendant was arrested on suspicion of violating the National Public Employees Law (NPEL) at the conclusion of an investigation that covered nearly a year. This must be seen as the result of the tenacity of the state security police. Tense images from the dramatic arrest were filmed by the mass media and broadcast into everyone's home

DOI: 10.4324/9781003193999-15

> as if it were a case of great importance. Why was the act of distributing flyers made into such a big issue? We continued our observation of the trial because we wanted to know the answer to this question.[1]

Ultimately, the students were unable to find an answer, but their published report does provide some flavor of the courtroom testimony. For example, their description of the 12th court hearing, held on June 25, 2005, reports the testimony of a police officer who operated a camera that recorded Horikoshi's movements on October 25, 2003. His videorecording was among the items of evidence released to the defense in response to Judge Nakatani's momentous order issued at the first court hearing. Defense counsel showed it in court and then questioned the man behind the camera. According to his testimony, a superior seemed to know of Horikoshi's expected movements that day with great precision. First, he ordered the witness to wait at the entrance to councilman Katsuhiko Mariko's office in the morning.[2] When the video begins at 9:20 a.m., it shows Horikoshi arriving at Mariko's office. Next, at 10:01, it shows Horikoshi departing with a brown handled bag. Then the video stops. For the next stage of his assignment, the superior instructed the witness to proceed directly to Harumi Garden No. 6 after recording Horikoshi's departure from Mariko's office. When it resumes at 10:10, the video shows Horikoshi entering the Harumi Garden No. 6 lobby. Then, at 10:10, when Horikoshi was in the lobby, the videorecording reproduces the officer's exultant voice: "*Yatta!*" ("Hurray!") when he observed Horikoshi depositing his material into the mailboxes. The recording stopped when Horikoshi departed the building. According to the witness, at this point the police entered the building and collected samples of Horikoshi's delivery voluntarily provided by residents.

Defense lawyer Kenji Kato explains that evidence released due to Judge Nakatani's order was vital in enabling his team to prepare for cross-examination of witnesses like this.[3]

The students' report presents just a thin slice of the full story revealed over the course of the long trial. The police officers' testimony—and the 29 items of evidence released by Judge Nakatani's order—told of police surveillance on an epic scale. As summarized by Professor Shirō Okubo, those reports say the police tailed Horikoshi every day without fail from October 11 through November 8, 2003. At times, they used as many as four vehicles and employed 11 officers on the assignment.[4]

Courtroom testimony concerned Horikoshi's flyer deliveries, but the police recorded much more. One member of the defense team described the attorneys' astonishment when they learned of the breadth of the surveillance: "When we saw the investigation record, every member of the defense team swallowed their breath."[5] At times, the surveillance continued all day and into the night. For example, a notation by one officer for Sunday, October 12, 2003, read:

> I picked him up departing his home at 12:08 PM. At 12:25, he came through the wicket at Yurakucho station and met an unidentified woman

> (height 150 cm., age about 35). They went to the XXX restaurant in the basement floor of the Ginza Inz building. They left the restaurant at 1:20 PM. Walking in the direction of Tsukiji, they entered the Chiyoda-ku Hall at 2–15–6 Ginza, Chuo-ku, where they saw the play "Toguchi." After the performance finished at 5:25 p.m., they went to a pub with about ten men and women who had attended the play. After they left the pub at 7:50 p.m., while holding hands with the woman, the suspect walked together with an unidentified man to the karaoke shop "Diana Ginza" (Ginza 3–9–6). I ended the surveillance at 10:30 p.m.[6]

Other police notations gave the times of his departures from home, details of the tickets he bought at train stations and stations where he alighted; license plate numbers for taxis; the gender, body type and estimated age of persons he met; the banks where he used cash machines; visits to medical clinics; a trip to the lost-and-found counter at a train station; and other precise details. The record showed surveillance of the daily round of an ordinary citizen that mostly had nothing to do with acts alleged in the indictment. The defendant's life was laid bare by government officials who either had no knowledge of privacy protections or simply felt empowered to disregard them.

Constitutional scholar Shirō Okubo raised another fundamental question: Why were the police involved at all? The law charges the National Personnel Authority (NPA) with enforcement of the NPEL and related regulations. After all, the NPA itself is the author of the very regulations the police accused Akio Horikoshi of violating. Professor Okubo even cites a longstanding directive by the first head of that agency which states that the restriction on political acts should be interpreted in the narrowest manner possible and the power to investigate possible violations must not be abused. Another regulation requires the heads of administrative agencies to report violations to the NPA and to take measures to stop violations.[7] There is no directive to call the police.

According to Professor Okubo, the Social Insurance Agency, the defendant's employer, made no complaint over his activities. It seems likely that officials at the Agency knew nothing of the police investigation of their colleague until a police team showed up at their offices with a search warrant. By criminalizing violations, Article 110 of the NPEL empowers the police and prosecutors to bypass the NPA and other administrative agencies and apply their own interpretations.

In light of the incredible scale of the police surveillance and the searches at the Japan Communist Party offices, Professor Okubo concluded that the obvious goal of the state security police had nothing to do with the purposes of the government personnel law; instead, their objective was to gather information on the JCP.[8]

The government called its final witness on September 30, 2005. At that hearing, a patrolman told the court how he and a partner had happened upon Akio Horikoshi by accident. According to the four college students, the witness testified that he first noticed Horikoshi's questionable activities on April 19, 2003, when he and his partner were in their car and observed Horikoshi dropping something into the central bank of mailboxes at Harumi Garden Building 6. He couldn't quite see what it was, but he suspected Horikoshi might be delivering political flyers.

The students found the testimony dubious:

> Sitting in his car, the patrolman saw the defendant was delivering "something like political flyers." If so, he would have also thought there's a possibility the defendant was delivering advertising or newspapers. If patrolmen conduct their watch like this … everyone who delivers something would be the object of suspicion. Can it be that every time a police officer sees someone delivering advertising or a newspaper, he suspects a violation of the election law?[9]

With the prosecution case complete, defense counsel prepared to call their first witnesses on October 14.

A Coordinated Appeal to the Public

Supporters of the defendants in all three cases were inflamed by what they saw as a gross abuse of police power. It became obvious that they should join forces in a common effort to alert the public to the threat posed to free speech. They organized joint events at central Tokyo locations with the defendants and their lawyers taking turns at the microphone. By working together at convenient venues in central Tokyo, they could gather much larger audiences than they could find in far-off Tachikawa and other arrest locations. Of even greater importance, the audiences might include news reporters and other writers in position to spread the word.

The national lawyers' federation (Nichibenren) hosted a number of symposia at its Tokyo headquarters building located next door to the courthouse in Kasumigaseki. There was no more important audience than the lawyers themselves, many of whom hold a deep commitment to protecting fundamental constitutional rights, especially freedom of expression. An event titled "Can this be a crime?" (*kore tte hanzai?*) staged on April 6, featured defendants and their lawyers from four cases.[10]

Three weeks later, a much larger event was held at a public hall in central Tokyo that demonstrated the organizational muscle of the JCP. Titled "Freedom of Speech in Danger, April 26 Gathering," the event filled a venue located just across the moat on the north side of the imperial palace with an audience of 900. Speakers from the three cases were joined by the defendant in an election case from Oita Prefecture and a senior officer of the JCP. Professor Okudaira, Japan's most acclaimed expert in the law of free speech and a co-founder of the Article 9 Association, delivered the keynote speech.[11]

The campaign also attracted the attention of many public intellectuals.[12] The monthly magazine *Tsukuru* organized public symposia in February and again in July that attracted around 400 attendees each under the title "Very Suspicious! Police, Prosecutors, Courts." The speakers' presentations were edited for publication in the monthly magazine and then again in a 235-page paperback that came out in August.[13] Japan's publishers work fast. Separate chapters carried the first-person accounts of Obora, Arakawa, Horikoshi, and defendants in three other cases, along with panel discussions and additional chapters by freelance journalists and others. As indicated in the title, the specific thrust of the project was to document and criticize the extreme police action and the failure of prosecutors and courts to rein them in. The editors highlighted Professor Okudaira's courtroom testimony regarding the prewar Peace Preservation Law in the book's introduction.

Back in Tachikawa, Tent Village supporters continued their spirited campaign throughout the year, delivering tens of thousands of flyers in the local area (while carefully avoiding the Self-Defense Force buildings), gathering signatures on petitions at tables set up in front of train stations, and holding public events including gatherings to commemorate the Iraq invasion on March 21 and to celebrate Constitution Day on May 3. By the time of the first Tokyo High Court hearing, supporters would submit demands to dismiss the appeal and uphold the not guilty verdict signed by more than 16,000 persons.

The Tent Village crew also continued its nationwide tour and the attorneys worked on their response to the government appeal brief filed on May 30. The

FIGURE 14.1 Tent Village supporters continued their campaign after the government appeal of the not guilty verdict. Here, they march through central Tachikawa in March 2005. (Photograph by Yutaka Osawa)

first appellate hearing was set for Wednesday, September 14. But as that day drew near, there was one more surprise.

On September 10, the state security police arrested a government official named Shin'ichi Ujihashi for delivering the *Akahata* and other political material, this time at apartments in Setagaya, a residential area of Tokyo just outside the Shibuya hub. Like Horikoshi, he would be prosecuted for violating the NPEL. This time a court rejected the prosecutors' request for detention, so the suspect was released after only two nights in jail.[14]

The Tent Village Case Arrives at the Tokyo High Court

The Tokyo High Court is one of eight intermediate appellate courts in Japan's judicial system, each responsible for appeals in a defined geographic area. It is the country's second most important and prestigious court after the Supreme Court because it resolves all appeals that arise from decisions of lower courts throughout the Tokyo judicial district, which includes ten prefectures and approximately 30% of Japan's population. Moreover, since it is located at the seat of the national government, the court also takes charge of most appeals in litigation against the government itself. The chief judge of the Tokyo High Court oversees the work of more than 150 High Court judges and is nearly always a candidate for elevation to the Supreme Court. The High Court conducts its work through 35 separate court divisions, ten of which specialize in criminal cases.[15]

The first hearing in the appeal of the Tent Village verdict took place on Wednesday, September 14 at 3:30, in courtroom No. 725 in the 19-story court tower in the Kasumigaseki district of central Tokyo.[16] The appeal was heard by a three-judge panel led by chief judge Taketaka Nakagawa, a veteran of 37 years on the bench who was promoted to the Tokyo High Court in 2001 after serving as the chief judge of district courts in the Niigata District.[17]

Under Japan's court procedure, lower courts are primarily charged with hearing witnesses and taking other evidence, but to some degree appellate courts are also empowered to accept evidence.[18] In the Tent Village case, both sides sought to add new material to the evidentiary record. The court denied defense requests for testimony by a constitutional scholar and the mayor of a small city, but did allow brief testimony by the defendants themselves.[19]

The prosecutors declared that they would stand on the case made in their appeal brief filed on May 30 with no additional argument, but they did request to submit one item of new evidence. This was a report that identified seven other trespass cases in which defendants were found guilty in 2003 and 2004. Their goal was to show that the government regularly prosecuted trespass cases and therefore Tent Village was not targeted for political reasons.

Defense counsel responded at the next hearing, on October 3. They argued that, in a country of more than 120 million people, seven cases over a two-year period did not shake the conclusion that despite the constant flow of commercial flyers from real estate agents, English-language schools, fast food joints, and other places, the police selected Tent Village for special treatment.[20]

After examining the prosecutors' list of seven cases, the defense noted two key characteristics. First, six concerned so-called "pink flyers," meaning solicitations for prostitution. Second, in five out of the seven cases, the defendants were foreigners. Moreover, only three of the cases went to a full trial. The other four were disposed of by summary proceedings with no court hearings.[21]

The evidence seemed to indicate that, in addition to flyers that criticize the government's war policy, prosecutors also sought criminal trespassing charges related to solicitation of sex acts and against foreign residents of such precarious existence that they resorted to the meager employment of flyer delivery. The prosecutors did not explain whether the focus on non-Japanese messengers reflected discrimination, a backdoor effort to enforce immigration law, or some other animus.

As for the general societal acceptance of door-to-door flyers, the defense noted that the practice was so commonplace and ordinary that there is an industry group, the "Japan Posting Association," accredited by the Ministry of Economy, Trade and Industry.[22] When defense counsel were done with their attack on the supplementary evidence, there were no comments from the court or the prosecutors.

Aside from the defendants' statements and the evidence offered by the prosecutors, the court felt no need to augment the record. After closing arguments, the court would be ready to deliver its judgment at the next session, scheduled for Friday, December 9.

The Tokyo High Court Issues Its Judgment (December 9, 2005)

The December 9 court proceeding began suddenly. Spectators had barely taken their seats when Judge Nakagawa abruptly announced, "We reverse the lower court judgment." With this simple statement, the Hachioji judgment was overturned and the three defendants were found guilty. Attorney Yamamoto said the judge's expression was so rigidly fixed when he delivered these words that his face resembled a *Noh* mask. When voices of protest arose from the spectators' gallery, however, Judge Nakagawa displayed some emotion for the first time, yelling, "Be quiet! If you are not quiet, I will order you removed from the court!"[23]

The good news for the defendants was that the High Court denied the prosecutors' request for six months imprisonment and imposed small fines instead. The court ruled that Obora and Takada delivered flyers on two dates and were required to pay fines of 200,000 yen (approx. US $ 17,000 in 2005) each. Onishi, who participated only once, was fined 100,000 yen.

With the hearing finished, the defendants and their attorneys moved to the courthouse press club where they spoke of their disappointment and fielded questions from reporters. The attorneys called the judgment unfair and pledged to secure ultimate victory with an appeal to the Supreme Court. They resorted to the cliché often repeated by Japan's human rights lawyers when the odds are against them: "The Tokyo High Court abandoned its role as a 'fortress of human rights'" (*jinken no toride*). Maybe they would find that fortress at the Supreme Court.[24]

The three defendants sat together at the center of the small stage in the press club conference space as they commented on the judgment. Expressing his extreme disappointment, Obora demanded, "What's the difference between everyday commercial flyers and our antiwar flyers? What is the content that justifies arrests? Today's judgment did not answer these questions." News reports also carried Sachimi Takada's passionate exclamation: "The right to free speech is important! This judgment is like the last nail in the coffin of Japan's democracy!" (*saigo no todome wo sashita*). Onishi was quoted to say

> The frightening thing is that people who do nothing more than distributing flyers can be arrested. This will give a boost to the high-handed attitude of the police. We must win at the Supreme Court with a judgment that says "people delivering flyers is an ordinary thing."[25]

In their brief reports on the judgment, all major papers quoted a single sentence from Judge Nakagawa's courtroom comments: "Even if the expression of political opinions through flyers is protected, this does not mean that it is acceptable to enter property against the will of the building managers."[26]

According to custom, the court released a summary of its decision to members of the press club as a reference for news reports.[27] The *Asahi* published a version of this summary in its evening editions. After a brief description of the facts and the court's judgment that the defendants had violated Article 130 by disregarding the will of the custodians, most of the summary concerned the High Court's dismantling of the Hachioji court's reliance on "insufficient illegality" to find the defendants not guilty. It listed the three elements of the Hachioji court's analysis: "legitimacy of motivation," the "propriety of behavior," and the "degree of injury resulting from their acts" followed by the High Court's rejection of each.

But the summary provided little insight into other fundamental aspects of the court's analysis. The court's full opinion carried much more. Of special significance, the High Court took a different approach from the Hachioji court in applying Criminal Code Article 130. Whereas Judge Hasegawa and his colleagues had ruled that the defendants had trespassed into a "residence," the High Court pushed this aside, selecting the alternate prong of Article 130. Instead of entering a residence, the High Court said they trespassed into the much broader "premises." The court stressed the importance of this distinction: "this court interprets the lot and common areas of the buildings to constitute part of the 'premises' and therefore only the intent of the managers is at issue."[28] At a stroke, the intentions or desires of the actual residents became irrelevant. Was the residents' "peaceful daily life" disturbed? Maybe, but this would only be relevant if the building managers thought so. According to the High Court, it was only the will of the managers that mattered.

Because the court selected premises and the will of the managers, it encountered the additional requirement that the property be "under guard." Although the court provided no definition of the phrase, it clearly set a very low bar. One might think that "under guard" implied the presence of uniformed guards or perhaps the manned entry points one sees at industrial sites or "gated communities," but the Tokyo High Court panel did not. The court was explicit: the premises were under guard "even though there is no gate or similar structure in place at the entrances." After all, it explained, "the paths that lead from these entrances are provided for the passage solely of persons related to the multifamily residences." Apparently, the fact that visitors could discern that the paths were intended for residents was sufficient to conclude that the premises were "under guard" as required by statute. Perhaps the most important fact was simply that the entire property was under the management of duly appointed SDF officers. The High Court panel provided no further indication of its reasoning.

In his review, Professor Kōji Adachi ridiculed this aspect of the judgment, pointing out that the lack of entrance gates enabled a free flow of uninvited visitors into the property, including not only commercial salespeople, but elementary school children who regularly passed through the grounds. He published a photo of school children walking through the property alongside his text for good measure.[29]

But the police did not arrest commercial salespeople or school children. They singled out only individuals who carried messages critical of the government's Iraq policy. In democratic societies, people rely on the courts to strictly monitor such selective enforcement of the law against government opponents. But Judge Nakagawa and the other members of the Tokyo High Court panel were unconcerned. After quoting Hachioji court language that stressed the importance of free political speech as a "pillar of democracy," the High Court judges wrote, "even if freedom of expression should be interpreted in such a way, it does not immediately allow violation of the rights of others."[30] As for selective enforcement based on content, it appeared that the court was in favor. The court was clearly disturbed by the message, writing "It is clear from the text of the flyers that … the defendants urged the SDF members to reject orders to deploy to Iraq, a so-called 'SDF member targeting operation'" (*jieikan kōsaku*). Other than that, there is no evidence in the court's opinion that it attempted any kind of balance between the alleged injury suffered by the building managers against the values protected by the constitutional guarantee of free speech or any other analytical approach that might afford particular importance to the constitutional right.

Regarding the defense claims of abusive prosecution, the High Court's opinion was clear:

> Upon review of the evidence, we do not agree that the prosecution in this case had the objective of suppressing the defendants' speech or limiting or shutting down the activities of the group of which they were members. This prosecution cannot be said to have violated Constitution Article 21. Of course, we cannot agree that the prosecution is such an extreme deviation of prosecutorial discretion as to fulfill the elements of a crime in exercise of their duties.[31]

The significance of the High Court's decision to shift the focus from building residents to building managers did not escape the notice of Professor Shōjirō Sakaguchi. His comments were quoted in both the *Asahi* and *Mainichi*.

> In a democratic society the free flow of a variety of opinions and the opportunity for us to hear them is of decisive importance. The judgment says that the flyer distribution was contrary to the will of the building managers, but the desires of the building managers and of the residents are not the same. Whether or not to receive information is something that should be decided by each individual; we must not allow others to cut the flow of information as they please.

In effect, he said the High Court granted the SDF managers censorship authority.[32]

The *Yomiuri*, the most conservative of Japan's major newspapers, sought to present a balanced view. In a sidebar comment, editors wrote that the case presented a "collision" between freedom of expression and the residents' right to peaceful daily life. The *Yomiuri* also pointed out that the Tent Village case was not alone; in fact, there were three similar prosecutions in 2003. After summarizing the District and High Court judgments, the authors wrote "On one hand, in a case like this where there was clearly no intent to cause damage to residents, one can say application of a criminal penalty is an 'overreaction.'" On the other hand, the conservative paper made no suggestion of a political motive behind the police action; instead, it found a justification in a police response to a supposed general decline in personal safety. Finally, the comment called upon the courts to strike a posture that reflects a balance between protection of peaceful daily life and freedom of speech.[33]

As commuters picked up evening editions on their way home and read these reports, Tent Village supporters gathered in Tachikawa to protest the guilty verdict. Yutaka Osawa was unable to attend the High Court proceeding due to city council business, but he joined others at Tachikawa station in the early evening to hand out flyers that attacked the judgment and then served as chairperson of the information session held at a public hall in Tachikawa that evening.

Osawa was joined at the microphone by several attorneys and supporters. Lead counsel Kuriyama contrasted the District Court's careful analysis with what she called the rough (*ranbō*) work of the High Court and repeated Professor Sakaguchi's complaint that the High Court erred by raising the interests of the building managers over those of the residents.

Defendants in three other flyer cases: Horikoshi, Arakawa, and a retired high school teacher named Katsuhisa Fujita—who was prosecuted for distributing printed material at a high school graduation ceremony—traveled to Tachikawa to deliver supporting comments of their own.[34]

Professor Ishizaki was also there and delivered a rather blunt assessment of the current state of affairs: "The High Court has just delivered a 'go-sign' to the police," he said. "You can become a criminal for carrying flyers. This judgment is far from the everyday feelings of the people."[35]

According to Osawa, the event was attended by 120 people. There was no doubt that he expressed the consensus of the gathering when he exhorted the crowd to keep fighting: "Looking toward the Supreme Court, let's continue our unwavering commitment to protecting freedom of speech!"[36]

Two Court Judgments in Summer 2006

District Court Judgment in the Horikoshi Case (June 29, 2006)

After a mammoth trial that consumed 27 court hearings and featured more than two dozen witnesses, on June 29, 2006, a Tokyo District Court panel led by Judge Haremitsu Mōri found Akio Horikoshi guilty.[37] The court's opinion lists seven separate objections to the prosecution made by defense counsel. The court readily dismissed challenges to the constitutionality of the statute on its face and as applied as well as the defense claim that the defendant's actions did not violate the statute at all.

Regarding commencement of the investigation, the court accepted the police explanation that it began serendipitously one day in Spring 2003, when a pair of officers spotted Akio Horikoshi at the Harumi Garden apartments and sensed something amiss. It rejected the defense claim that this was part of an ongoing police surveillance scheme directed at the JCP.

The court encountered slightly more difficulty in assessing evidence collected in the enormous police investigation, especially the videorecording of the defendant's movements. For the most part, the court did accept what amounted to police stalking and videorecording, but it also ruled there are limits.

In addressing Horikoshi's claim that the investigation violated his right to privacy, the court first considered whether the police were required to obtain a warrant. Because the police teams followed Horikoshi while he walked on public streets and in other public areas such as apartment building lobbies, the court ruled no warrant was necessary.[38]

Regarding videorecording, however, the court confronted a hurdle presented by a 1969 Supreme Court judgment that involved police photos of a demonstrator taken on the streets of Kyoto. It was the first time the Supreme

Court recognized a constitutional right to control one's likeness and placed limits on the circumstances in which police may take photos or other images of persons in a public place.[39] In order for such photography to be lawful, the Court said it must fulfill three conditions: a crime was in progress or had recently occurred, it was necessary to preserve evidence or for another emergency purpose, *and* the police employed methods that did not go beyond generally accepted limits.

Judge Mōri and his colleagues found that all three conditions were present. Horikoshi's movements to and from the Mariko office where he picked up flyers and the residences where he delivered them fulfilled the first requirement. The second condition was fulfilled because the videos preserved important evidence. Finally, the court ruled that despite the grand scale of the surveillance and the large number of undercover police involved, none of this violated its view of the "common sense of society" (*shakai tsūnen*). With all three conditions fulfilled, the court ruled that the police did not require a warrant for video recording.[40]

But the court did not accept all of the video evidence presented by the government. Proximity to the crime scene was a key factor. The judges accepted the videos taken by police teams as they tailed Horikoshi around the Chuo district of Tokyo: from his home to the office of Assemblyman Mariko and to the Harumi Garden and other apartments where he dropped his material. However, the court did not accept videos from the police tails that extended beyond this area to the JCP office in neighboring Chiyoda-ku that were not directly related to flyer deliveries. Nonetheless, this improper surveillance of the defendant's trips to Chiyoda-ku had no effect on the court's judgment: "Even though a part of the videorecording was unlawful, it cannot be said that this illegality was sufficiently important to cause the entire investigation to lose legality."[41]

The District Court had found Akio Horikoshi guilty, but the penalty was extraordinarily light: a small fine with sentence suspended. Why such a light penalty? In the court's words, "The defendant committed the act on his day off without any relation to his duties and there was no impact on the workplace, there was no concrete risk of immediate infringement of any protected legal interests."[42]

For the defense, this final passage was the most important in the entire judgment. In the court's own words, Akio Horikoshi had not caused any of the harms the NPEL was intended to prevent. His attorneys quickly appealed the verdict.

District Court Judgment in the Arakawa Case (August 28, 2006)

Meanwhile, the trial of Yōsei Arakawa also continued. It was of particular interest to the Tent Village defendants because the trespassing charges in the two cases were identical. Although the Arakawa trial did not approach the scale of Horikoshi's case, there were twice as many hearings as the Tent Village trial in Hachioji. The seventh hearing took place on December 8, just a day before the

High Court judgment in the Tent Village case. This was the final day for prosecution evidence, with the defense yet to begin.

Defense counsel made a strenuous effort spread over the next five hearings. Witnesses included two local assembly members who described the reports Arakawa delivered and how important they are for assembly members to communicate with their constituents. Other witnesses included a resident of the building where Arakawa was apprehended who told the court that he wished to continue receiving the reports and two constitutional scholars who testified that punishing Arakawa would violate the constitutional guarantee of free speech.[43]

When prosecutors made their final plea to the court on June 23, 2006, they retreated from any demand for prison time, instead requesting only that Arakawa be judged guilty and made to pay a fine of 100,000 yen. The trial was completed with closing arguments on July 10.

Chief Judge Takaaki Oshima delivered the judgment on the morning of August 28, 2006. His announcement of "not guilty" was greeted with applause and cries of joy from the spectators' gallery. A young lawyer dashed from the room to display a "Not Guilty" banner to more than fifty supporters gathered outside the courthouse doors.[44] Defendant Arakawa removed his glasses to wipe away tears as he listened to the chief judge read from the court's opinion.

Court observers would be surprised again as Judge Oshima and his colleagues took an entirely different route to the not guilty verdict from the Hachioji court. It appeared they had learned from the High Court's reversal of Judge Hasegawa's ruling. Although the court's opinion ticked off some of the same factors that drove Judge Hasegawa's not guilty verdict such as the defendants' purpose in entering the property and their conduct on the scene, it avoided the "punishable illegality" theory the High Court had found unacceptable.

At the foundation of the court's opinion Judge Oshima declared,

> The commonly accepted sense of society is the standard to determine the times that entry to property should be allowed, in light of the purpose and conduct of that entry. There is no alternative to the commonly accepted sense of society viewed from the legal structure as a whole in determining whether acts are allowable or not.[45]

Thus, Judge Oshima used the same abstract expression as the District Court in the Horikoshi case: "commonly accepted sense of society." But whereas the Horikoshi Court applied the phrase in a manner that upheld broad police power, Judge Oshima turned the tables and used the same words to curtail police power.

According to celebrated Japan law scholar John Owen Haley, "expressions for 'the sense of society' are among the most frequently used phrases in Japanese judicial opinions. In judgment after judgment, Japanese judges invoke 'the sense of society' as a controlling source of value and standard for their decisions."[46] It's hard to imagine a more subjective rule of law than this. The two cases clearly showed that different judges could apply this amorphous standard in very different ways.

In support of his common-sense approach to the problem, Judge Oshima noted various details of Arakawa's behavior. His actions caused a minimal disturbance to residents, if any. He spent no more than seven or eight minutes in a building as he quietly dropped his material through mail slots. His actions were no different from the messengers from pizza shops and other commercial operations who were not arrested or prosecuted. And, according to the court's opinion, he had followed this practice for more than 40 years without encountering a complaint. To top it off, the court also wrote that notices prohibiting trespassers at the property were not particularly clear.[47]

Even retired prosecutor Takeshi Tsuchimoto, who complained about the not guilty verdict in Hachioji a year and a half before, struggled to uphold the government's action in this case. He *did* support appeal of the Arakawa judgment, but he was not enthusiastic: "Although the illegality in this case was thin, it was not zero."[48]

Whatever one thinks of the result, Judge Oshima's assessment of the "common sense of society" is hard to challenge. Few ordinary Japanese people would think that someone like Yōsei Arakawa should be tossed in the clink for more than three weeks and then subjected to a criminal trial just because a resident didn't like material found in his mailbox. On an inside page, *Mainichi* reporters made precisely this point by gathering comments from local residents. One woman in her thirties said, "You can just throw away flyers you don't need. An arrest is excessive." A man in his fifties said, "We also get advertising from pizza shops and other businesses. The arrest is too much." On the other hand, they found a woman in her fifties who said, "For someone you don't know to come right up to your door leaves a bad feeling (*kimochi warui*). They should drop flyers at the central post boxes on the ground floor."[49]

But constitutional scholars—experts who spend their lives elucidating the meaning of Japan's democratic constitution—could hardly be satisfied by the court's resort to an unwritten "sense of society" to decide such a fundamental question of constitutional law. Professor Masahiro Usaki of Dokkyo University Law School complained that the court "said almost nothing about the importance of freedom of political speech in a democratic society" and thus failed to adequately address the chilling effect on free speech.[50] Hokkaido University professor Yūji Shiratori, who had denounced the prosecutors when commenting on the Tent Village verdict, also faulted the court's failure to condemn the political nature of the prosecutions: "Even though the judgment was not guilty, the indictments caused great social harm to the defendants and a chilling effect on citizen movements. The prosecutors should be held accountable for filing indictments targeted at specific political activities."[51]

Tokyo Shimbun reporters quoted other commentators who linked the arrests of government critics to broader issues such as the nationalist campaign to compel public school teachers to stand and sing the national anthem and the longstanding drive for a new "conspiracy law" that would empower police to cast a broader net and arrest individuals who did not actually commit criminal acts, but were involved in related planning or communications.[52]

The prosecutors filed an appeal three days later. Another defendant would have to fight to preserve a not guilty verdict.

15

TENT VILLAGE ARRIVES AT THE "STONE FORTRESS"

(2005–2008)

Tent Village lawyers quickly filed notices of appeal and began work on a memorandum of law that set out their arguments for reversal of the High Court judgment.[1] While the lawyers did their work, others were also busy.

The High Court judgment was a hot topic in the editorial pages. Readers across Japan, including prosecutors and judges with responsibility for the Tent Village case, saw editorials that challenged it.[2] Their primary theme was an appeal to common sense: flyer delivery is an everyday matter and even if there was a technical violation of the trespass law, criminal prosecution is not the proper response. Many writers expressed their fear of chilling effects on political activities and citizen activism. Similar comments were found in letters to the editor from ordinary citizens that were published alongside editorials.

Aggressive police action also made the evening news. In a program that broadly addressed the police crackdown following the Iraq deployment, the news documentary series "Sunday Project" featuring journalist Akihiro Otani even broadcast police footage of Akio Horikoshi delivering the *Akahata* and other materials.[3] Foreign correspondents also did their part, inviting the Tent Village appellants to a press conference at their central Tokyo club on March 13.

Takato Narisawa, Manabu Ishizaki, and other constitutional scholars were busy, too. On January 6, they released a lengthy statement critical of the High Court judgment that was signed by 115 scholars. In the scholars' opinion, the appellants' actions did not violate the criminal code and did not cause sufficient injury to justify prosecution; moreover, the High Court erred by failing to accord adequate weight to the free speech interests at stake.

Tent Village members and followers continued their customary mini protests, flyer distributions, signature gathering at train stations, and other activities. Small groups even began to make the trip downtown to deliver speeches and hand out flyers to passersby before the Supreme Court compound.

DOI: 10.4324/9781003193999-16

Thirty joined the attorneys when they filed their memorandum of law on May 31.[4] The memorandum covered 117 pages, including appendices with statements by the three appellants, five legal scholars, and 12 separate petitions by Tent Village supporters. The primary task for counsel was to persuade the Supreme Court that Judge Nakagawa and his colleagues had erred in the judgment they delivered in December 2005. Regarding elements of Criminal Code Article 130, this meant they would have to confront the High Court's conclusions that the appellants had entered "premises" "under guard" and that it was the will of the building managers rather than the residents that mattered.

They would try to shift the Supreme Court's focus away from the building managers and toward the residents. Failing that, they would have to follow Professor Adachi's lead and persuade the Court that the flow of uninvited visitors through the property—including elementary school children—showed the property was *not* "under guard." Of course, they would be overjoyed if they could revive Judge Hasegawa's "punishable illegality" thesis, but this appeared to be the least likely road to success.

Finally, they would make an impassioned plea based on the most fundamental right in a democratic society: the right to speak, especially regarding a matter of such great public interest as a march to war. Regarding this issue, they called upon Professor Sakaguchi and Professor Tōru Mōri of Kyoto University to draft their own pleas to be appended to the attorneys' work.

Defense counsel believed that legal arguments alone would not be enough. As explained by Attorney Yamamoto, "In order for the Supreme Court to truly understand the influence this case would have on the future shape of society, it was necessary to make an energetic presentation to the Court."[5] The attorneys relied on the supporters to help deliver this "energetic presentation." Those who accompanied the attorneys sought to provide more than just moral support. In fact, many had written messages of their own to the Supreme Court justices in the form of petitions (*jōshinsho*) similar to the ones they delivered at the Tachikawa Self-Defense Force bases. Tent Village supporters had been gathering signatures on statements protesting the arrests since three members were taken away in February 2004, but these petitions were different. Each one was unique and carried the personal, political, and sometimes emotional feelings of its author.

Japan's courts do not accept the "friend of the court" briefs that are common in the United States, but the Supreme Court does accept petitions filed by anyone concerning specific cases. Tent Village supporters began gathering the petitions soon after the High Court judgment. Supporters who accompanied the attorneys to the Supreme Court on May 31 brought 172 separate petitions along with a statement with 7095 signatures. A Tent Village pamphlet explains the source of so much enthusiasm: "If we can express what we are after, the fight against suppression can gain new life!"[6]

The petitions came from all over the country. Some authors wrote sophisticated legal arguments citing the right to free speech or stressing the great significance of Constitution Article 9, the antiwar clause. Others wrote of their personal experiences delivering or receiving flyers at their homes. Some of the older writers had experienced the horror of war themselves; they stressed the importance of protecting voices that call for peace. Of course, many were written by people with very strong opinions, including some who participated in antiwar protests or even joined as plaintiffs in litigation that challenged the constitutionality of the SDF deployment to Iraq. The collection included petitions from Katsuko Kato and other Tent Village members.

Kato described the source of her lifelong commitment to antiwar activism—childhood in an American military base town. She even wrote of her sympathy for the thousands of prostitutes who worked there at the time, only a few years older than herself, and of how those women and other residents only narrowly survived the extreme poverty of the early postwar era.

Then she told the court of the police attack on the Tent Village and the indignity of suffering a police search of her home and belongings when she personally experienced "the police enforcing the will of the state." She explained the government logic: "At this moment when the SDF is going to the battlefields of Iraq, it is necessary to crush opposing voices." But Kato wrote that the state sometimes errs and reminded the Court of its duty to correct those errors. She pleaded for a judgment that would not "throw Japan away."

Kato had lived alongside soldiers and military bases for her entire life and she wrote that she saw the SDF members as ordinary people, like herself. "The SDF is not like the emperor's army of the past," she wrote. "First of all, SDF members are citizens; in that regard, they share the same platform with us." Kato believed that many of the residents in the Tachikawa SDF apartments were eager to read the messages from Tent Village. Like other citizens, they had the right to receive opinions of all kinds, not just those delivered by their commanders. And for them, it was even more important, for they might be sent to the war zone.

Finally, she requested the justices to restore the not guilty verdict, urging them to read the Hachioji judgment, "written after a thorough inspection of the site of the flyer deliveries that took a half-day on a hot day in August."[7]

Entering the Supreme Court Compound

When supporters arrived at the Supreme Court compound at 2 p.m. on May 31, court personnel allowed a maximum of 17 in to present the petitions. They followed a winding path through an inner courtyard and maze-like corridors that led to a small room where two clerks waited. The clerks would notify the Second Petty Bench justices and the research judges who support them that petitions had arrived and then the judges themselves would decide whether to read them.[8] Hearing this explanation, the supporters' reaction was immediate: "So you mean the justices might not read them at all?" When the clerks confirmed this was the case, they demanded to talk directly to the justices or research judges. After this was denied, they appealed to the attorneys for help, to no avail. Blocked at the very threshold to the Supreme Court, some supporters said the slogan that appeared in news accounts of recent judicial reforms touting "a judicial system open to the people" was a sham.[9]

That evening around 150 supporters gathered at a big public hall not far from the Supreme Court compound. When it was done, many joined in a march that passed by the Supreme Court and then continued down a broad boulevard to the Yotsuya district. When they passed the Supreme Court compound after 8 p.m., marchers were surprised to see that lights were still on.

The May 31 petition delivery was the first of eight that would take place in coming months. A Tent Village delegation appeared at the Court each time and followed the path to an inner room where clerks waited. The visitors read some of the petitions aloud, just as they did when they confronted guards at entrances to the SDF bases in Tachikawa. At each visit, they asked about progress on the case and requested that the Court hold a public hearing, but the clerks had no authority to respond.

We don't know if any of the justices or research judges read them, but the petitions would take on a life beyond the courthouse. Supporters gathered 168 for publication in a book released in October. When a Tent Village delegation traveled to the Court to deliver a new batch of signatures and petitions on November 22, 2006, they also brought a package of eight copies of the book, one copy intended for each of the judges involved and for the clerks they met during their periodic visits.[10] The editors' motivation for producing the book was clearly stated:

> We cannot stand the thought that these petitions would be left in a corner of a room at the Supreme Court to gather dust. We want them to be read by many people who lived in the same era as a jointly-owned property.[11]

There would be one more significant event before the end of the year. The attorneys returned to the Court on December 22 to deliver a supplementary memorandum of 23 pages with no fewer than 45 appendices that illustrated the wide breadth of opposition to prosecution in the flyer cases. The package included copies of 11 editorials that condemned the High Court guilty verdict. According to defense counsel, the editorials showed, "it is clear that society has not recognized that flyer delivery ('posting') is a problem for application of criminal penalties."[12]

Appendices also included eight news stories. According to defense counsel, they reported "a huge chilling effect on citizen movements … citizen groups other than Tent Village have stopped delivering flyers with political content and government residences and other places."[13] The memorandum also introduced the Arakawa case and appended 20 editorials that applauded the not guilty verdict in that case delivered just four months earlier, on August 28. On the academic front, they reproduced the scholars' declaration in full with a list of 115 signatories along with two formal opinions by law professors.[14]

During the Hachioji trial, there were numerous public hearings with live testimony, so supporters enjoyed a regular rhythm of court sessions followed by group meetings with reports from defense counsel and inspirational words from the defendants and other speakers. But that show was over. The Tokyo High Court's first hearing did not take place until ten months after the trial court judgment. The second hearing would be its last. The High Court reversal fueled the outrage of Tent Village supporters and they were joined by most editorial writers in the immediate aftermath of the judgment. But once the appellants' memorandum of law was filed on May 31, 2006, there would be no real action in the case until the Supreme Court decided either to hold oral argument or to render its judgment. Oral argument at Japan's Supreme Court is exceedingly rare. When it is scheduled, appellants have a chance. The Court's failure to hold oral argument is a clear indication that the appeal will be rejected.[15]

As the months passed by with no new developments, attention wandered and Osawa and other leaders worked hard to keep their movement together. Gathering signatures at tables set up in front of train stations and petitions from individuals willing to write them served as the core activity of the ongoing campaign. Leaders also organized small demonstrations in the Tachikawa area on the anniversaries of the arrests and on other occasions. A march held on October 15, 2006 that was joined by 80 people and covered the full 12 kilometers between the Tachikawa and Yokosuka military bases was accompanied by a marching band.[16]

2007

Documents Reveal Government Surveillance of Tent Village

In early 2007, Tent Village mailed opinion surveys to 60 SDF members who had resided in the Tachikawa compound that sought their opinions on the flyer deliveries. They received two responses. Each one agreed that mailslot deliveries should not constitute a crime and one even commented on the flyers' content. Tent Village members were overjoyed. At long last they had made a real connection with SDF members who saw their flyers and agreed the messengers should not be jailed.[17]

The story took another unexpected turn that summer. On June 6, *Akahata* reported the leak of documents that described the surveillance of antiwar groups by a secretive SDF counterintelligence unit called the "Intelligence Security Corps" (ISC). Later news stories would say that the ISC had even tracked the Tent Village and collaborated with the police in planning the arrests of the Tent Village suspects.[18]

The leaked documents found their way to the Tent Village attorneys who composed a 24-page memorandum they delivered to the Supreme Court on

December 25, 2007. They appended copies of 14 so the justices could see them with their own eyes.

The ISC documents cited large demonstrations against the Iraq war in 2003 in Tokyo, Kyoto, and Hiroshima that had been reported in the press. According to defense counsel, "the SDF feared this would spread and affect the SDF itself."[19] The demonstrations triggered an ISC investigation of the antiwar movement that lasted from August 1, 2003 through February 29, 2004. Unfortunately for Tent Village, this period overlapped almost precisely with the plan to deliver five monthly flyers at the SDF apartments.

According to these records, ISC agents were on the scene at several Tent Village events that winter, including a regular monthly demonstration against the C-1 flights on November 25, 2003, "antimilitary broadcasts" on January 16 and February 21, 2004, and another demonstration on February 29.

Just as the state security police tracked the movements of Akio Horikoshi, these records showed SDF counterintelligence spying on Tent Village in the weeks leading to the arrests. For the records to affect the outcome of the appeal, Supreme Court justices would have to share the Tent Village outrage at secret government surveillance of political speech activities obviously protected by Article 21 of the Constitution.

A document dated December 17, 2003, recorded the police requesting help in arresting individuals distributing antiwar flyers at the SDF apartments. Specifically, it said the police requested calls to their hotline and preparation of complaints indicating that residents were troubled by the flyers. SDF managers posted "no trespassing" signs on December 18 and submitted their first formal complaint to the police on December 22. Although it was common to see no trespassing signs at apartment buildings in Tokyo, no such signs had been posted at the SDF residential compound prior to the police request.[20]

The police originally sought to arrest the defendants in the act, so they had SDF managers instruct residents to telephone the police emergency number (110) immediately if they spotted anyone delivering the flyers.[21] But no arrests were made on the scene and the police changed strategy to *ex post facto* arrests based on warrants. As defense counsel explained it, the police turned ordinary procedure upside down. Instead of acting to prevent a crime or investigate a crime that had already taken place, the police planned arrests for acts that had not yet occurred. Defense counsel wrote that "The police and the SDF put up the notices in order to build a stage with the purpose of arresting the defendants."[22] In other words, they set a trap.

The story told in these documents matched the testimony of SDF witnesses in Hachioji in the summer of 2004. Under cross-examination, SDF managers confirmed that the complaints they submitted to the police were prepared by the police themselves, typed on police typewriters and presented to them for signature.[23]

Like the 2004 testimony of the government's own witnesses, the new documentary evidence clearly undermined the logic of the High Court's guilty verdict. The High Court ruled that the defendants violated Article 130 because they acted contrary to the will of the building managers and the managers' will was shown by their complaints to the police and other actions. But the evidence showed that these measures were initiated by the police, not the managers. As for the residents, government witnesses could not specify the details of any complaints prior to the arrests.[24] The lawyers concluded that there was no injury or violation of the residents' "peaceful daily lives" caused by the flyers.[25]

As for the rights of the Tent Village messengers, the memorandum asserted that the surveillance and the arrests and detentions violated their constitutional rights to freedom of speech, of association, and assembly, as well as their constitutional right to privacy. These claims were supported by many constitutional experts, the national bar association, and others.[26]

Kato and others had expected a Supreme Court judgment by year-end, but there was still no word. There was ominous news on another front, however. On December 11, 2007, the Tokyo High Court reversed the acquittal of Yōsei Arakawa. As Supreme Court justices pondered the Tent Village appeal, they now had not one, but two guilty verdicts from High Courts in flyer cases.

2008

A Message from the Supreme Court

On February 27, 2008, supporters gathered again to commemorate the arrests that occurred four years earlier. Then, on March 20, the three appellants each received a formal notice from the Supreme Court stating that judgment would be issued three weeks hence. There would be no oral argument. This meant the High Court guilty verdict would be upheld. Obora told reporters he was filled with anger and bitter disappointment.[27]

When she heard the news, Kato wrote,

> For almost two and a half years after the High Court judgment, every time we delivered petitions with lists of names demanding a not guilty judgment, we asked for an oral argument. But our requests did not get through. Suddenly there is a "Pronouncement of Judgment." We are allowed entry to the Supreme Court, which sets the standards for freedom of speech and freedom of expression in this country, only to hear a "Pronouncement of Guilt" … . Freedom of speech and expression can only be realized when we exercise them ourselves. Did we survive the suppression? Did we make an effective fight in the courts? Answers to questions like these will be left to the future.[28]

When they learned of the March 20 notice, Osawa and others gathered quickly to plan their response. They decided to hold a demonstration before the Supreme Court on the day of the judgment, an information session at a labor hall near Tachikawa that evening, and a protest march in the Tachikawa area on April 19.[29]

The Supreme Court of Japan

Fifteen justices occupy seats on Japan's Supreme Court. They are all appointed by the Cabinet, without review by the Diet or other body, so evaluations and appointments are made in secret. The Japanese people learn of Supreme Court appointments only after the fact, through brief notices in the news. By custom, the seats are generally allocated by career backgrounds, with five or six occupied by career judges, three or four by career attorneys and the remainder filled by prosecutors, bureaucrats, and usually a single career academic. Also, by custom, appointees are of advanced age, typically in their mid-60s. Because retirement at age 70 is mandatory, they tend to serve relatively brief terms.[30]

Although there are 15 justices, nearly all cases are decided by five-judge panels, so-called "Petty Benches." The Tent Village appeal was assigned to the Second Petty Bench, led by Nirō Shimada, the chief justice of the entire Court. But Justice Shimada did not join his colleagues in reviewing the Tent Village appeal. Preoccupied with his duties as the chief administrative officer of the entire judicial system, Justice Shimada generally excused himself from Petty Bench cases.[31] Another member of the Second Petty Bench, Justice Yūki Furuta, had served as a senior officer in the Supreme Prosecutors' Office from 2002 through 2004. In that position he may have had access to privileged information regarding the Tent Village case or even participated in deciding strategy. Although justices rarely disclose reasons for recusing themselves, Justice Furuta had obvious reasons to step back. So, among the 15 justices of Japan's Supreme Court, the Tent Village case was heard by only three.

All three were appointed by the Koizumi Cabinet, around the time the SDF were dispatched to Iraq and the police went after the Tent Village. In the absence of Justice Shimada, the panel was led by Isao Imai, an elite member of the judiciary who had served as chief of the Tokyo High Court before his promotion. Perhaps the best-known member was Osamu Tsuno, a career bureaucrat who had served for three years as head of the Cabinet Legislation Bureau, one of the most prestigious positions in Japan's government. The terror attacks of September 11, 2001, occurred during his term, so he advised the Koizumi Cabinet on such issues as constitutional limitations on anti-terrorism legislation and the legality of military collaboration with the United States and other allies. The third member was career attorney Ryōji Nakagawa, who had served as the chairperson of one of the Tokyo bar associations.

The Supreme Court compound is located across the street from the expansive imperial palace grounds, at the top of a long slope that leads down to the huge cluster of government buildings in Kasumigaseki. The Court's main entrance is tucked into a somewhat recessed space, separated from the street by a small courtyard, with a driveway ordinarily roped off from public access. From the top of the staircase, one looks out toward the imperial palace moat, the palace grounds, and the city beyond.

First-time visitors are struck by the radical design of the buildings, especially when viewed from the south. From this angle, visitors see what appears to be a jumbled pile of huge, startlingly white granite blocks rather than modern offices of government. It is said that construction required ten thousand tons of granite. The design was selected at the end of the turbulent 1960s, when mass protests shut down many of the nation's universities, explosions rocked central Tokyo, and young attorneys like Uchida and Koto were busy representing protesters in court.[32] Japan's leaders were undoubtedly searching for symbols of stability and power. Celebrated architect Shin'ichi Okada responded with a design that projects awesome power and permanence. He rejected traditional western structures, with their broad staircases and stout white pillars looking down upon public squares. Instead, he produced a multifaceted cluster of seven buildings that present an array of starkly different faces to the outside world. Often called the "Stone Fortress," the location and forbidding appearance match the Court's status as the nation's final arbiter clothed with the great power to determine even the constitutionality of laws passed by the Diet.[33]

Kato herself was intimidated by this Stone Fortress. Frustrated by the clerks' refusals to comment on progress in the justices' deliberations during a visit to the Court, she thought their cold response matched the chilling image projected by Okada's creation, "like a medieval fortress that looms above you as if to drive people away." The cold exterior fit well with the silence of the clerks and the absolute secrecy that surrounded the proceedings. Mysteriously, Kato heard the unspoken message that "We already know the result." Yes, the powerholders knew, but she and her friends remained in the dark. In her despair, she felt that neither the well-honed arguments of lawyers nor the passionate cries of the supplicants could make a difference.[34]

"Necessary and Reasonable Restrictions"

Formal pronouncement of the final judgment was set for 3 p.m. on Friday, April 11, 2008. Supporters arrived early to make speeches, hand out flyers to passersby and, when the time came, to get in line to pull straws for entry to the Second Petty Bench courtroom. Once inside, some were intimidated by the oppressive air of authority projected by the grandiose courtroom.[35] The justices entered through a door that was twice as tall as themselves and then proceeded to a bench raised on a pedestal so they could look down on the advocates and spectators below. Some were surprised to see that this courtroom was not equipped with a witness stand.[36] Japan's highest court relies on the lower courts to hear testimony and create the evidentiary record. Its role is generally limited to deciding whether the lower courts correctly applied the law. The rare oral arguments are generally limited to presentations by advocates, so there is no need for a witness stand.

Because the Court did not schedule an oral argument, the appellants already knew the disheartening result. Nonetheless, they clung to hope for a dissenting opinion.[37] It would count for a victory if they had persuaded even one judge to vote "not guilty." There was also hope that even though the final verdict was

FIGURE 15.1 Spectators wait for entry to the Supreme Court on April 11, 2008. (Photograph by the author)

guilty, the Court would lay down clear guidelines for balancing claims to free speech against the rights of residents and others.

After a sergeant-at-arms called for all to rise, the three justices filed into the courtroom at 3 p.m. No sooner had the appellants and spectators taken their seats than Justice Isao Imai announced that the Court rejected the Tent Village appeal. He read key portions of the judgment aloud, including the Court's curt dismissal of the defendants' claims to constitutional protection:

> The first clause of Constitution Article 21 does not guarantee absolutely unlimited protection for free expression; it recognizes necessary and reasonable restrictions for the public welfare. Even if an act serves to express one's thoughts to others, if that act improperly injures the rights of others, it cannot be allowed.[38]

Then the justices stood up to leave. The proceeding was over in two minutes.[39] Thus ended the sole opportunity for the defendants to see the faces of the men who ultimately decided their fates.

For Obora and the others, surely the press conference that followed was more significant than the actual court hearing. When he got there, Obora told reporters that he wondered why he and the others had bothered to come to the court for such a superficial proceeding.

FIGURE 15.2 Toshiyuki Obora outside the Supreme Court compound on April 11, 2008. (Photograph by the author)

With his reference to "necessary and reasonable restrictions for the public welfare," Justice Imai summarized the jurisprudence that had decided more than six decades of free speech litigation at Japan's Supreme Court. Through all those years, the Court consistently rejected claims that the police or another agency of government violated free speech rights protected by the Constitution.[40] The Court frequently holds that government action serves the public welfare and therefore is immune from constitutional challenge. The term "public welfare" appears in four places (Articles 12, 13, 22, and 29) in Japan's Constitution. It is of special importance in Articles 12 and 13, where it serves as a limitation on other rights.[41] The Supreme Court has not defined what this term means, but it has applied it in case after case, holding that laws or government actions challenged on free speech grounds serve the public welfare and are therefore constitutional.

The Second Petty Bench closely followed the model set by the court below. Like the Tokyo High Court, it ruled that the defendants violated Article 130 by trespassing into the "premises" against the will of the building managers. The Second Petty Bench also ruled that the posting of warning signs served multiple purposes: it was sufficient to show the intent of the managers, to give adequate warning to the defendants, and to constitute evidence of significant injury. Also like the High Court, it said nothing about the witness testimony or other evidence that showed the SDF managers responding to prodding by the police—not building residents—when they chose to sign police complaints and take other action that set the stage for the arrests.

In its dismissal of the defendants' claims to free speech protections, the Second Petty Bench provided slightly more detail than the High Court, stressing that "it is not the constitutionality of the expression itself that is under question, it is the method of entering 'guarded premises' without the approval of property managers." If the police were concerned with the "method," however, they might have also arrested others who entered the property without permission to deliver flyers, or at least warned them off. But they did not. The single-minded focus of the police on the Tent Village messengers is undeniable. Commentators would say their special treatment proved that the goal of the police was to stop criticism of the government and broadcast a loud warning to others who might consider doing so.[42]

There was also a somewhat technical reason for the Court to insert this reference to method. By ruling that the police action did not constitute a restriction on speech itself, the Court avoided the need to apply the so-called "strict scrutiny" standard (*genkaku na kijun*) in its analysis. Under the strict scrutiny standard, it would be much more difficult to uphold the police action.[43]

In an apparent attempt to display their concern for "public welfare," the three justices wrote that

> for someone to enter this kind of place contrary to the will of the building managers is not only a violation of the managers' rights, but also a violation of the right to peaceful daily life of those who live there.[44]

Since the Court had followed the lead of the Tokyo High Court in choosing the will of the managers as the required element, this reference to the residents was superfluous. As noted in Chapter 14, the Tokyo High Court explicitly declared the residents' will irrelevant.

Reactions to the Supreme Court Judgment

Editorial reaction took varied approaches. Predictably, the *Asahi* was most strident in its criticism. Its editorial primarily addressed police conduct rather than the actual Supreme Court judgment, stating unequivocally that the police action "smacked of a targeted crackdown by the authorities against any movement that opposed the SDF deployment to Iraq." The authors did admonish the defendants for insisting on door-to-door delivery, suggesting that they should have dropped their flyers at the central mailboxes on the ground floor instead. Either way, they wrote, the defendants' actions did not "merit the harsh treatment they received" The *Asahi* concluded that "We are greatly disappointed at the Supreme Court ruling, which effectively endorsed and took no issue with an investigation and prosecution that far overstepped the bounds of common sense."[45]

Regarding the *Asahi's* advice to drop flyers at ground-floor central mailboxes, Professor Sakaguchi later suggested that the *Asahi* editors should read the judgment one more time. Because the Supreme Court followed the Tokyo

High Court in ruling that the defendants had broken the law by trespassing into "premises," a broad concept that includes the entire lot, buildings, and all of the common areas, dropping flyers at central mailboxes clearly violates the Court's view of the law as much as door-to-door delivery.

The *Asahi* also reminded readers that the Supreme Court decision was not an isolated event; it took place at a time of great controversy concerning not only the SDF deployment, but also more deeply rooted issues of Japan's history and military tradition. The *Asahi* cited two recent examples in which threats of violence from ultranationalists forced the cancellation of events that contradicted their vision of Japan's history. One was a film that concerned the Yasukuni shrine. Distributors found it impossible to show the film because theater owners feared potential violent attacks.[46] The other involved the cancellation of a Tokyo hotel's agreement to host the annual meeting of the national teachers' association due to such threats. The teachers' organization is a frequent target of rightwing attack because of its commitment to the liberal education principles declared in the postwar fundamental law of education.

The *Nikkei*, Japan's financial and business daily, also criticized the decision, stressing its business aspects. No trespassing signs are posted at many multifamily residences and the *Nikkei* was concerned that the Court's judgment could be interpreted to mean that anyone could be criminally prosecuted for disregarding such signs. If so, it could have a significant impact on those businesses that rely on mailbox flyers to get their word out. *Nikkei* writers expressed their disappointment that "Today's judgment does not provide a clear standard to determine in what kinds of cases residents and managers have expressed their opposition (to flyer deliveries)."

For expert comment, the *Nikkei* carefully selected spokesmen for both sides. Nagoya University Professor Noriho Urabe expressed the disappointment of most constitutional experts regarding the Court's failure to recognize the potential impact of its judgment on free speech. After his criticism of the Court's legal analysis, he was quoted to say "This appears to be a decision in which the result was predetermined because the defendants opposed the SDF deployment to Iraq, a very important policy of the administration."[47]

For the contrary view, the *Nikkei* selected Tōyō Atsumi, a senior professor of criminal procedure who said it was a mistake to view the case as one of restricting free speech at all. The defendants could have freely delivered their message at countless other places. To do so against the wishes of residents or building managers was nothing more than "harassment" (*iyagarase*). He likened this to unwanted telephone solicitations, which he would presumably also subject to criminal prosecution.

For their part, the *Yomiuri* writers expressed their satisfaction with the Court's judgment: "Delivering flyers at a place where entry is strongly prohibited is a crime. This is a judgment that provides a rule for daily life." Moreover, the paper endorsed the notion of differential treatment depending on flyer content. As for "general flyers and advertising," the *Yomiuri* said that some residents see these items as "treasures" and therefore police intervention is not appropriate. The Tent Village flyers were another matter entirely:

> The flyers said such things as "those who do the killing and those who are killed are SDF members." When SDF members and their families read them, their mental anguish must not have been slight. When you consider this, it is an appropriate judgment.[48]

So the *Yomiuri* approved differential treatment based on content, with commercial messages given greater protection than political ones, the very reverse of the order upheld by constitutional scholars, the Hachioji court, and others who see protection of political messages of higher importance as a "pillar of democracy." The *Yomiuri's* conclusion appeared to be that the building managers' authority to control flyer distribution and the authority of the police to enforce managers' decisions is absolute and that they are free to pick and choose the items that appear in residents' mailboxes.

Whatever one thought of the Court's decision, one thing was certain. The decision was final. The defendants would forever bear the mark of a criminal conviction. The Supreme Court ruled in favor of the government and said nothing at all about the extreme police measures that put the defendants behind bars.

16

THE SUPREME COURT DECIDES THE ARAKAWA AND HORIKOSHI CASES

(2009–2012)

Final Judgment in the Arakawa Case (November 30, 2009)

The Tokyo High Court judgment that overturned the acquittal of Yōsei Arakawa was condemned by all major newspapers, including the conservative *Yomiuri*, which attacked the court's application of Article 130 as "formalistic" and concluded that "The investigating authorities should carefully consider that arrests that go beyond the citizens' understanding are connected to limitations on 'freedom of expression.'"[1] The defendant, a shaven-headed Buddhist monk in his fifties who invariably appeared in court and other public gatherings in refined monk's robes, was a very appealing, even charismatic figure. Ordinary people who learned of the case would surely think, "They must have gotten something wrong. What could possibly motivate the government to haul this man into court on criminal charges?"

The police had carefully planned the Tent Village arrests, but the Arakawa case appeared to be an accident. Prosecutors must have been truly nonplussed to learn that some Buddhist monk had been arrested for delivering Japan Communist Party materials. Unlike the Tent Village case, here the government had no real interest. The defendant did not enter a Self-Defense Force residential compound, did not directly challenge the government's Iraq war policy, and was not the subject of any complaints from residents prior to the day of his arrest. If not for the Tent Village case, especially the acquittal just a week before his arrest, the police would have paid no attention to Yōsei Arakawa and if they did, the prosecutors would have refused to take such a trivial case to court.

With Arakawa's arrest, the prosecutors were stuck with a parallel case that looked even more absurd than the capture of three harmless antiwar activists in Tachikawa. But if they let the monk slide this time, they were mired in a

DOI: 10.4324/9781003193999-17

contradiction: How to justify releasing a man arrested on the very same charge as the Tent Village defendants?

So they plowed ahead. On the plus side, Arakawa's arrest offered them a new opportunity. Now they could pursue the initiative against the troublesome anti-government flyers simultaneously on two separate tracks and if the appeal of the Hachioji judgment somehow went awry, they could focus their energies on this new case.

Prosecutors could also console themselves with the thought that this time they would not confront the confusing distinction between residents and building managers that affected the Tent Village case. Here there was no SDF or other government authority involved and no SDF managers who made decisions on building security and negotiations with the police. Instead, the key player was the condo association that controlled the building where Arakawa was arrested. The association was responsible for matters like "no solicitation" signs and there was no doubt that the association represented the residents.[2] Residents could object to the signs if they wished, but none did. Who would? Such warnings were common at residential buildings throughout Tokyo.

But no one expected such prohibitions to be enforced against visitors like Arakawa. Uninvited messengers walk past such warning signs every day to deliver commercial flyers from real estate agents, English language schools, fast-food shops, and other businesses. Judge Takaaki Oshima and his colleagues at Tokyo District Court relied on common sense—their "sense of society"—to find Arakawa not guilty. They were so confident in their common sense that they felt free to disregard the guilty verdict by the High Court in the Tent Village case that appeared nearly a year before.

But the Tokyo High Court overruled Judge Oshima's common-sense approach and found Arakawa guilty on December 11, 2007. As Arakawa's attorneys set to work on their appeal to the Supreme Court, they labored in the shadow of the Tent Village case, which had lain quietly on the Court's doorstep since the Tent Village defendants lodged their appeal two years before. Any appeal in either case would rely heavily on claims to constitutional protection for free speech, even though all Japanese attorneys are aware of the Supreme Court's impregnable record in free speech cases. Defense counsel knew they faced very long odds. As members of the *Jiyū Hōsōdan*, however, they had pledged to take cases just like this and do their utmost for victims of political suppression. So they pounded away on their draft appeal with one eye on progress of the Tent Village case. As they worked, that case hung over them like a dark cloud that could burst at any time.

Then suddenly, the word came down. The Supreme Court's March 20, 2008, notice to the Tent Village defendants ended any hope that the Court would rule in their favor. This was a heavy blow to the Arakawa team as well. The Supreme Court had followed the path to a guilty verdict set by one Tokyo High Court panel. Everyone in the Arakawa camp feared the Court would do it again in their case.

Defense counsel would not see the text of the Court's Tent Village judgment for several weeks. Once it was released, they would comb through its curt dismissal in search of some expression they could turn to their advantage, some indication that the Court might recognize significant differences between the two cases. Sure, the antiwar protesters who delivered disturbing messages at the homes of SDF families caused much anxiety to those who received them. In contrast, Arakawa had delivered less controversial material door-to-door for decades without complaint. The local assembly report that Arakawa delivered concerned commonplace daily life issues like milk provided in the public schools, not political controversies such as the overseas deployment of the SDF. Even those recipients who disagreed with the JCP program could not say the deliveries disrupted their daily lives.

Defense counsel ultimately filed their appeal on May 20, 2008, a little over a month after the Supreme Court judgment in the Tent Village case. The case was assigned to the Second Petty Bench, the same court that had just decided the Tachikawa case. On September 29, 2009, Arakawa received notice that the Court was ready to issue its judgment.[3] Like the Tent Village defendants, Arakawa was denied the opportunity to address the Court in oral argument.

Before the Court issued its decision, there were some changes in personnel. Judge Osamu Tsuno retired and was replaced by Yukio Takeuchi, a career bureaucrat from the Ministry of Foreign Affairs. Justice Yūki Furuta, who did not participate in the Tent Village judgment, joined this one. So, when the Court issued its judgment on November 30, 2009, the case was decided by a panel of four judges rather than three and only two of the four had participated in the Tent Village judgment.

Despite the similarity of the two cases, the Second Petty Bench did not decide the Arakawa case until 19 months after the Tent Village judgment.[4] The Court declined to hear oral argument, but when Shigeaki Matsui, chief counsel of the Arakawa team, requested to speak on the day of judgment, Justice Imai relented and allowed him to briefly address the Court. Matsui called upon the Court to respect the free speech provision of the Constitution, to reject the police suppression of the JCP, and issue a judgment that accorded with Japan's obligations under international law.[5] The judicial panel listened politely, but their work was already finished. When Matsui was done, Justice Imai announced that the appeal was dismissed and the High Court's guilty judgment confirmed. Thus, Yōsei Arakawa's case ended on November 30, 2009.

Arakawa's attorneys received another shock when they read the Court's judgment. The text was nearly identical to the Tent Village judgment issued 19 months before. There were a few wording changes such as substitutions of "condo association" for "building managers" and "condo residents" for "Self-Defense Force members and their families." Otherwise, the text was the same. The Court reaffirmed its interpretation of Article 130 and repeated the same formulation that doomed the Tent Village appellants' claims to constitutional protection.[6]

The arrest and prosecution of Yōsei Arakawa appeared to be an accident. In the end, the Supreme Court put the case to rest with as little fuss as possible. The case would be an embarrassment for Japan's prosecutors. The mighty government agency with the power to investigate and put anyone behind bars, including the nation's most powerful politicians and government officials, decided to direct its fire at a local monk who served one of Tokyo's poorest neighborhoods. According to the Supreme Court, however, they did no wrong.

Tokyo High Court Judgment in the Horikoshi Case (March 29, 2010)

The prosecution of Akio Horikoshi was fundamentally different from the Tent Village and Arakawa cases. Whereas defendants in the latter were charged with violating a standard provision of the criminal law, the government claimed that Horikoshi violated a special statute that does not apply to ordinary citizens at all. Adopted in 1947, the same year Japan's democratic Constitution took effect, the National Public Employee Law (NPEL) reflected the desire of Occupation authorities to assert control during the chaotic conditions of the immediate postwar era.[7] In addition to the prohibition of political activities that provided grounds for Horikoshi's arrest, a 1948 revision to the NPEL also took away the rights to strike and bargain collectively. The 1948 revision was especially controversial because Constitution Article 28, authored by Occupation officials, expressly guarantees workers' rights to bargain and act collectively.

The validity of laws that limit the rights of government employees was the object of a fierce struggle in the Supreme Court of the 1960s and 1970s. Liberal judges and the great majority of scholars thought the severe restrictions on political activities and collective bargaining went too far and violated constitutional protections for free speech and political activity. But a new conservative Supreme Court majority upheld the NPEL's universal ban on political activities in the *Sarufutsu* judgment of 1974. That judgment came down in the shadow of the violent upheavals of the 1960s and the early 1970s, not long after the final blocks were set in place at the Supreme Court's "Stone Fortress." The nation was on edge and, like the Occupation authorities in the 1940s, a hardline Supreme Court majority led by Chief Justice Kazuto Ishida was determined to preserve order. The Court reversed a trend of court judgments that favored the activists, especially labor union members. One result was the absolutist *Sarufutsu* rule, which would remain the unchallenged law of the land until the arrest of Akio Horikoshi 30 years later.[8]

The District Court panel that found Horikoshi guilty felt bound to honor the strict *Sarufutsu* rule, even though the court concluded that "The defendant committed the act on his day off without any relation to his duties and there was no impact on the workplace and there was no concrete risk of immediate infringement of any protected legal interests."[9]

These words surely invigorated defense counsel as they prepared their appeal. They would deliver an extended presentation that continued through 14 court hearings over a period of more than two years. In addition to the more than two dozen witnesses who had appeared before the District Court and whose testimony was already in the court files, the defense team called another ten, including eight university professors who attacked the *Sarufutsu* standard from various angles, including comparisons with more lenient rules that prevail in other democracies and the charge that Horikoshi's prosecution conflicted with Japan's obligations under international law.

Well aware of the historic nature of the case, Chief Judge Takao Nakagawa allowed all of this testimony to go forward. Of equal importance, the court also ruled in favor of the defendant regarding the government's store of video recordings collected during the police surveillance that led to the arrest. Defense counsel drew the court's attention to the recordings at the very first appellate hearing on October 10, 2007, when they screened a video compiled from the nine recordings released by Judge Yūjirō Nakatani's order issued more than three years before. They demanded that the court direct the government to hand over an additional 24 video recordings. Nearly two years would pass before the court ruled on the request, ordering disclosure of 22 at the 11th court hearing on September 16, 2009.[10] This record of the intense police surveillance would surely color the court's view of the entire case.

"The Legal Consciousness of the People Has Changed"

Judge Nakagawa declared the verdict on the morning of March 29, 2010. After ordering Horikoshi to step forward, the judge intoned "The judgment below is reversed. The defendant is not guilty." The audience in the spectators' benches burst into applause and cries of joy. Judge Nakagawa silenced everyone with the simple statement that "You must not rejoice at something like this."[11]

With the defendant seated again and order restored, Nakagawa proceeded to read selected portions of the judgment aloud. Underscoring its momentous nature, he continued for an hour and 20 minutes. The defendant, news reporters, and other spectators scribbled furiously to capture the judge's words.

Although the High Court found Horikoshi not guilty, it declined to say that the *Sarufutsu* case had been wrongly decided. Instead, Judge Nakagawa told his audience that "with the progress of time and changes in political and social circumstances, the legal consciousness of the people has changed." According to the judge, Japanese democracy had "matured" since the *Sarufutsu* judgment. These days, he said, "the complete prohibition of political activities by national government employees is unnecessarily broad." As for Horikoshi's particular actions,

> There was no possibility that ordinary people would recognize that he was a government official engaging in a political act; it was clearly the

> defendant's independent act made at his own judgment … Applying ordinary common sense, it would be difficult to find an abstract danger to the legal interest of maintaining neutrality of administration and the trust of the people.[12]

After he finished reading from the court's opinion, Judge Nakagawa called Horikoshi to stand before the court once more. Then the judge made an extraordinary statement that can be read as an apology. He told the defendant there was a strong likelihood that the government would appeal to the Supreme Court. For this reason, he said,

> We conducted a very thorough examination of the issues, the thinking of academic experts, and the historical circumstances in which the law was adopted, not only for our own judgment, but also for the Supreme Court. I want you to understand that for these reasons the proceedings took time.[13]

Because the Supreme Court does not gather new evidence, the High Court proceeding was the last opportunity to build the case record. Judge Nakagawa and his colleagues had allowed defense counsel to make the most of it.

Most commentary applauded Horikoshi's acquittal and repeated the High Court's theme that times had changed.[14] The changes concerned not only the passage of time since the tumultuous era of the 1960s and the early 1970s in Japan, but larger geopolitical issues as well. The court referred to Cold War conditions when "ideologies were in conflict." One might interpret this as a veiled suggestion that it may have been acceptable to crack down on the JCP and labor activists in the old days, but not anymore.

Even the conservative *Yomiuri* recognized that Horikoshi presented no threat to "government neutrality," but also fretted that things could get out of hand. The paper called upon the Supreme Court to articulate a new standard that enabled government workers to clearly understand which political activities are allowed and which are not.[15]

As Judge Nakagawa predicted, the government appealed. Prosecutors declared that the court's judgment was an illegal violation of a leading Supreme Court precedent and filed on April 7, eight days after the High Court judgment.

Tokyo High Court Judgment in the Ujihashi Case

Just five weeks later, on May 13, 2010, a Tokyo High Court panel led by Chief Judge Kōichi Ideta issued its judgment in the Ujihashi case.[16] The court's approach was quite different from the Horikoshi court. The Ideta panel not only found the defendant guilty, but also denied defense requests to call witnesses and convened only three hearings before issuing judgment.

Like Akio Horikoshi, Shin'ichi Ujihashi was a national government employee at the time of his arrest for delivering the JCP newspaper *Akahata* and other political materials. But he held a position slightly higher in the bureaucratic hierarchy. The court decided he was more likely to influence the behavior of others and therefore, in his case, the ban on all political activities was appropriate. Ujihashi appealed.

Like other cases described in this book, the Horikoshi and Ujihashi cases were assigned to the Second Petty Bench. But only the full 15-justice Grand Bench holds authority to reverse its own precedents. Because the *Sarufutsu* judgment was a Grand Bench precedent, transfer to that Court was required if the appellants were to have any hope of overthrowing the *Sarufutsu* standard. Defense counsel filed requests for transfers to the Grand Bench on September 22, 2010.

After the High Court's rejection of Ujihashi's appeal, support groups for the two defendants joined forces with the goal of creating a mass movement to demand not guilty rulings from the Supreme Court. On November 6, leaders announced the formation of an umbrella group of 22 organizations that formally declared support, a number later increased to 40. The group was led by nine chairpersons including the heads of several labor organizations and Professor Okudaira along with other public intellectuals. It would sponsor monthly events, including demonstrations before the Supreme Court and gatherings for speeches by lawyers, academic experts and other writers, and the defendants themselves. Supporters also began a signature-gathering campaign with the audacious goal of collecting 200,000 names on petitions to the Court.

This campaign continued throughout 2011 and most of 2012.[17] Then, on November 9, 2012, the Second Petty Bench announced it had fixed a date for final judgment.[18] There would be no transfer to the Grand Bench and no oral arguments. Whatever the Second Petty Bench might do with the two cases, the 1974 *Sarufutsu* precedent would stand.

Supreme Court Judgments in the Horikoshi and Ujihashi Cases (December 7, 2012)

On December 7, 2012, four justices filed into the Second Petty Bench courtroom to announce the final results. Due to the brief tenure of Japan's Supreme Court justices, the lineup had changed since the Court issued the Arakawa judgment three years earlier. Of the four justices who decided that case, only Justice Yukio Takeuchi remained. The new panel was led by Justice Katsumi Chiba, a 66-year-old career judge who had been appointed to the Supreme Court in 2009. It was Justice Chiba who pronounced the result: a split decision that upheld the judgments of both High Courts, not guilty for Horikoshi and guilty for Ujihashi.[19]

The Court announced that criminal prosecution under the NPEL is appropriate only concerning acts that cause "substantive (*jisshitsuteki*) damage to political neutrality in the exercise of official duties." To determine whether such damage is present, the court conducted a comprehensive analysis that relied on examining several factors, including whether the defendant holds a managerial position and exercises discretion in that position, whether the political acts were committed during working hours or at the workplace, and whether others would recognize that the defendant is a government employee. None of these factors applied in Horikoshi's case.

On the other hand, the Court decided that Ujihashi, who held the title of deputy section head (*kachō hosa*) and coordinated the work of eight people in his group held sufficient authority to influence the actions of others and therefore was guilty of violating the NPEL prohibition of political activities.[20] According to the Court, even though he acted during his free time away from the workplace, because he was in a position to influence others, Ujihashi's delivery of the *Akahata*, an act of support for a specific political party, went too far. The Court wrote "there is a high possibility that this tendency could affect his work duties and it was unavoidable that it would affect his subordinates' work duties and management of the organization." Therefore, Ujihashi violated the Court's "substantive damage" standard.

The Horikoshi decision was unanimous, but the vote was 3-1 in the Ujihashi case, with a dissent by Justice Masahiko Sudō, a career attorney, who would have ruled Ujihashi not guilty. In his opinion,

> Because his actions would be seen as those of one individual, one citizen, I do not see any rational explanation that indicates his political attitude would be reflected in his work duties. Even if we consider that he held a managerial position and exercised discretion at the work place, the defendant should be found not guilty.[21]

In a separate opinion, Justice Chiba went out of his way to explain there was no conflict between the Horikoshi and *Sarufutsu* judgments. He did not repeat the High Court's "times have changed" rationale. Instead, according to Justice Chiba, the facts of the underlying cases were sufficiently different that there was no conflict.[22]

For Akio Horikoshi, this was a clear victory. The record would show that he was not guilty of crime. For the attorneys and supporters motivated by their interest in Japanese law, it was also a victory but a much smaller one. Their dream was to see the *Sarufutsu* standard struck down by the Grand Bench and replaced by a more lenient rule. This did not happen. Today the *Sarufutsu* judgment remains the leading precedent for limitations on the political rights of national government employees. But the Horikoshi judgment added an appendix. Justice Chiba and his colleagues did not have the power to overturn the *Sarufutsu* standard, but they did modify it.

Prior to the decision in the Horikoshi case, the *Sarufutsu* rule imposed an absolute prohibition on political activities as defined in the NPEL and related regulations. The Horikoshi judgment changed this to prohibit only those acts that cause "substantive damage to political neutrality in the exercise of official duties." In assessing whether "substantive damage" is present, future courts can compare the different results in the two cases.

As one might expect, some prosecutors grumbled that this would make bringing cases under the NPEL more difficult. On the other hand, the *Asahi* quoted two former prosecutors who said that going after Horikoshi was overkill.[23] His actions were just too insignificant to bother with prosecution. They spoke anonymously, of course.

CONCLUSION

Dissent in Wartime

All governments seek to block dissent in wartime. Many lives and sometimes the survival of the nation may be at stake. But Japan is a special case. Because Article 9 of its "Peace Constitution" outlaws participation in war, one might think that those who speak out against war engage not in dissent but in expressing support for the Constitution itself. But leaders of Japan's Liberal Democratic Party have campaigned against Article 9 since the party's founding. When U.S. President George W. Bush launched war in the Middle East, Prime Minister Jun'ichi Koizumi saw his chance to strike a major blow against Article 9. By deploying a small Self-Defense Forces contingent, he could achieve several goals at once: demonstrate the impracticality of extreme limitations on Japan's military, appease the Bush Administration demands that Japan put "boots on the ground" in Iraq, and even share in the spoils of a victorious campaign in the oil-rich Middle East. The cost was trivial: deployment of a few minor units kept well away from the fighting.

But the move was unpopular. A majority of the Japanese people have consistently supported Article 9 and opposed Japan's return to the battlefield. This made suppression of dissent against the Koizumi Iraq policy especially important. If antiwar protests spread, the political damage to the otherwise popular Prime Minister could be significant. By raiding the Tent Village office before waiting television cameras and by locking the suspects away for an extended period, the police sought to halt public dissent and thus perform a valuable service to the Administration.

The police campaign against Tent Village was a success. SDF members would no longer find paper messages from Tent Village and other activists in their mailboxes. Anyone with the nerve to deliver such messages risked a stay of 75 days—or more—in a jail cell. For most Japanese people, jail time like this would mean the loss of employment and orderly family life. The police raid was also a success

DOI: 10.4324/9781003193999-18

on a more strategic front. Police executives confirmed that in cases with large political issues at stake, the prosecutors and courts would do their bidding.

This book is focused on the Tent Village case, with brief references to the Horikoshi and Arakawa prosecutions. But there were other cases around the same time in which police took extremely aggressive actions against persons accused of trivial offenses. Among them: the prosecutions of government official Shin'ichi Ujihashi, high school teacher Katsuhisa Fujita, and the author of anti-war graffiti in a public park.[1] Although the fact patterns in these cases differed, as did the laws applied, Professor Okudaira points out that they share a common characteristic: "The issue in all of these cases was whether writings or spoken words that carried a political message should be the target of suppression by governmental power."[2] The political message the government feared most was opposition to Japan's participation in the Iraq War.

There is another side to the story. The reaction to the arrests and prosecution revealed the underlying forces that support Japan's democratic Constitution and the limits it sets on government power. A broad range of supporters quickly rose to the defense of Tent Village and the right to free political speech that the case represented. Within days of the arrests, young scholars crafted a powerful condemnation of the police action. It quickly attracted the signatures of more than 50 colleagues, laying the foundation for a sharply worded editorial that appeared in one of the country's premier publications two days later. This message was delivered to millions of readers who had never heard of Tent Village or imagined that dropping a flyer into someone's mailbox could lead to arrest.

At the same time, an elected member of the city council stepped forward to lead a campaign to support the three messengers who suddenly found themselves in jail cells and would stay there for more than ten weeks. His personal website became the key tool for spreading the word to supporters. The press conference he called one week after the arrests enabled reporters to alert the Japanese people to the significance of the events taking place in Tachikawa. Along with other volunteers, he took on the task of documenting the story through the Internet, interviews and articles in the news media, and even full-length books.

Criminal prosecutions must be tried in court. Supporters of the rule of law look to the courts to ensure that police and prosecutors respect limitations on their power. In both the Tent Village and Arakawa cases, the trial court judges who heard the testimony of witnesses and the pleas of the defendants found them not guilty. But in Japan, the government holds a right to appeal such verdicts, and the Supreme Court has the final word. The Court ruled the defendants guilty in both cases. It made no complaint about government surveillance of Tent Village prior to the arrests, the manner in which the police set a trap to capture the suspects, the intensive searches of individual homes, and the 75-day jail term based on such trivial charges. Through its silence, Japan's Supreme Court approved all of these measures.

In his review of the Supreme Court judgment, Manabu Ishizaki issued a stark warning:

> The investigative authorities, the prosecutors and the courts have sent a clear and forceful message to the people. They will use whatever laws they can find to shut down the activities of citizens who express opposition to important government policies.[3]

Only days after the Supreme Court judgment in the Tent Village case, an unrelated group of antiwar activists achieved an important victory in the Nagoya High Court. That court issued a historic opinion that declared the actions of an Air Self-Defense Forces (ASDF) unit in support of the Iraq War effort in violation of Constitution Article 9 and the Special Measures Law that authorized SDF action in the Middle East. The Nagoya High Court's opinion on the ASDF activities had no legal force, however, because the court dismissed the case for lack of standing. Government spokesmen declared it would have no effect on Japan's Iraq policy. Nonetheless, news of the Nagoya court's statement was on the front page of every newspaper and clearly expressed the opinions of many Japanese. With the Nagoya court judgment, popular opposition to the SDF deployment may have reached a tipping point: the government decided against extending the ASDF assignment in the Middle East when its authorized term ended three months later.

The Iraq deployment and the Tent Village prosecution occurred at a crossroads in Japan's recent history. After decades of LDP criticism of Article 9, Prime Minister Koizumi took decisive action, ordering the SDF into a war zone. A decade later, another LDP Prime Minister, Shinzo Abe, led his party in passing legislation that explicitly authorizes offshore deployment of the SDF, so the next time Japanese forces are sent into action abroad, they will likely be acting with the authority of the Diet at their backs. If protesters deliver flyers door-to-door or otherwise cross some line drawn by the police, they will risk arrest, lengthy detention, and prosecution. And this will happen with the approval of Japan's Supreme Court. Japan's first "prisoners of conscience" may not be its last.

We may look to the Supreme Court's Horikoshi judgment as ground for hope that the Court will take a more aggressive stance in protecting individual rights in the future. However, even though it upheld a not guilty verdict, the Court was careful to avoid finding fault with restrictive precedent or clearly basing its judgment on the Constitution. The particular nature of that case, involving a statutory ban on political activity left over from the Occupation era that had been criticized for decades, makes it a poor platform to support fundamental change.

The primary source for optimism is the Constitution itself. Despite the long-running efforts of nationalistic politicians, the Constitution that took effect in 1947 remains unaltered. Every student learns that it is the supreme source of law that serves as the central pillar of Japan's democracy. The attorneys, scholars, editorialists, and others who stepped forward to defend the activists described in this book uniformly grounded their pleas in the language of the Constitution. As long as those words remain unchanged, the people can continue to draw from a great source of strength.

CHRONOLOGY

2003

March 17 The United States and its allies begin bombing attacks in Iraq.

March 18 Prime Minister Koizumi declares unequivocally that Japan will support U.S. military action in Iraq and criticizes Japan's antiwar demonstrators. Opinion polls would show his Iraq policy is very unpopular.

July 26 Japan's Diet passes a Special Measures Law authorizing the deployment of Self-Defense Forces (SDF) to Iraq.

August The Tachikawa "Tent Village" antiwar group meets to plan its response to potential deployment of Japan's SDF in the Iraq War zone.

October 12 Tent Village members make their first flyer delivery at the SDF apartments in Tachikawa.

November 9 In general elections for the House of Representatives, the opposition Democratic Party of Japan gains 40 seats, but the Liberal Democratic Party retains power. Prime Minister Koizumi declares the results to be a confirmation of his Iraq policy.

November 30 Tent Village members make their second flyer delivery at the SDF apartments in Tachikawa.

December 9 The Cabinet approves the fundamental plan for Iraq support. Prime Minister Koizumi announces plans to deploy SDF units to Iraq in a nationally televised press conference.

December 13 Tent Village members make their third flyer delivery at the SDF apartments in Tachikawa.

December 18–22 Managers at the SDF apartments post signs prohibiting trespassing and file complaints with police.

December 26 Air Self-Defense Force advance units depart for the Middle-East.

2004

January 1 Prime Minister Koizumi makes a formal visit to the Yasukuni Shrine.

January 16 Ground Self-Defense Force advance teams depart for Samawah, Iraq.

January 17 Tent Village members make their fourth flyer delivery at the SDF apartments in Tachikawa. There are confrontations with residents who warn them to stay away.

February 27 The police raid six locations in the Tachikawa area including the Tent Village office and residences of five members. The police arrest three Tent Village members and confiscate personal computers, files, datebooks, and other material.

March 3 Tachikawa City Council member Yutaka Osawa holds a press conference at the city hall concerning the Tent Village arrests. A formal declaration that criticizes the arrests signed by 56 law professors is released to the news media at the event.

March 3 Akio Horikoshi is arrested on the charge of unlawfully distributing Japan Communist Party political material. State security police raid six locations, including Japan Communist Party (JCP) offices.

March 5 The *Asahi Shimbun* publishes an editorial that sharply criticizes the Tent Village arrests.

March 6 Horikoshi is indicted for violating the National Public Employees Law.

March 18 Amnesty International declares the Tent Village suspects to be Japan's first "Prisoners of Conscience."

March 19 and **31** The Tent Village suspects are indicted on criminal trespass charges.

May 6 The first public hearing in the Tent Village trial is held at the Hachioji courthouse.

May 11 The three Tent Village defendants are released on bail, 75 days after the arrests.

June 3—July 8 Prosecutors present courtroom testimony of three witnesses during the second to fourth hearings in the Tent Village trial.

June 10 Nine prominent intellectuals, including Tokyo University Professor Emeritus Yasuhiro Okudaira launch the "Article 9 Association."

July 20 At the first public hearing in the Horikoshi trial the court orders disclosure of 29 items of evidence over prosecutors' objections.

September 9–30 Defense counsel present the courtroom testimony of three witnesses, including Professor Okudaira, in the fifth and sixth hearings in the Tent Village trial.

November 4 The prosecution and defense make final arguments in the Tent Village trial. Prosecutors demand six-month prison terms for the three defendants, plus fines.

December 16 Tokyo District Court, Hachioji branch, issues its judgment finding all three Tent Village defendants not guilty.

2005

December 9 Tokyo High Court overturns the not guilty verdict in the Tent Village case, finding the three defendants guilty of criminal trespass. The Court orders payments of fines, but no imprisonment.

2006

June 29 Tokyo District Court rules Akio Horikoshi guilty of violating the National Public Employees Law and liable to pay a fine of 100,000 yen.
July Japan's Ground Self-Defense Forces are removed from Iraq.
August 28 Tokyo District Court rules Yōsei Arakawa not guilty of criminal trespass.

2007

December 11 Tokyo High Court overturns the District Court ruling in the Arakawa case, finding the defendant guilty of criminal trespass and liable to pay a fine of 50,000 yen.

2008

April 7 Nagoya High Court issues a judgment declaring Japan's Air Self-Defense Force activities in the Iraq war zone in violation of Constitution Article 9, but dismisses the case due to the plaintiffs' lack of standing.
April 11 The Supreme Court upholds the guilty verdict in the Tent Village case.
July Japan's Air Self-Defense Forces end operations in the Iraq war zone.

2009

November 30 The Supreme Court upholds the guilty verdict in the Arakawa case.

2010

March 29 Tokyo High Court overturns the District Court ruling in the Horikoshi case, finding the defendant not guilty.
May 23 Tokyo High Court upholds the guilty verdict in the Ujihashi case.

2012

December 7 The Supreme Court upholds both the not guilty verdict in the Horikoshi case and the guilty verdict in the Ujihashi case in judgments issued the same day.

A NOTE ON SOURCES

I relied on a wide range of publications, court documents, and interviews to piece together the Tent Village story. Japan's mainstream news media produced extensive reports concerning court judgments, but not much during the trial or intervals between court judgments. Some of the gaps were covered by weekly magazines and other publications.

Nearly all of the source material is in Japanese. My translations of the original material appear throughout the text. There was very little reporting on the case in English.

Fortunately, many Tent Village members and their supporters are skillful writers and they produced an extensive record of their experiences. Much of this appeared in very minor publications or was self-published, so is not generally available to the broader public. One of the most valuable sources is a blog maintained by Yutaka Osawa, who served as a member of the Tachikawa City Council at the time of the arrests. Written in real time, his blog provides an invaluable guide to the events as they unfolded, beginning with the arrests and continuing through the not guilty verdict in the District Court and beyond. (As I write this, Osawa's blog remains live.)

Regarding the Tent Village trial, the most authoritative source is the court record, but in Japan public access to court records in criminal cases is generally prohibited. Denied access to this official record, I assembled a collection of documents from the fragments that remained in the files of participants many years after the trial concluded. Another important source was a website maintained by Tent Village during the trial that carried detailed reports for each trial hearing with summaries and quotations from courtroom testimony. I label this the "Tent Village Trial Reports" in the endnotes. (Unfortunately, this website is no longer available.) Freelance writer Mitsuru Munakata was one of the main authors of these reports and he also produced a full-length book on the Tent Village story, which includes many details from the courtroom. All three courts that heard the case produced written judgments, but only the District Court—the trial court that heard witnesses and considered other evidence—created a document with great detail concerning the facts of the case. The appellate court judgments addressed narrow legal issues and did not add to the factual record.

The best comprehensive sources for the Tent Village story appear in two books published in 2005, soon after the not guilty verdict. Mitsuru Munakata's book, *When Voices Against War Leave Town—The Tachikawa Antiwar Flyer Suppression Case, [Machi Kara Hansen no Koe ga Kieru Toki—Tachikawa Hansen Bira-ire Dan'atsu Jiken]* is a dramatic retelling of the story. The author was an active Tent Village supporter and present at many of the protests and strategy sessions and at all of the court hearings. He provides aliases for all the main characters, driven by his desire to protect their privacy during a time of great controversy. The second book, *The Tachikawa Antiwar Flyer Case [Tachikawa Hansen Bira Jiken]*, is a compendium of articles by ten different authors, transcripts of roundtable discussions, and appendices that include primary materials such as copies of the flyers, a map of the area where the incident took place, and other material.

Defendants in all three cases benefited from the support of groups of sympathetic individuals who spoke out on their behalf and attended court hearings and other events. Each group memorialized its work by publishing lengthy and detailed pamphlets that provide a rich source of factual details and opinions. Useful commentary by legal professionals appeared in the monthly periodicals *Hōgaku Seminar* and *Hō to Minshushugi*.

Other sources, including more generally available commercial publications, are identified in the bibliography and notes.

NOTES

Introduction

1. See "The Forgotten Prisoners," at https://www.theguardian.com/uk/1961/may/28/fromthearchive.theguardian (viewed April 5, 2019).
2. For general Amnesty International history, see https://www.amnesty.org/en/who-we-are/. In 2019, the organization claimed more than 7 million members.
3. Lawrence Repeta and Colin P.A. Jones, "State Power Versus Individual Freedom: Japan's Constitutional Past, Present, and Possible Futures," in *Japan: The Precarious Future*, Frank Baldwin and Anne Allison (eds.) (New York and London: New York University Press, 2015); Lawrence Repeta, "Nationalism and the Law: Japan's Tale of Two Constitutions," in *Asian Nationalisms Reconsidered*, ed. Jeff Kingston (Oxon and New York: Routledge, 2016).

Prologue

1. "Koizumi Pays Surprise Visit to Yasukuni Shrine," AFP Tokyo, January 2, 2004, http://www.taipeitimes.com/News/world/archives/2004/01/02/2003086040.
2. "Press Conference by Prime Minister Jun'ichiro Koizumi," *Speeches and Statements by Prime Minister*, December 9, 2003, http://japan.kantei.go.jp/koizumispeech/2003/12/09press_e.html (accessed September 17, 2020). Quoted in Michael Penn, *Japan and the War on Terror* (I. B. Tauris, 2014), 92.
3. For a brief note in English and some photos from the Prime Minister's visit to Komaki air base, see "Prime Minister Encourages Japan Air Self-Defense Force (JASDF) to Be Dispatched to Iraq," December 24, 2003, http://japan.kantei.go.jp/koizumiphoto/2003/12/24komaki_e.html. See also Penn, *Japan and the War on Terror*, 94.
4. Penn, *Japan and the War on Terror*, 93.

Chapter 1

1. There were two other residential buildings at the site, marked 9 and 10, but the District Court noted that they were little used and completely empty by December 2004. Tokyo District Court, Hachioji Branch, Judgment of December 16, 2004. *Hanrei Jihō 1892*, 150. *Hanrei Times 1177*, 133.

2. Tent Village members also delivered flyers at the SDF residences on November 30, December 13, January 17, and February 22. Copies of all flyers are appended to the Tokyo District Court judgment. Tokyo District Court, Hachioji Branch, Judgment of December 16, 2004.
3. Bush visited Tokyo on October 19–20, 2003. Office of the Historian, "George W. Bush," https://history.state.gov/departmenthistory/travels/president/bush-george-w. According to a *CBS News* story, "Japan is reportedly considering sending the forces to Basra and Nasiriya, two relatively stable cities in southern Iraq. But the timing of the deployment remains a matter of debate, in part because of Japan's Nov. 9 national elections. Military involvement of any kind is controversial in Japan, where the electorate contains a strong pacifist streak." "Bush Has Yen for Japan Help," CBS News, October 18, 2003, https://www.cbsnews.com/news/bush-has-yen-for-japan-help/.
4. Quotations are from the October 12, 2003, flyer, titled, "To Members of the Self-Defense Forces and Their Families: What Will SDF Deployment to Iraq Lead To?"
5. Dustin Wright, *The Sunagawa Struggle: A Century of Antibase Protest in a Tokyo Suburb* (Ph.D. thesis, University of California at Santa Cruz, June 2015), 16–17. The Tokugawa shoguns were the dominant leaders in Japan from 1600 to 1868. Edo was the Tokugawa-era name for Tokyo.
6. Wright, *Sunagawa Struggle*, 26–27.
7. Wright, *Sunagawa Struggle*, 40.
8. Wright, *Sunagawa Struggle*, 48–49.
9. Wright, *Sunagawa Struggle*, 37.
10. Wright, *Sunagawa Struggle*, 51.
11. Wright, *Sunagawa Struggle*, 50.
12. Wright provides descriptions of local victims of the U.S. bombing, with quotations from survivors, *Sunagawa Struggle*, 50–55.
13. Dustin Wright, "'Sunagawa Struggle' Ignited Anti-U.S. Base Resistance Across Japan," *Japan Times*, May 3, 2015, https://www.japantimes.co.jp/community/2015/05/03/issues/sunagawa-struggle-ignited-anti-u-s-base-resistance-across-japan. As summarized by the historian Thomas R. H. Havens, by mid-1968 "American bases had become unwelcome to a majority of Japanese because of their connection with a bogged-down war in Vietnam, their record of local frictions from Sasebo to Sunagawa, and their affront to national pride." *Fire Across the Sea: The Vietnam War and Japan 1965–1975* (Princeton, NJ: Princeton University Press, 1987), 163.
14. Wright reports the dates of the four expansions at *Sunagawa Struggle*, 100.
15. The eviction order would affect 140 families. Many traced their roots in Sunagawa to the early Edo Period. Wright, "Sunagawa Struggle Ignited."
16. Wright, "Sunagawa Struggle Ignited."
17. Wright, "Sunagawa Struggle Ignited." Seven protesters were arrested in 1957 and charged with trespassing onto the U.S. military base. The resulting criminal trial ultimately reached the Supreme Court and led to the most important court interpretation of Constitution Article 9. Wright describes the case in *Sunagawa Struggle*, 204–212.
18. Seisaku Shimada served on the Tachikawa city council from 1966 through 1998. Wright describes his career in *Sunagawa Struggle*, 233–241.
19. According to 1970 data from the Embassy in Tokyo, the United States maintained more than 120 separate facilities covering more than 75,000 acres. John K. Emmerson, *Arms, Yen, and Power* (North Clarendon, VT: Tuttle, 1971), 93.
20. Havens, *Fire Across the Sea*, 162.
21. Havens, *Fire Across the Sea*, 162.
22. Havens, *Fire Across the Sea*, 199. The "reversion" agreement was signed by representatives of the two governments on June 17, 1971, and ratified by the House of Representatives on November 24, 1971. Japan regained full sovereignty over Okinawa the following spring.

23. Havens, *Fire Across the Sea*, 193.
24. The Defense Agency was elevated to ministry status in 2006.
25. Katsuko Kato, "Why We Hand Out Flyers to Self-Defense Force Members" [Watakushitachi ha naze jieikan ni bira wo kubaru no ka], in *The Tachikawa Antiwar Flyer Case* [*Tachikawa Hansen Bira Jiken*] (Tokyo: Akashi Shōten, 2005), 15. Noboru Minowa and Masatoshi Uchida, *Constitution Article 9 and Exclusive Self-Defense* [*Kenpō Kyūjō to Senpu Bōei*] (Tokyo: Nashinoki, 2004), 4.
26. Kato, "Why We Hand Out Flyers," 15–16. There is additional background on conditions in Tachikawa at this time in the District Court Judgment.
27. Kato, "Why We Hand Out Flyers," 16.
28. Kato, "Why We Hand Out Flyers," 16.
29. Wright, *Sunagawa Struggle*, 247–249.
30. *Tachikawa Tent Village 30-Year Commemorative Pamphlet* [*Tachikawa Tentō-Mura 30 Nen Shūnen Kinen Panfu*] (2002).
31. Tokyo District Court, Hachioji Branch, Judgment of December 16, 2004.
32. Tokyo District Court, Hachioji Branch, Judgment of December 16, 2004.

Chapter 2

1. Hiroaki Nakajima, "Reporting that Cheers the 'Not Guilty Verdict' but Excuses Suppression" [Dan'atsu wo menzai suru 'muzai hanketsu' banzai hōdō], in *The Tachikawa Antiwar Flyer Case* [*Tachikawa Hansen Bira Jiken*] (Tokyo: Akashi Shōten, 2005), 129.
2. According to the District Court judgment, the headcount included the three members arrested on February 27, so the police raid wiped out nearly half of the group's total strength. Members were said to be supported by an unknown number of people who sometimes attended meetings, made monetary contributions or otherwise helped out. To finance their operations, the group raised between 100,000 and 400,000 yen per month (approximately US $1,000 to $4,000). Tokyo District Court, Hachioji Branch, Judgment of December 16, 2004. *Hanrei Jihō 1892*, 150. *Hanrei Times 1177*, 133.
3. Toshiyuki Obora, "75 Days in Detention for Dropping Antiwar Flyers in Mail Boxes at Self-Defense Force Housing" [Jieitai kansha he no hansen-bira tōkan de 75-nichikan no kōryu], in *Very Strange! Police, Prosecutors, Courts—The Freedom of Civil Society is in Danger* [*Okashii zo, Keisatsu, Kensatsu, Saibansho—Shimin Shakai no Jiyū ga Abunai*], eds. Akira Uozumi et al. (Tokyo: Tsukuru Shuppan, 2005), 13.
4. Sachimi Takada describes the police raid in "Jail Diary: 75-Day Fight from Inside the Walls" [Goku-chu Nikki: Kabe no naka de tatakatta 75-nichikan], in *The Tachikawa Antiwar Flyer Case* [*Tachikawa Hansen Bira Jiken*] (Tokyo: Akashi Shōten, 2005), 45.
5. Takada, "Jail Diary," 45. Takada's description of approximately three television cameras in front of the Tent Village building matches *Kyodo News* reporter Hiroaki Nakajima's account.
6. Takada expressed her sense of desolation in the police vehicle: "As I looked out the window at the very familiar scene, I thought my feeling of riding my bike here was far away." Takada, "Jail Diary," 46.
7. Takada, "Jail Diary," 46.
8. Tachikawa Antiwar Flyer Suppression Support Group [Tachikawa Hansen Bira Dan'atsu Kyūenkai], *The Complete Record 2004–2009* [*Zenkiroku 2004–2009*] (Tokyo, 2009), 8. The police were required to obtain judicial approvals for warrants for arrests and for each of the six places searched. They served arrest warrants only on the three members who participated in the January 17 flyer deliveries.
9. Katsuko Kato's interview, "Urgent Interview—We Won't Allow Suppression of Antiwar Flyer Deliveries!" [Kinkyū intabyū—Hansen bira ire he no dan'atsu wo yurusanai!], *War and Sex* [*Sensō to Sei*] 22 (Spring 2004), 10.

10. Kato, "Urgent Interview," 11. Regarding such searches, Article 35 of the Constitution requires search warrants to be issued for "adequate cause and particularly describing the place to be searched and the things to be seized." The search warrant for Kato's residence indicates that the police fulfilled this requirement by appending a very long list of "things to be seized."
11. Kato, "Urgent Interview," 11–12.
12. In addition to the Tent Village apartment and the homes of the members they arrested, the police also searched the homes of Tent Village members Mori Inoue and Tamaki Kōno. Kōno was in charge of bookkeeping and allowed to take copies of the accounts before the police took the originals away. Kato, "Urgent Interview," 14.
13. Kato, "Urgent Interview," 12.
14. Tachikawa Support Group, *Complete Record*, 12. Mitsuru Munakata describes the February 27 gathering of supporters, *When Voices Against War Leave Town—The Tachikawa Antiwar Flyer Suppression Case* [*Machi Kara Hansen no Koe ga Kieru Toki—Tachikawa Hansen Bira-ire Dan'atsu Jiken*] (Tokyo: Jushinsha, 2005), 14, and protests immediately after the arrests, 47–51 and 74–75. Tent Village member Mori Inoue describes the demonstration at the police station, "Looking Back on the Year Following the Arrests" [Taiho kara no ichinen wo furikaeru], in *The Tachikawa Antiwar Flyer Case* [*Tachikawa Hansen Bira Jiken*] (Tokyo: Akashi Shōten, 2005), 26. Yutaka Osawa provides photos from protests that immediately followed the arrests, Osawa, *Homepage for Peace* [Heiwa no Peiji], blog, February 29, 2004, http://osawa-yutaka.my.coocan.jp/heiwa-top.htm.
15. Tachikawa Support Group, *Complete Record*, 12.
16. Tachikawa Support Group, *Complete Record*, 12. Yutaka Osawa, "Final Comment" [Owari ni], in *The Tachikawa Antiwar Flyer Case* [*Tachikawa Hansen Bira Jiken*] (Tokyo: Akashi Shōten, 2005), 180.
17. Munakata, *Voices Against War*, 74–75. Tent Village members told me there have never been arrests for the "anti-military broadcasts." Broadcast dates are recorded in the Tent Village newsletter.
18. Osawa, *Homepage for Peace*, February 29, 2004. The common term used by the activists for petitions under Constitution Article 16 is "*moshi-ire*."
19. According to the published record of the support group, supporters made protests outside the jail cells more than 20 times during the Tent Village members' detention. Tachikawa Support Group, *Complete Record*, 14.
20. Kato, "Urgent Interview," 2004, 15. The same sentiments were expressed by Inoue and Osawa. See Inoue, "Looking Back," 27, and Osawa, "Final Comment," 181.
21. The term *Santama* refers to the area encompassed by three small adjacent cities: Tachikawa, Kunitachi, and Kokubunji. Activists residing in the three cities often joined together. Some Tent Village members live in Kunitachi, which shares a border with Tachikawa.
22. Osawa's comment in the roundtable discussion in *The Tachikawa Antiwar Flyer Case* [*Tachikawa Hansen Bira Jiken*] (Tokyo: Akashi Shōten, 2005), 82.
23. Osawa, "Final Comment," 183–84. Kato describes Osawa contributions, "Urgent Interview," 15.
24. Osawa retired from the city council in 2018. The section of his website devoted to the Tachikawa case remained accessible at least until spring, 2022. Osawa, *Homepage for Peace*, http://osawa-yutaka.my.coocan.jp/heiwa-top.htm.
25. Osawa's comment in the roundtable discussion in *The Tachikawa Antiwar Flyer Case* [*Tachikawa Hansen Bira Jiken*] (Tokyo: Akashi Shōten, 2005), 82.
26. Osawa said he had coordinated protests with Tent Village for more than ten years. Osawa's comment in the roundtable discussion, 82.
27. Osawa, *Homepage for Peace*, February 27, 2004.
28. The complete text of the message is at Osawa, *Homepage for Peace*, February 28, 2004.

29. The Tent Village declaration is reproduced in *The Tachikawa Antiwar Flyer Case* [*Tachikawa Hansen Bira Jiken*] (Tokyo: Akashi Shōten, 2005), 212–13 and Osawa, *Homepage for Peace,* February 28, 2004.
30. When arrests are made by the police as in this case, the police can maintain custody up to 48 hours before transferring suspects to prosecutors, who can continue custody for another 24 hours before seeking a court order to extend the detention.
31. According to defense attorney Hirotatsu Kojima, opinions among defense counsel were divided on whether the suspects would be indicted. Kojima, "Trial Proceedings Until We Won the Not Guilty Verdict" [Muzai hanketsu wo kachitoru made no saiban shinri], in *The Tachikawa Antiwar Flyer Case* [*Tachikawa Hansen Bira Jiken*] (Tokyo: Akashi Shōten, 2005), 61.
32. Tachikawa Support Group, *Complete Record,* 8; Obora, "75 Days," 13.
33. Code of Criminal Procedure Article 81 empowers courts to prohibit visits to detainees when there is a risk of flight or destruction of evidence. The common Japanese term for this practice is *sekken kinshi.*
34. The Supreme Court ruled that criminal suspects must submit to interrogations even though they have declared a right to remain silent in a 1999 judgment issued by the full 15 justice bench. These practices have been repeatedly decried by international human rights panels to no effect. David Johnson describes several cases of violent assaults by prosecutors during interrogation sessions. David T. Johnson, *The Japanese Way of Justice: Prosecuting Crime in Japan* (New York: Oxford University Press, 2002), 253–63.
35. Regarding interrogations, Atsuko Muraki, a high-ranking female bureaucrat who was the victim of a false prosecution commented that it's like a boxing match with a professional fighting an amateur—and the attorney is not allowed in the ring. Jeff Kingston, "Justice on Trial: Japanese Prosecutors Under Fire," *The Asia-Pacific Journal* 9, issue 10, no. 1 (March 7, 2011).
36. These practices attracted the attention of the international news media with the arrest of former Renault-Nissan CEO Carlos Ghosn in 2018. Following Ghosn's arrest, more than 1,000 Japanese experts signed a declaration that attacks Japan's "hostage justice" system. An English translation is available at Human Rights Watch, "Call to Eliminate Japan's 'Hostage Justice' System by Japanese Legal Professionals," April 10, 2019, https://www.hrw.org/news/2019/04/10/call-eliminate-japans-hostage-justice-system-japanese-legal-professionals#.
37. "Suppression of Antiwar Flyers—Our Battle" [Hansen bira dan'atsu—Watakushitachi no tatakai], *War and Sex* [*Sensō to Sei*] 24 (Summer 2005), 13.
38. Author's interview with Nobuhiro Onishi, July 3, 2019.
39. Takada was held in a part of the facility reserved exclusively for female detainees. Attorney Shizu Yamamoto (a woman) told me there are very few such facilities in Tokyo. Therefore, they are larger and the procedures may be more bureaucratic than the men's facilities, which are smaller and very numerous, allowing more autonomy. Author's interview with Shizu Yamamoto, April 22, 2019.
40. Takada, "Jail Diary," 48.
41. Obora, "75 Days," 13–14.
42. Takada, "Jail Diary," 46.
43. Yutaka Osawa's comment in the roundtable discussion in *The Tachikawa Antiwar Flyer Case,* 84.
44. Osawa describes his frenzied activities after the arrests in the roundtable discussion in *The Tachikawa Antiwar Flyer Case,* 82–84. Specific actions are recorded in *Homepage for Peace.*
45. Osawa describes the press conference at *Homepage for Peace,* March 4, 2004. There are also brief descriptions in Inoue, "Looking Back," 27, and Munakata, *Voices Against War,* 49–50.
46. Muneo Narusawa provides this description of the 1991 dispatch of minesweepers to the Persian Gulf: "The SDF's first dispatch overseas: the sending of six minesweepers and auxiliary vessels to the Persian Gulf. After the Gulf War, they set about clearing

the mines launched during the war. In the Diet, there was criticism that 'the dispatch of SDF overseas is unconstitutional,' but the Kaifu Cabinet forced through the rubrics of 'police action' and 'international contribution.' This became one important step in the ever-growing overseas dispatch of the SDF thereafter." Muneo Narusawa, "The Overseas Dispatch of Japan's Self-Defense Forces and U.S. War Preparations," *Asia-Pacific Journal* 12, no. 31 (July 28, 2014), https://apjjf.org/2014/12/31/Narusawa-Muneo/4158/article.html.

47. Author's interview with Manabu Ishizaki, April 26, 2019. The 1991 deployment of minesweepers was followed in 1992 by the Diet passage of a "peacekeeping operations" (PKO) law in 1992 that authorized deployments to support United Nations peacekeeping operations abroad. Ishizaki and many others feared that this step would lead to other foreign deployments without UN sponsorship, as occurred with the SDF deployment to Iraq.
48. Ishizaki had met Osawa when they both volunteered to support the Diet candidacy of Etsuko Kawada, who became well known as the mother of the first AIDS patient to come out publicly. Author's interview with Ishizaki, April 26, 2019. Jeff Kingston describes the Kawada case in Kingston, *Japan's Quiet Transformation* (London: Routledge, 2004), 161–63.
49. The issue exploded in the spring of 2004 when hundreds of Tokyo school teachers refused to stand and sing the *kimigayo* anthem at school ceremonies. Nezu's repeated refusals led to repeated punishments. Her support group included Takato Narisawa, Katsuko Kato, and other local antiwar activists. Kato and Narisawa met through their support for Nezu. Kato, "Urgent Interview," 15. Munakata discusses the Nezu case in *Voices Against War,* 155–59. (He uses the alias "Ono-san" for Nezu.)
50. Author's interview with Ken'ichiro Okada, January 26, 2021.
51. Manabu Ishizaki, *Examining Democracy* [*Demokurashii Kentei*] (Tokyo: Ōtsuki Shōten, 2006), 80.
52. E-mail from Takato Narisawa, May 18, 2019.
53. Ishizaki, *Examining Democracy,* 79–80.
54. The declaration was signed by 56 scholars in time for the public release on March 3. Nationally famous scholars included Shōjirō Sakaguchi of Hitotsubashi University and Asaho Mizushima of Waseda. The most prominent name on the list was that of Yasuhiro Okudaira, a retired Tokyo University professor revered in Japan's legal community as the nation's foremost expert on the constitutional right to free speech. Narisawa had studied with Okudaira at Waseda University.
55. Author's interviews with Manabu Ishizaki, April 26, 2019, and Takato Narisawa, November 14, 2019. See also Ishizaki, *Examining Democracy,* 79–80.
56. For a thorough discussion of the LDP 2005 constitutional proposals, see Christian G. Winkler, *The Quest for Japan's New Constitution: An Analysis of Visions and Constitution Reform Proposals, 1980–2009* (London: Routledge, 2011).
57. "Law Scholars' Declaration Against Suppression of the Tachikawa Self-Defense Force Surveillance Tent Village" (*Tachikawa Jietai Kanshi Tento-Mura he no Dan'atsu ni Kōgi suru Hōgakusha Seimei*), March 3, 2004. Reproduced in *The Tachikawa Antiwar Flyer Case* [*Tachikawa Hansen Bira Jiken*] (Tokyo: Akashi Shōten, 2005), 214–15.
58. Osawa describes the news reporters and the visit to Tachikawa police headquarters in Osawa, *Homepage for Peace,* March 4, 2004.

Chapter 3

1. Details of the arrest and presence of television cameras are from Tokyo Southern District Law Office, *Trials and Human Rights* [*Saiban to Jinken*] (Tokyo: Nihon Hyōronsha, 2009), 146–47. See also *Suppression Under National Public Law—The Horikoshi Case Record of Battle, 2004–2013* [*Kokkōhō dan'atsu horikoshi jiken tatakai no kiroku 2004–2013*] (Tokyo: Group to Prevent Suppression Under National Public Law and Protect Freedom of Speech, 2013), 4.

2. The Ministry of Health was merged with the Ministry of Labor in 2001 to form the current Ministry of Health and Labor.
3. Max M. Ward, *Thought Crime* (Durham, NC, and London: Duke University Press, 2019).
4. Author's interview with Akio Horikoshi, July 3, 2018.
5. The organization's URL is http://www.dylj.or.jp.
6. Details of Horikoshi's life are recorded in an affidavit prepared by police and signed by Akio Horikoshi, with fingerprint affixed, dated March 5, 2004. The government employs millions of workers, and the role of labor unions in the public sector was a controversial topic through much of the early postwar period. The Supreme Court issued a series of decisions in the early 1970s that reinforced restrictions on political activities by public sector unions. See Lawrence Repeta, "Reserved Seats on Japan's Supreme Court," *Washington University Law Review* 88, no. 6 (2011), 1728–41.
7. National Public Employees Law [*kokka kōmuin hō*], Law no. 120 of 1947.
8. National Personnel Authority Rules [*jinjiin kisoku*] 14–17 (1949).
9. There are brief English language descriptions of these cases in Lawrence W. Beer, *Freedom of Expression in Japan* (Tokyo: Kōdansha, 1984), 236.
10. *Japan v. Osawa*, Supreme Court Grand Bench judgment of November 6, 1974, *Keishū* vol. 393, 28. English translations of the justices' opinions appear in Lawrence W. Beer and Hiroshi Itoh, *The Constitutional Case Law of Japan, 1970 through 1990* (Seattle, WA: University of Washington Press, 1996), 522.
11. Nobuyoshi Ashibe, "Japan: The United States Constitution and Japan's Constitutional Law: Human Rights and Judicial Power," in *Constitutional Systems in Late Twentieth-Century Asia*, Lawrence W. Beer (ed.) (Seattle, WA: University of Washington Press, 1992), 224, 245–46. Professor Ashibe explains that prior to the *Sarufutsu* decision, many lower courts had adopted a "strict scrutiny" doctrine requiring the state to show that it had used the "least restrictive alternative" method (commonly referred to as the "LRA standard" in Japan) in restricting speech. The *Sarufutsu* judgment, which overturned the lower courts' decisions and held that a complete and uniform ban on political activities was constitutional, stopped this movement in its tracks.
12. Yasuhiro Okudaira, "Once Again Under Threat—Freedom of Expression" [Ima futatabi odokasareru hyōgen no jiyū], *Hōgaku Seminar* 615 (March 2006), 46.
13. Akio Horikoshi, "The First Indictment in 37 Years Under the National Public Employees Law for Delivering Political Flyers" [Seitō bira haifu de 37nenburi no kokkōhō ihan kiso], in *Very Strange! Police, Prosecutors, Courts* [*Okashii zo, Keisatsu, Kensatsu, Saibansho*], eds. Akira Uozumi et al. (Tokyo: Tsukuru Shuppan, 2005), 53.
14. A report on the Japan Communist Party's activities is a feature of the annual police "White Paper." The White Paper does not carry reports on other political parties. The 2021 edition includes the regular section titled, "Developments concerning the Japan Communist Party" (*Nihon kyōsantō no dōkō*), available online here: https://www.npa.go.jp/hakusyo/r03/honbun/index.html. Of course, this is a brief public document that cannot be expected to cover the full range of police activities.
15. Indictment, March 5, 2004.
16. *Mainichi Shimbun*, March 6, 2004.
17. He knew that delivering a publication with a photo of the JCP chairman calling for a big turnout at the coming election would be illegal if distributed after the formal announcement of the candidates, scheduled for October 28. Because that date was rapidly approaching, he anxiously awaited delivery of the materials and when they arrived on October 16 or 17, he acted quickly to distribute his allotment. Regarding Japan's elections laws, see Masahiro Usaki, "Restrictions on Political Campaigns in Japan," *Law and Contemporary Problems* 53, no. 2 (1990), 133, Dan Rosen, "Policing Political Speech: Japan's Mistrust of the Marketplace," *Michigan State International Law Review* 22 (2014), 799, and Shigenori Matsui, *The Constitution of Japan* (Oxford: Hart Publishing, 2011), 200.
18. Horikoshi's affidavit, March 5, 2004.
19. Author's interview with Akio Horikoshi, July 3, 2018.

20. The organization's history is recorded in *The Jiyū Hōsōdan Story 2 vols.* [Jiyū Hōsōdan Monogatari, 2 vols.] (Tokyo: Nihon Hyōronsha, 2002).
21. Details are from the indictment of Akio Horikoshi, reproduced in *Trial Materials from the Suppression Under National Public Law Case, vol. 1* [*Kokkōhō dan'atsu jiken—saiban shiryō—1*] (Tokyo: Group to Prevent Suppression Under National Public Law and Protect Freedom of Speech), 237. Also, Horikoshi affidavit, March 5, 2004.
22. The police energetically enforce election laws against selected violators. Elections are commonly followed by arrests. One of the most infamous cases attracted coverage in the *New York Times*. Norimitsu Onishi, "Pressed by Police, Even Innocent Confess in Japan," *New York Times*, May 11, 2007, https://www.nytimes.com/2007/05/11/world/asia/11japan.html.

Chapter 4

1. Nic Newman et al., *Reuters Institute Digital News Report 2018*, Reuters Institute for the Study of Journalism, https://www.digitalnewsreport.org/survey/2018, 130.
2. A prosecutor later suggested the government was after a chilling effect in published comments. The speaker served as deputy head of the Hachioji prosecutors' office at the time. *Mainichi Shimbun*, June 3, 2004.
3. *Asahi Shimbun*, March 5, 2004.
4. They would learn that the tents disappeared after someone set fire to the Tent Village shack in 1975 and authorities blocked access to the area.
5. Tachikawa Antiwar Flyer Suppression Support Group [Tachikawa Hansen Bira Dan'atsu Kyūenkai], *The Complete Record 2004–2009* [*Zenkiroku 2004–2009*] (Tokyo, 2009), 8. By Osawa's count, 93 people joined the protest. Osawa, *Homepage for Peace* [*Heiwa no Peiji*], blog, March 6, 2004, http://osawa-yutaka.my.coocan.jp/heiwa-top.htm.
6. Tokyo District Court, Hachioji Branch, Judgment of December 16, 2004. *Hanrei Jihō 1892*, 150. *Hanrei Times 1177*, 133.
7. Katsuko Kato interview, "Urgent Interview—We Won't Allow Suppression of Antiwar Flyer Deliveries!" [Kinkyū intabyū—Hansen bira ire he no dan'atsu wo yurusanai!], *War and Sex* [*Sensō to Sei*] 22 (Spring 2004), 14.
8. Katsuko Kato (ed.), *Blown by the Wind: The 101 Years of En Suda* [*Kaze ni fukaretsu—Suda En hyakuichinen*], self-published pamphlet (2017).
9. According to Kato, among her exploits En Suda traveled to China during the war years to demand that her husband be sent home to Japan. Kato, *Blown by the Wind.*
10. Kato, *Blown by the Wind*, and author's interview with Kato, October 18, 2018.
11. Kato, *Blown by the Wind*, and author's interview with Kato, November 29, 2018.
12. John W. Dower provides extended descriptions of dismal postwar conditions, including food shortages, black markets, prosecution, and other details in Dower, *Embracing Defeat: Japan in the Wake of World War II* (New York: W. W. Norton, 1999). Dustin Wright describes such conditions in the Tachikawa area. Wright, *The Sunagawa Struggle: A Century of Antibase Protest in a Tokyo Suburb* (Ph.D. diss., University of California at Santa Cruz, June 2015).
13. The 1960 protests have been described well in several histories, most recently in Nick Kapur, *Japan at the Crossroads: Conflict and Compromise After Anpo* (Cambridge, MA: Harvard University Press, 2018). See also Justin Jesty, "Tokyo 1960: Days of Rage and Grief," *MIT Visualizing Cultures*, 2012, https://visualizingcultures.mit.edu/tokyo_1960/anp2_essay05.html.
14. Kato has said that she accompanied Kamba to the hospital where she died. *Sekai*, June 2004, 199.
15. Sachimi Takada has written, "A lawyer arrived that night. She told me that I was under a *sekken kinshi* order; I would not be allowed to see anyone but my lawyers, so I would only be able to communicate to others through them. I asked the lawyer to notify my bandmates, my workplace and others about my situation." Takada, "Jail

Diary: 75-Day Fight from Inside the Walls" [Goku-chū nikki: kabe no naka de tatakatta 75-nichikan], in *The Tachikawa Antiwar Flyer Case* [*Tachikawa Hansen Bira Jiken*] (Tokyo: Akashi Shōten, 2005), 46.

16. Takada identified the cellmate who made this comment as "No. 630." After the lawyer's visit, she received some items from her friends. At this point, she writes that her feelings changed to "a commitment to believe in my friends and fight my way through." Takada, "Jail Diary," 46.
17. Author's interview with Katsuko Kato, November 29, 2018.
18. West Tokyo Kyōdō Law Office, https://nt-law.info. Some founders of the Hachioji office, including Yamahana, had previously worked at the Tokyo Kyōdō Law Office in central Tokyo.
19. Sadao Yamahana became an important player during the political upheaval that followed the LDP's loss of power in 1992. He served as a member of the national Diet and briefly as a Cabinet Minister during the first brief interregnum when the LDP was out of power. History of the West Tokyo Kyōdō Law Office, https://nt-law.info/officeinfo.
20. Author's interview with Tadashi Nishibatake, July 3, 2019.
21. Nishibatake recalls that there were around 30 lawyers in the area in the late 1970s when the West Tokyo Kyōdō Office was launched. Author's interview with Nishibatake, July 3, 2019.
22. Author's interview with Kato, November 29, 2018.
23. Author's interview with Kato, November 29, 2018.
24. The attorney who accompanied her ultimately did not join the defense team.
25. Japan Federation of Bar Associations, *2016 Attorneys' White Paper* [*Bengoshi Hakusho 2016*] (Tokyo, 2016), 30.
26. In a memoir published in 2001, Uchida describes many cases but especially highlights his work on behalf of victims of forced labor during the war years, commonly known as the Hanaoka case. Masatoshi Uchida, *Born in the Year of Defeat* [*Haisen no Toshi ni Umarete*] (Tokyo: Ohta Shuppan, 2001).
27. Author's interviews with Masatoshi Uchida, July 4, 2019, and Akira Koto, October 26, 2018. For a full account of the Sanrizuka conflict, see William Andrews, *Dissenting Japan* (London: Hurst, 2016), chapter 8.
28. Author's interviews with Masatoshi Uchida, July 4, 2019, and Takato Narisawa, November 14, 2019.
29. "The Suppression of Antiwar Flyers—Our Battle" [Hansen bira dan'atsu—watakushitachi no tatakai] (roundtable discussion), *War and Sex* [*Sensō to Sei*] 24 (Summer 2005), 27.
30. According to Nishibatake, he and Kato first met working at a part-time job when they were students. Author's interview with Nishibatake, July 3, 2019.
31. Author's interview with Kato, November 29, 2018. Miyaoka wrote a book that tells the story of the Sunagawa Struggle. Wright provides a detailed description of Miyaoka and his writings. *Sunagawa Struggle*, 210–30.
32. For background and citations to these cases, see John Owen Haley, "Waging War: Japan's Constitutional Constraints," *Constitutional Forum* 14, no. 2 (2005), 18, https://papers.ssrn.com/sol3/papers.cfm?abstract_id=821504.
33. Author's interview with Yamamoto, November 27, 2018.
34. Johnson discusses the typical profile of criminal defense attorneys in this era and their poor compensation in David T. Johnson, *The Japanese Way of Justice: Prosecuting Crime in Japan* (New York: Oxford University Press, 2002), 72–82.
35. Author's interview with Yamamoto, November 27, 2018.
36. Article 39, Paragraph 1 of the Code of Criminal Procedure (Right of a Detainee to Communicate with his Lawyer Without Officer Present). Mayu Arimoto, "Is There Attorney–Client Privilege in Japan?" *LLM Law Review*, June 16, 2018, http://www.llmlawreview.com/2018/06/16/is-there-attorney-client-privilege-in-japan.

37. This section is based on unpublished notes by support group members. Also, author's interview with Yamamoto, November 27, 2018.
38. Toshiyuki Obora, "75 Days in Detention for Dropping Antiwar Flyers in Mail Boxes at Self-Defense Force Housing" [Jieitai kansha he no hansen-bira tōkan de 75-nichi-kan no kōryu], in *Very Strange! Police, Prosecutors, Courts—The Freedom of Civil Society Is in Danger* [*Okashii zo, Keisatsu, Kensatsu, Saibansho—Shimin Shakai no Jiyū ga Abunai*], eds. Akira Uozumi et al. (Tokyo: Tsukuru Shuppan, 2005).
39. Code of Criminal Procedure, Article 82. Colin P.A. Jones and Frank S. Ravitch, *The Japanese Legal System* (St. Paul, MN: West Academic Publishing, 2018), 256. Professor Jones provides a detailed history of the failed attempt to create a habeas corpus practice similar to the common law tradition in Colin P.A. Jones, "From Great Writ to Tuning Fork: How Habeas Corpus was Tamed in Japan," *University of Pennsylvania Asian Law Review* 12 (2019), 407.
40. "According to the Ministry of Justice, only 583 of 104,529 detainees requested that a court explain their cause of detention in 2017." Motoko Rich, "Carlos Ghosn Emerges to Say He Was 'Wrongly Accused and Unfairly Detained,'" *New York Times*, January 7, 2019.
41. Mori Inoue, "Looking Back on the Year Following the Arrests" [Taiho kara no ichinen wo furikaeru], in *The Tachikawa Antiwar Flyer Case* [Tachikawa Hansen Bira Jiken] (Tokyo: Akashi Shōten, 2005), 27–28; Munakata, *Voices Against War*, 110–11. Regardless of the nature of the alleged crime or the history of the defendant, the standard practice is to lead each defendant into the courtroom on a rope, in handcuffs. In recent years, attorneys have mounted a challenge to this practice. See Shunsuke Abe, "Lawyers in Call to End Practice of Handcuffs, Ropes in Courtrooms," *Asahi Shimbun*, August 15, 2021, https://www.asahi.com/ajw/articles/14407268.
42. Munakata, *Voices Against War*, 110–11. "Destruction of evidence" is interpreted to include communication with potential witnesses.

Chapter 5

1. Osawa describes a small protest march held on March 13. Yutaka Osawa, *Homepage for Peace* [*Heiwa no Peiji*], blog, March 16, 2004, http://osawa-yutaka.my.coocan.jp/heiwa-top.htm.
2. Japan's bar associations accept petitions for investigations of human rights violations. Committees made up of members gather information, question witnesses, and prepare reports. They do not commence litigation or take other formal legal action. According to Munakata, five supporters traveled to the attorneys' building in central Tokyo to file a request for an inquiry by the bar association, where they were met by Uchida. Munakata, *When Voices Against War Leave Town—The Tachikawa Antiwar Flyer Suppression Case* [*Machi Kara Hansen no Koe ga Kieru Toki—Tachikawa Hansen Bira-ire Dan'atsu Jiken*] (Tokyo: Jushinsha, 2005), 111–12. Mori Inoue also reports the approach to the bar association in Inoue, "Looking Back on the Year Following the Arrests" [Taiho kara no ichinen wo furikaeru], in *The Tachikawa Antiwar Flyer Case* [Tachikawa Hansen Bira Jiken] (Tokyo: Akashi Shōten, 2005), 28–29.
3. Munakata, *Voices Against War*, 112.
4. Uchida also told the crowd about a plan to challenge the constitutionality of the SDF deployment through lawsuits filed in courts around the country. *Voices Against War*, 116. Uchida was a primary organizer of the Tokyo litigation, which featured separate suits filed by different individuals on a daily basis.
5. "Arrest and Prosecution for Antiwar Graffiti on a Public Park Outhouse" [Kōen toire de hansen rakugaki de taiho/kiso], in *Very Strange! Police, Prosecutors, Courts—The Freedom of Civil Society Is in Danger* [*Okashii zo, Keisatsu, Kensatsu, Saibansho—Shimin Shakai no Jiyū ga Abunai*], eds. Akira Uozumi et al. (Tokyo: Tsukuru Shuppan, 2005), 58.

6. Munakata describes the speakers in *Voices Against War,* 112–16. Masatoshi Uchida provides a detailed overview of several cases of dubious arrests during this period in Uchida, *Is This a Crime? Thinking About "Arrests for Handing Out Flyers" [Kore ga hanzai? "Bira kubari de taiho" wo kangaeru], Iwanami Booklet 655* (Tokyo: Iwanami Shōten, 2005). He wrote this 71-page booklet as he worked on the Tent Village case, the SDF constitutional litigation, and other cases.
7. The speaker was a 28-year-old activist named Kanako Burukitch. She and her husband began their protests in April 2002 against violent attacks on Palestinians. Munakata, *Voices Against War,* 115. (Munakata gave her the alias Kayako Kudo). Kanako Burukitch, "Protest Rally Against American Embassy 2003," http://www.mkimpo.com/diary/2003/american_embassy_03-03-01.html. See also Toshihiro Yoshida, *Refusing to Cooperate in War [Sensō Kyōryōku Kyōhi]* (Tokyo: Iwanami Shinsho, 2005), 179–82. Others spoke, including some who had traveled from afar like Hiroshi Niikura, an antiwar activist well known for continuing protests at the giant U.S. naval base at Yokosuka. Munakata, *Voices Against War,* 113. Yutaka Osawa describes the March 15 meeting agenda and calls for action from the audience to stop the pending indictment. Osawa, *Homepage for Peace,* March 16 or March 17, 2004. (No date indicated.)
8. Kato's words are reported in "We Won't Allow the Unfair Arrests for the Tachikawa Antiwar Flyer Deliveries" [Tachikawa hansen bira-ire futō taiho wo yurusanai!], Japan Revolutionary Communist League [Nihon kakumeiteki kyōsanshugisha dōmei] Kakehashi, blog, March 22, 2004, https://jrcl.info/web/frame040322a.html.
9. The letter relied on the reasoning of the law scholars' declaration to assert that the Tent Village members had committed no crime. It also cited Article 248 of the Code of Criminal Procedure, which provides that even though the elements of a crime are present, prosecutors may choose not to act, based on the factors like the factual circumstances, the characters, and previous records of the suspects. The letter concluded that if the prosecutors chose to indict the three detainees, they would surely lose the trust of the Japanese people. Osawa, *Homepage for Peace,* March 16 or March 17, 2004.
10. Osawa called upon participants at the March 15 meeting to join the protest at the prosecutors' national headquarters on March 17. He posted a map to guide protesters to the site. About 20 persons gathered. Osawa, *Homepage for Peace,* March 16 or March 17, 2004.
11. Munakata, *Voices Against War,* 120.
12. Inoue, "Looking Back," 28–29.
13. See Peter Benenson, "The Forgotten Prisoners," *Guardian,* May 28, 1961, https://www.theguardian.com/uk/1961/may/28/fromthearchive.theguardian. For general Amnesty International history, see Amnesty International, "Who We Are," https://www.amnesty.org/en/who-we-are. In 2019, the organization claimed more than 7 million members worldwide.
14. As Amnesty International grew, the range of its human rights campaigns also expanded. Today it is probably best known for its global campaign against the death penalty. But the "Prisoners of Conscience" initiative continues. When Amnesty designates someone as a Prisoner of Conscience, it frequently calls upon the membership to send letters in support of the detainee. Repressive regimes may suddenly receive dozens, hundreds, or even thousands of letters from all over the world, demanding that the prisoner be released or accorded other beneficial treatment.
15. Author's interview with Teranaka, April 23, 2019.
16. For an overview of Japan's human rights issues, see Saul Takahashi (ed.), *Civil and Political Rights in Japan* (London: Routledge, 2019), and Lawrence Repeta, "The Struggle for Individual Rights Protection in Japan -- Seven Decades of Progress," in *The Cambridge History of Japan, Volume 3 The Modern Japanese Nation and Empire,* ed. Laura Hein (London: Cambridge University Press, 2023). The world would become aware of the harsh treatment accorded to persons accused of crime as described in this book with the arrest and detention of the senior business executive Carlos Ghosn in 2018–19.

17. Teranaka's comments in the roundtable discussion in *The Tachikawa Antiwar Flyer Case* [*Tachikawa Hansen Bira Jiken*] (Tokyo: Akashi Shōten, 2005), 79.
18. See, e.g., Daniel H. Foote, "Confessions and the Right to Silence in Japan," *Georgia Journal of International and Comparative Law* 21 (1991), 415. For a recent highly publicized example, see David McNeill, "Death Row Miscarriage Case Puts Spotlight on Japanese Justice," *Irish Times,* February 19, 2019.
19. Mori Inoue relates the events of March 19 in "Looking Back," 29–30. See also Munakata, *Voices Against War,* 120.
20. Inoue reports the donations collected on March 20 in "Looking Back," 31. World Peace Now had organized big rallies at the park on January 25, March 8, and other dates in 2004. Many photos from the March 20 rally and march appear at "World Peace Now 3.20," March 20, 2004, http://www.mkimpo.com/diary/2004/wpn_04-03-20.html.
21. Osawa, *Homepage for Peace,* March 17, 2004.
22. Critics among labor activists seemed especially disturbed because the police took away the laptops with all the information they contained. Katsuko Kato, "Urgent Interview—We Won't Allow Suppression of Antiwar Flyer Deliveries!" [Kinkyū intabyū—Hansen bira ire he no dan'atsu wo yurusanai!], *Sensō to Sei* [*War and Sex*] 22 (Spring 2004), 17.
23. Japan's activists use the English term "posting" to mean delivery of flyers to post (mail) boxes and slots.
24. Kato, "Urgent Interview," 18–19.
25. Kato, "Urgent Interview," 20.

Chapter 6

1. John Owen Haley, the most prominent foreign expert on Japanese law for decades, has praised Japan's approach to criminal justice throughout his career. He consolidated these ideas in Haley, *Authority Without Power* (New York: Oxford University Press, 1991), see especially 129–38. He updated his argument in Haley, "Punish or Prevent: The Night and Day of Criminal Justice," *Virginia Journal of Criminal Law* 7 (2019), 119. Daniel H. Foote also broke new ground in this area with Foote, "The Benevolent Paternalism of Japanese Criminal Justice," *California Law Review* 80 (1992), 316, and other writings. David T. Johnson provides great insight into the prosecutors' role in the policy of leniency in *The Japanese Way of Justice: Prosecuting Crime in Japan* (New York: Oxford University Press, 2002), 104–16.
2. Prosecutors have full authority to decide whether or not to file an indictment. Code of Criminal Procedure, Art. 248 provides guidance for their decisions. "Suspended prosecution" (*kiso yūyo*) is not a formal legal term, but is commonly used to describe the actual practice.

   Although prosecutors have authority to withhold prosecution, they did not have formal plea bargaining power similar to the American practice in 2004. They obtained such power in a limited range of cases with amendments to the Code of Criminal Procedure in 2016.
3. Johnson, *The Japanese Way of Justice,* 109.
4. Mori Inoue, "Looking Back on the Year Following the Arrests" [Taiho kara no ichinen wo furikaeru], in *The Tachikawa Antiwar Flyer Case* [*Tachikawa Hansen Bira Jiken*] (Tokyo: Akashi Shōten, 2005), 30.
5. Details of the meeting are from a contemporary memorandum by a participant.
6. Defense counsel Hirotatsu Kojima wrote a detailed account of procedural aspects of the trial. Kojima, "Trial Proceedings Until We Won the Not Guilty Verdict" [Muzai hanketsu wo kachitoru made no saiban shinri], in *The Tachikawa Antiwar Flyer Case* [*Tachikawa Hansen Bira Jiken*] (Tokyo: Akashi Shōten, 2005), 61–76.
7. Code of Criminal Procedure, Article 88; Colin P.A. Jones and Frank S. Savitch, *The Japanese Legal System* (St. Paul, MN: West Academic Publishing, 2018), 257.

8. Moreover, each had appointed a friend or family member to serve as guarantor.
9. Kojima, "Trial Proceedings," 62.
10. Kojima, "Trial Proceedings," 62.
11. In fact, the police had gathered many photos of the flyer deliveries and other information that left the identities of the suspects unmistakable.
12. Details of the meeting from an unpublished contemporary memorandum by a participant.
13. Yutaka Osawa, *Homepage for Peace* [*Heiwa no Peiji*], blog, April 3, 2004, http://osawa-yutaka.my.coocan.jp/heiwa-top.htm.
14. The letter also called on anyone who had experience in distributing flyers at the SDF apartments to contact Tent Village. Mitsuru Munakata, *When Voices Against War Leave Town—The Tachikawa Antiwar Flyer Suppression Case* [*Machi Kara Hansen no Koe ga Kieru Toki—Tachikawa Hansen Bira-ire Dan'atsu Jiken*] (Tokyo: Jushinsha, 2005), 155; Inoue, "Looking Back," 32.
15. Osawa, *Homepage for Peace,* April 19, 2004.
16. Michael Penn, *Japan and the War on Terror* (London and New York: I. B. Tauris, 2014), 97–104. The kidnappings are also described in Munakata, *Voices Against War,* 159–60.
17. Penn, *Japan and the War on Terror,* 102–103. Because Constitution Article 22(2) guarantees the freedom to move abroad, few people thought this threat realistic.
18. The text of the statement is reproduced in Penn, *Japan and the War on Terror,* 104.
19. Munakata, *Voices Against War,* 160.
20. The speaker, Nobutaka Watanabe, was himself kidnapped and briefly detained in Iraq when he sought to investigate wartime conditions. Osawa, *Homepage for Peace,* April 26, 2004. For the "hotline," see "Trans-Pacific GI/SDF Rights Hotline" [Beihei Jieikan Jinken hotline], February 15, 2006, https://www.jca.apc.org/gi-heisi. The Japanese language has adopted the English word "bashing" to describe the phenomenon of countless voices attacking a targeted individual, often unfairly.
21. Kojima, "Trial Proceedings," 63.
22. Kojima, "Trial Proceedings," 62–63.
23. Osawa, *Homepage for Peace*, April 21, 2004.
24. Inoue, "Looking Back," 34.
25. Mori Inoue provides these details: "At this time (the second half of March), aside from the activities of the support organization itself, many individuals and groups became active on their own. There was a demonstration from the neighboring city of Kunitachi to the SDF buildings on March 13. On March 14, the 'Do Not Send the SDF to Iraq—Tachikawa Joint Action' distributed flyers and joined a protest at the police station. Support groups that gathered donations and sent messages of encouragement and support were formed in Iwate and Fukuoka. There were even large individual donations sent by post (*furikomi*) from addresses we had never heard of." Inoue, "Looking Back," 29.
26. Shun-ichi J. Watanabe, "The Historical Analysis of the 'Kunitachi Machizukuri Movement': Its Nature and the Role of Professor Shiro Masuda," paper presented at the *15th International Planning History Society Conference,* http://www.usp.br/fau/iphs/abstractsAndPapersFiles/Sessions/36/WATANABE.pdf.
27. Alexander Brown, *Anti-Nuclear Protest in Post-Fukushima Tokyo: Power Struggles* (New York: Routledge, 2018).
28. Munakata, *Voices Against War,* 161.
29. Munakata and Osawa both reported 360 attendees. Munakata, *Voices Against War,* 162; Osawa, *Homepage for Peace*, April 26, 2004.
30. Shigematsu's comment and Akio Kotō's quotation are from "We Oppose the Iraq Deployment! We Denounce the Unfair Indictments and Long Detentions!" [Iraku hahei hantai! Futō kiso to chōki kōryu kyūdan], Japan Revolutionary Communist League [Nihon kakumeiteki kyōsanshugisha dōmei], *Kakehashi*, blog, May 3, 2004, https://jrcl.info/web/frame0453c.html.
31. Author's interview with Makoto Teranaka, April 23, 2019.

32. Osawa, *Homepage for Peace*, April 26, 2004.
33. Osawa's statements are reported in Japan Revolutionary Communist League, "We Oppose the Iraq Deployment."
34. The defendants' appeal included discussion of some of the other hot topics of the day, such as the government's proposal for a "conspiracy law" that would criminalize discussion of prohibited actions even though the actions do not occur. (The Diet passed such a law more than a decade later, on June 15, 2017.)
35. Inoue, "Looking Back," 34; Munakata, *Voices Against War*, 161–63; Osawa, *Homepage for Peace*, April 26, 2004.
36. Osawa, *Homepage for Peace*, April 26, 2004.

Chapter 7

1. Mitsuru Munakata, *When Voices Against War Leave Town—The Tachikawa Antiwar Flyer Suppression Case* [*Machi Kara Hansen no Koe ga Kieru Toki—Tachikawa Hansen Bira-ire Dan'atsu Jiken*] (Tokyo: Jushinsha, 2005), 164–65.
2. Takada's comment in Sachimi Takada, "Jail Diary: 75-Day Fight from Inside the Walls" [Goku-chu nikki: kabe no naka de tatakatta 75-nichikan], in *The Tachikawa Antiwar Flyer Case* [*Tachikawa Hansen Bira Jiken*] (Tokyo: Akashi Shōten, 2005), 58.
3. The Hachioji courthouse was constructed in 1959. Due to its location so far from the center of Tokyo, most Tokyo attorneys tried to avoid taking cases there. The court would be moved from Hachioji to Tachikawa in 2009. Construction of the new Tachikawa courthouse commenced in 2006. *Hachioji Keizai Shimbun*, January 28, 2009. https://hachioji.keizai.biz/headline/213.
4. His next posting was in Shizuoka. The regular reassignments often require that judges depart while trials are midstream, to be replaced by others who have not heard preceding live testimony and must rely on the documentary file to catch up. The Tachikawa trial was relatively fast and all three judges were present throughout the trial.
5. John Owen Haley, *The Spirit of Japanese Law* (Athens, GA: University of Georgia Press, 2006), 56. For assistant judges, Colin P.A. Jones and Frank S. Savitch use the expression "judge in training." Jones and Savitch, *The Japanese Legal System* (St. Paul, MN: West Academic Publishing, 2018), 104. Courts Act Article 26–27.
6. Yutaka Osawa wrote that there were 78 spectators. Osawa, *Homepage for Peace* [*Heiwa no Peiji*], blog, May 7, 2004, http://osawa-yutaka.my.coocan.jp/heiwa-top.htm.
7. Osawa, *Homepage for Peace*, May 7, 2004.
8. Takada describes struggling to twist around to see her friends. "Jail Diary," 58. Osawa wrote that he caught her eye and waved. Osawa, *Homepage for Peace*, May 7, 2004.
9. In recent years, Japanese lawyers have campaigned to eliminate handcuffs and shackles in courtrooms. Shunsuke Abe, "Lawyers in Call to End Practice of Handcuffs, Ropes in Courtrooms," *Asahi Shimbun*, August 15, 2021, https://www.asahi.com/ajw/articles/14407268.
10. Munakata, *Voices Against War*, 167.
11. Judge Hasegawa's statement is quoted by both Osawa and Munakata. Osawa, *Homepage for Peace*, May 7, 2004; Munakata, *Voices Against War*, 169.
12. Osawa published the text of the indictment in *Homepage for Peace*, May 7, 2004.
13. Hirotatsu Kojima, "Trial Proceedings Until We Won the Not Guilty Verdict" [Muzai hanketsu wo kachitoru made no saiban shinri], in *The Tachikawa Antiwar Flyer Case* [*Tachikawa Hansen Bira Jiken*] (Tokyo: Akashi Shōten, 2005), 64.
14. Osawa published the texts of the three defendants' May 6 court statements in *Homepage for Peace*, May 8, 2004.
15. Muneo Narusawa, "The Overseas Dispatch of Japan's Self-Defense Forces and U.S. War Preparations," *Asia-Pacific Journal* 12, no. 31 (July 28, 2014), https://apjjf.org/2014/12/31/Narusawa-Muneo/4158/article.html.
16. Renunciation of the right to wage war as declared in Constitution Article 9 is obviously a core characteristic of Onishi's "ideal state."

17. Nobuhiro Onishi, "Statement of Opinion" [Iken chinjutsu], May 6, 2004, in Osawa, *Homepage for Peace*, May 8, 2004.
18. Sachimi Takada, "Statement of Opinion" [Iken chinjutsu], May 6, 2004, in Osawa, *Homepage for Peace*, May 8, 2004.
19. Takada, "Jail Diary," 59.
20. Toshiyuki Obora, "Statement of Opinion" [Iken chinjutsu], May 6, 2004, in Osawa, *Homepage for Peace*, May 8, 2004.
21. Obora, "Statement of Opinion."
22. For a recent study of "*tenkō*," see Max M. Ward, *Thought Crime: Ideology and State in Interwar Japan* (Durham, NC: Duke University Press, 2019).
23. Obora, "Statement of Opinion."
24. Obora, "Statement of Opinion."
25. Obora, "Statement of Opinion."
26. Kuriyama read the Defense Counsel Statement of Opinion [Bengonin iken chinjutsu] May 6, 2004, to the court. Quoted in Munakata, *Voices Against War*, 169.
27. "Defense Counsel Statement of Opinion."
28. "Defense Counsel Statement of Opinion."
29. "Defense Counsel Statement of Opinion." The brief *Asahi* report on the hearing focused on the issue of "just cause." *Asahi Shimbun*, May 7, 2004.
30. Code of Criminal Procedure, Article 248: "Where prosecution is deemed unnecessary owing to the character, age, and environment of the offender, the gravity of the offense, and the circumstances or situation after the offense, prosecution need not be instituted."
31. The quotation and details from Kuriyama's statement are from "Defense Counsel Statement of Opinion." Co-counsel Hirotatsu Kojima discusses the charge of abuse of prosecutorial power in Kojima, "Trial Proceedings," 66.
32. Frank Upham discusses the case in *Law and Social Change in Postwar Japan* (Cambridge, MA: Harvard University Press, 1987), 52, and in *Law in Japan, An Annual*, vol. 13 (1980), 141. See also, David T. Johnson, *The Japanese Way of Justice: Prosecuting Crime in Japan* (New York: Oxford University Press, 2002), 63–64.
33. Osawa, *Homepage for Peace*, May 11, 2004. Takada wrote that she could see the supporters in the alley and hear the cheers and loud blasts from a bullhorn. Takada, "Jail Diary," 59.
34. Kojima, "Trial Proceedings," 66.
35. Munakata, *Voices Against War*, 170.
36. Munakata, *Voices Against War*, 170; Kojima, "Trial Proceedings," 69.
37. Kojima, "Trial Proceedings," 66. Supporters raised the 4.5 million yen bail money through donations and loans. Osawa, *Homepage for Peace*, May 11, 2004.
38. Munakata, *Voices Against War*, 171–72. Osawa published this petition in *Homepage for Peace*, May 11, 2004.
39. Osawa, *Homepage for Peace*, May 11, 2004.
40. Munakata, *Voices Against War*, 172–73.
41. Details of release in Osawa, *Homepage for Peace*, May 11, 2004. Tent Village published a statement describing the release of the three defendants here: https://jrcl.info/web/frame04524m.html. See also, Kojima, "Trial Proceedings," 67.

Chapter 8

1. *Shimbun Akahata*, July 21, 2004. Supporters complained about the tight courthouse security. They were required to pass through a metal detector and leave behind all briefcases, cameras, and other devices. *Suppression Under National Public Law—The Horikoshi Case Record of Battle, 2004–2013* [*Kokkōhō dan'atsu horikoshi jiken tatakai no kiroku 2004–2013*] (Tokyo: Society to Prevent Suppression Under National Public

Law and Protect Freedom of Speech [Kokkōhō Dan'atsu wo Yurusazu Genron no Jiyū wo Mamoru Kai], 2013), 5.

2. All statements in this section are from the text of the indictment of Akio Horikoshi, reproduced in *Trial Materials from the Suppression Under National Public Law Case, vol. 1* [*Kokkōhō dan'atsu jiken—saiban shiryō—1*] (Tokyo: Society to Prevent Suppression Under National Public Law and Protect Freedom of Speech), 237.
3. Constitution Article 38(3) states that a confession alone is insufficient to support a guilty verdict. Prosecutors must show additional evidence to prove their case.
4. Hiroshi Fukurai, "A Step in the Right Direction for Japan's Judicial Reform," *Hastings International and Comparative Law Review* 36, no. 2 (2013), 544. Fukurai cites David T. Johnson, *The Japanese Way of Justice: Prosecuting Crime in Japan* (New York: Oxford University Press, 2002), 40–41.
5. Shirō Okubo, "The Current Stage of the Trial and Points at Issue" [*Soshō no gendankai to sōten*], *Hōgaku Seminar* 615 (March 2006), 53. At the time, Okubo was a professor of law at Ritsumeikan University. He took emeritus status in 2020.
6. Retrials following lengthy incarcerations are described in Daniel H. Foote, "From Japan's Death Row to Freedom," *Pacific Rim Law & Policy Journal* 1 (1993), 11. For a recent highly publicized example, see David McNeill, "Death Row Miscarriage Case Puts Spotlight on Japanese Justice," *Irish Times,* February 19, 2019, https://www.irishtimes.com/news/world/asia-pacific/death-row-miscarriage-case-puts-spotlight-on-japanese-justice-1.3798279.
7. Johnson, *Japanese Way of Justice,* 41.
8. As it took up its duties, the Council itself declared that "what we must do is transform both the spirit of the law and the rule of law into the flesh and blood of this country, so that they become the shape of the country." For an overview of the Council's work, see Daniel H. Foote, "Introduction and Overview," in *Law in Japan: A Turning Point,* ed. Daniel H. Foote (Seattle, WA, and London: University of Washington Press, 2007), xix.
9. Fukurai, "A Step in the Right Direction," 543.
10. "When the court recognizes that a prosecutor has not disclosed evidence. ... it shall issue an order requiring the disclosure of such evidence as requested by the defense." Code of Criminal Procedure, Art. 316–26.
11. Naoto Sasayama, "A Great, Historic Case: Suppression Under National Public Law in the Horikoshi Case, Report from the First Court Hearing" [Rekishiteki daijiken—kokkōhō dan'atsu Horikoshi jiken dai-ikkai kōhan no hōkoku], *Jiyū Hōsōdan Report* [Jiyū Hōsōdan tsūshin] 1139 (September 1, 2004), https://www.jlaf.jp/old/tsushin/2004/1139.html. Okubo, "Current Stage," 53.
12. Okubo, "Current Stage," 53.
13. Sasayama, "A Great, Historic Case."
14. *Asahi Shimbun,* July 21, 2004.
15. Akio Horikoshi, "Statement of Opinion," in *Trial Materials vol. 1,* 1.
16. National Personnel Authority, Annual Report for Fiscal 2018, https://www.jinji.go.jp/en/recomme/annual2018/index.html. As the government has pursued a privatization policy, the number of employees has gradually decreased since 2004 but remained over a half million in 2018.
17. The opening statement continued throughout the remainder of the first hearing, which ended at 5:00 p.m. and then consumed all four hours of the second hearing, on September 14.
18. Defense Counsel Opinion in Response to the Indictment [kisōjō ni taisuru bengodan no iken], *Trial Materials vol. 1,* 2.
19. *Trial Materials, vol. 1,* 3.
20. *Trial Materials, vol. 1,* 4.
21. As a signatory of the International Covenant on Civil and Political Rights, Japan is bound to uphold the freedom of expression provision, which does not provide an

exception for government employees. "International Covenant on Civil and Political Rights," https://www.ohchr.org/en/professionalinterest/pages/ccpr.aspx.

22. *Trial Materials, vol. 1*, 31.
23. *Trial Materials, vol. 1*, 19.
24. Defense counsel also cited Article 19 of the International Covenant on Civil and Political Rights for support. *Trial Materials, vol. 1*, 193.
25. *Trial Materials, vol. 1*, 26. See also, Johnson, *Japanese Way of Justice*, 57, for another example of police wiretapping of a JCP politician.
26. Labor union activists, JCP staff, and other supporters had worked hard to mobilize supporters during the four months since the arrest. For example, an event that was held at a conference hall in the Nihonbashi district on April 22 was attended by representatives of 75 different labor and political organizations. *Record of Battle*, 4–5.

Chapter 9

1. A lay judge system was introduced in 2009 that allows ordinary citizens to join professional judges in deciding cases that involve serious crimes. See Dimitri Vanoverbeke, *Juries in the Japanese Legal System: The Continuing Struggle for Citizen Participation and Democracy* (London: Routledge Law in Asia, 2015). The lay judge system does not apply in less serious criminal cases like trespass.
2. Despite stiff sentences provided by statute, in cases where defendants admit guilt and express contrition, Japan's prosecutors and judges commonly show lenience, with light penalties. Leniency is discussed by many foreign authors, including John Owen Haley, in *Authority Without Power* (New York: Oxford University Press, 1991), 129–38 and more recently in "Punish or Prevent: The Night and Day of Criminal Justice," *Virginia Journal of Criminal Law* 7 (2019), 119. Daniel H. Foote also broke new ground in this area in "The Benevolent Paternalism of Japanese Criminal Justice," *California Law Review* 80 (1992), 317, and other writings. David T. Johnson provides great insight into the prosecutors' role in leniency policy in *The Japanese Way of Justice: Prosecuting Crime in Japan* (New York: Oxford University Press, 2002), 104–16 and 192–201. Of course, the Tent Village defendants would neither confess nor show contrition, so they would not benefit from this practice. In recent years, the Diet has responded to political pressure by passing laws that increase penalties. See Setsuo Miyazawa, "The Politics of Increasing Punitiveness and the Rising Populism in Japanese Criminal Justice Policy," *Punishment & Society* 10, no. 1 (January 2008), 47–77.
3. Judgment of the Supreme Court, March 4, 1976, *Keishū* 30, no. 2, 79. The case is discussed in Kōji Adachi, "The Criminal Law Issues in the Case" [*Jiken no keijihōteki mondaiten*], *Hōgaku Seminar* 596 (August 2004), 65.
4. In addition to court testimony, the government presented a large volume of documentary evidence. Prosecutors delivered a long list of exhibits at the May 6 hearing.
5. Detailed accounts of GSDF Officer A's testimony at the June 11 hearing appear in several sources. *Tent Village Trial Report, Hearing No. 2*; Hirotatsu Kojima, "Trial Proceedings Until We Won the Not Guilty Verdict" [Muzai hanketsu wo kachitoru made no saiban shinri], in *Tachikawa Antiwar Flyer Case* [*Tachikawa Hansen Bira Jiken*] (Tokyo: Akashi Shōten, 2005), 67–68; Mitsuru Munakata, *When Voices Against War Leave Town—The Tachikawa Antiwar Flyer Suppression Case* [*Machi Kara Hansen no Koe ga Kieru Toki—Tachikawa Hansen Bira-ire Dan'atsu Jiken*] (Tokyo: Jushinsha 2005), 189–94. *Shūkan Kinyōbi 511* (June 11, 2004), 5. See also *Asahi Shimbun*, June 4, 2004.
6. Munakata, *Voices Against War*, 189–90; *Trial Report, Hearing No. 2*.
7. *Mainichi Shimbun*, June 3, 2004. The speaker served as deputy head of the Hachioji prosecutors' office at the time.
8. Munakata reports "audible gasps" from the gallery, *Voices Against War*, 190.

9. Munakata, *Voices Against War*, 190; *Trial Report, Hearing No. 2*.
10. Munakata reports Judge Suzuki's intervention in *Voices Against War*, 192.
11. Kojima, "Trial Proceedings," 67–68; *Shūkan Kinyōbi 511* (June 11, 2004); *Trial Report, Hearing No. 2*.
12. Detailed accounts of ASDF Officer B's testimony at the June 17 hearing appear in several sources. *Trial Report, Hearing No. 3*; Kojima, "Trial Proceedings," 68; Munakata, *Voices Against War*, 195–98; *Shūkan Kinyōbi 513* (June 25, 2004).
13. Munakata reports Judge Hasegawa's questioning of ASDF Officer B, *Voices Against War*, 196–97.
14. *Trial Report, Hearing No. 3*.
15. *Asahi Shimbun*, July 14, 2004. Japan Federation of Bar Associations, *It's Time to Think About Freedom of Expression and the Right to Know* [*Ima Hyōgen no Jiyū to Shiru Kenri wo Kangaeru*], in Proceedings from the *52nd Human Rights Conference*, November 5, 2009, 67. The performance of Liberal Democratic Party candidates in the July 11 elections was disappointing, but the Party held on to its majority in the House of Councilors. Norimitsu Onishi, "Majority Party in Japan Retains Power in Parliament," *New York Times*, July 12, 2004. https://www.nytimes.com/2004/07/12/world/majority-party-in-japan-retains-power-in-parliament.html. The July 4 incident and others around that time are discussed in *The Complete Record*, 20. World Peace Now became well known for organizing protests that gathered more than 30,000 participants in the weeks preceding the launch of the Iraq War in March 2003.
16. Detailed accounts of ASDF Officer C's testimony at the June 17 hearing appear in several sources. *Trial Report, Hearing No. 4*; Kojima, "Trial Proceedings," 68–69; Munakata, *Voices Against War*, 202–205; *Shūkan Kinyōbi 516* (July 8, 2004), 4–5.
17. *Trial Report Hearing No. 4*; Munakata, *Voices Against War*, 202–206; *Shūkan Kinyōbi 516* (July 16, 2004), 4–5; Kojima, "Trial Proceedings," 68–69.
18. *Trial Report Hearing No. 4*; Kojima, "Trial Proceedings," 68–69.
19. Norimitsu Onishi, "After 8-Year Trial in Japan, Cultist Is Sentenced to Death," *New York Times*, February 28, 2004, https://www.nytimes.com/2004/02/28/world/after-8-year-trial-in-japan-cultist-is-sentenced-to-death.html.
20. There was a strong consensus that the most significant result of the election was consolidation of opposition forces behind the Democratic Party of Japan, leading many commentators to say that Japan was evolving toward a two-party system.
21. Manabu Ishizaki, "Freedom of Expression and 'Distortions' in Constitutionalism," [Rikkenshugi no 'yugami' to hyōgen no jiyū], *Hōgaku Seminar* 596 (August 2004), 60–61. These campaigns supported police efforts to maintain and expand budgets despite Japan's status as the most crime-free country in the developed world. See, e.g., David McNeill, "Japan's Crime Problem? Too Many Police, not Enough Criminals," April 6, 2018, https://www.irishtimes.com/news/world/asia-pacific/japan-s-crime-problem-too-many-police-not-enough-criminals-1.3451997.
22. Lawrence Repeta, "'Personal Information,' Media Control, and Government Power: Legislative Battles in Japan, 1999–2003," *Meiji Law Journal* 22 (March 2015), 25.
23. *Asahi Shimbun*, English edition, April 26, 2002; Repeta, "Personal Information," 25.
24. Tomoko Ohji, the journalist who made the scoop was awarded a prestigious prize for investigative reporting, the first woman to be so honored.
25. Ishizaki, "Freedom of Expression," 60.
26. For Manabu Ishizaki, the prosecution of the Tent Village defendants for the purpose of creating a chilling effect was a clear abuse of the prosecutorial power.
27. The August edition of "Legal Studies Seminar" also carried articles by Kōji Adachi, an expert in criminal law who reported the history of "trespass" under the Criminal Code, and Masato Ichikawa, a constitutional expert who addressed free speech issues.

Chapter 10

1. Hirotatsu Kojima, "Trial Proceedings Until We Won the Not Guilty Verdict [Muzai hanketsu wo kachitoru made no saiban shinri], in *Tachikawa Antiwar Flyer Case* [*Tachikawa Hansen Bira Jiken*] (Tokyo: Akashi Shōten, 2005), 69.
2. Tachikawa Antiwar Flyer Suppression Support Group [Tachikawa Hansen Bira Dan'atsu Kyūenkai], *The Complete Record 2004–2009* [*Zenkiroku 2004–2009*] (Tokyo, 2009), 20. Munakata, *When Voices Against War Leave Town—The Tachikawa Antiwar Flyer Suppression Case* [*Machi Kara Hansen no Koe ga Kieru Toki—Tachikawa Hansen Bira-ire Dan'atsu Jiken*] (Tokyo: Jushinsha, 2005), 222. Osawa, *Homepage for Peace* [*Heiwa no Peiji*], blog, September 2, 2004, http://osawa-yutaka.my.coocan.jp/heiwa-top.htm.
3. Opening Statement for the Defense (*bōtō chinjutsu*), September 9, 2004. Summary in *Tent Village Trial Report, Hearing No. 5*; Kojima, "Trial Proceedings," 69–71.
4. Attorney Kojima informed colleagues of a phone conversation with Judge Suzuki in which she stressed that the court was especially interested to know more about the Tent Village history and activities to confirm whether the group engaged in unlawful activities or was an ordinary citizens group. Fax message, August 17, 2004. *Trial Report, Hearing No. 5.*
5. The defendants testified at three separate court sessions, on July 8, September 9, and September 30.
6. Regarding Professor Okudaira's testimony on constitutional issues, Uchida told me, "We were surprised that the court approved his appearance. After all, the judges themselves are legal professionals. They don't need experts to explain rules of law." Uchida's interview, July 4, 2019.
7. Yasuhiro Okudaira, *Living the Constitution* [*Kenpō wo Ikiru*] (Tokyo: Nihon Hyōronsha, 2007), 33.
8. A list of Okudaira's "major publications" that appears in a 2017 volume published in his honor runs to nearly 40 pages in rather fine print. Yōichi Higuchi, Tōru Nakajima, and Yasuo Hasebe, eds., *The Dignity of Constitutionalism: Themes from the Constitutional Philosophy of Yasuhiro Okudaira* [*Hō no Songen—Okudaira Kempōgaku no Keishō to Tenkai*] (Tokyo: Nihon Hyōronsha, 2017).
9. Okudaira's opposition to war and commitment to defend Constitution Article 9 were underscored when he joined eight other prominent intellectuals to form the "Article 9 Association" on June 10, 2004. See Hisashi Inoue et al., *Constitution Article 9 Is Still Fresh* [*Kempō Kyūjō Ima Koso Shun*], Iwanami Booklet 639 (Tokyo: Iwanami Shōten, 2004).
10. Okudaira, *Living the Constitution*, 16.
11. Quotations from Okudaira's testimony are from the court transcript, September 9, 2004.
12. For a complete report on this era and enforcement of the Peace Preservation Law, see Max M. Ward, *Thought Crime: Ideology and State Power in Interwar Japan* (Durham, NC: Duke University Press, 2019). See also the writings of Patricia Steinhoff.
13. See, e.g., Yasuhiro Okudaira, *A Brief History of the Peace Preservation Law* [Chian Ijihō Shoshi], (Tokyo: Chikuma Shobō, 1977; republished, Tokyo: Iwanami Shōten, 2006).
14. In their zeal to silence opposition to the Iraq deployment, the police charged people with otherwise minor violations in a number of cases. For example, a student in Kyoto was arrested for making a false statement on his apartment lease because he did not notify the landlord that he might be making antiwar flyers in that space. Another was arrested for making a false statement to the police because he presented a driver's license that showed a previous and no longer accurate address. Other cases included the prosecutions of Akio Horikoshi and of a retired high school teacher charged with causing a delay of a few minutes at a graduation ceremony. There were others. See Masatoshi Uchida, *Is This a Crime? Thinking About "Arrests for Handing Out Flyers"* [*Kore ga hanzai? "Bira kubari de taiho" wo kangaeru*], Iwanami Booklet 655 (Tokyo: Iwanami Shōten, 2005).

15. Quotations from Minowa's testimony are from the court transcript, September 9, 2004.
16. Noboru Minowa and Masatoshi Uchida, *Constitution Article 9 and Exclusive Self-Defense* [*Kenpō Kyūjō to Senpu Bōei*] (Tokyo: Nashinoki, 2004).
17. Noboru Minowa v. Japan, complaint filed on January 28, 2004, in Sapporo District Court seeking a judgment that declared the Iraq deployment unconstitutional.
18. Under the "three non-nuclear principles," announced by the Sato administration in 1967, Japan may not make, use, or introduce nuclear weapons into the country. https://www.mofa.go.jp/policy/un/disarmament/nnp/index.html. Disavowal of the right to collective self-defense meant that Japan could not join in the defense of an allied country under attack. This limitation was modified by legislation adopted in 2015 that allows collective self-defense operations in defined circumstances. John Owen Haley, "Article 9 in the Post-Sunakawa World: Continuity and Deterrence Within a Transforming Global Context," *Washington International Law Journal* 26, no. 1 (January 2017), 1.
19. Quotations from Minowa's testimony are from the court transcript, September 9, 2004.
20. Kojima, "Trial Proceedings," 71–72.
21. Author's interview with Masatoshi Uchida, July 4, 2019.

Chapter 11

1. In one example, Osawa successfully advocated for the installation of elevators at Tachikawa train station to assist those who had difficulty with stairs.
2. Hirotatsu Kojima, "Trial Proceedings Until We Won the Not Guilty Verdict" [Muzai hanketsu wo kachitoru made no saiban shinri], in *Tachikawa Antiwar Flyer Case* [*Tachikawa Hansen Bira Jiken*] (Tokyo: Akashi Shōten, 2005), 72.
3. *Shūkan Kinyōbi 527* (October 8, 2004), 5. Additional details are from an undated attorneys' memorandum regarding Osawa's preparation for his testimony.
4. *Tent Village Trial Report*, Hearing No. 6.
5. *Shūkan Kinyōbi 527* (October 8, 2004), 5.
6. Attorney Kojima's fax message to the defense team, August 17, 2004.
7. *Trial Report,* Hearing No. 5 reports the judges' questions. In most criminal prosecutions, suspects respond to police interrogations and then sign off on formal statements prepared by interrogators. Because the Tent Village defendants refused to do so, the court did not have this source of information. Instead, the court would have to rely on the defendants' direct testimony.
8. *Shūkan Kinyōbi 524* (September 17, 2004), 5; *Trial Report*, Hearing No. 5.
9. *Trial Report,* Hearing No. 6; *Shūkan Kinyōbi 527* (October 8, 2004), 6.
10. *Trial Report,* Hearing No. 6; *Shūkan Kinyōbi 527* (October 8, 2004), 6; Yutaka Osawa, *Homepage for Peace* [*Heiwa no Peiji*], blog, November 4, 2004, http://osawa-yutaka.my.coocan.jp/heiwa-top.htm.
11. *Shūkan Kinyōbi 527* (October 8, 2004), 6.
12. Takada sought to deliver a petition opposing construction when the incident occurred. *Trial Report,* Hearing No. 6.
13. Osawa, *Homepage for Peace*, November 4, 2004.
14. Tachikawa Antiwar Flyer Suppression Support Group [Tachikawa Hansen Bira Dan'atsu Kyūenkai], *The Complete Record 2004–2009* [*Zenkiroku 2004–2009*] (Tokyo, 2009), 22–23.
15. Kojima, "Trial Proceedings," 73.
16. Kojima, "Trial Proceedings," 74.
17. Frank Upham discusses the case in *Law and Social Change in Postwar Japan* (Cambridge, MA: Harvard University Press, 1987), 52, and in *Law in Japan, An Annual*, vol. 13 (1980), 141. See also, David T. Johnson, *The Japanese Way of Justice: Prosecuting Crime in Japan* (New York: Oxford University Press, 2002), 63–64.

18. Article 248 reads "Where prosecution is deemed unnecessary owing to the character, age, environment, gravity of the offense, circumstances or situation after the offense, prosecution need not be instituted."
19. Quotations are from *Summary of Prosecutors' Closing Arguments* [ronkoku yōshi], submitted to court, November 4, 2004. Foreign commentators who praise Japan's criminal justice system invariably point to leniency shown to suspects and defendants who express remorse and seek forgiveness. Unfortunately, this policy is of little benefit to those who refuse to confess, like the Tent Village defendants. Haley acknowledges the dilemma presented by "political dissidents who steadfastly refuse to acknowledge wrongdoing." John Owen Haley, *Authority Without Power* (New York: Oxford University Press, 1991), 133. Johnson describes categories of defendants who do not obtain leniency in *The Japanese Way of Justice*, 192–99. Despite the well-established leniency policy, over the past two decades the Diet has responded to political pressure by passing laws that increase penalties. See Setsuo Miyazawa, "The Politics of Increasing Punitiveness and the Rising Populism in Japanese Criminal Justice Policy," *Punishment & Society* 10, no. 1 (January 2008), 47.
20. They cited an October 31, 1995 judgment of the Nagoya District Court. *Hanrei Jihō 1552,* 153.
21. Regarding the lot, the prosecutors pointed out that the boundaries were very clearly defined, especially by the chain-link fence that surrounded most of the property. Within the grounds parking areas were designated for bicycles and cars that were clearly for the exclusive use of the residents. Although there are openings in the fence to allow the entry of residents on foot, bicycle, or in their cars, these openings are relatively small when compared with the total length of the fence and cause no confusion regarding the boundary between the SDF residential property and the public rights of way outside. Moreover, warnings posted at these entrances unambiguously declare that entry is limited to residents and others with proper business (*kankeisha*). Accordingly, they argued, there is no doubt that the entire SDF property is protected by Article 130.
22. The government position seems to accept an undefined range of visitors whose presence is presumed to be lawful such as first responders in emergencies. Such a range might also include solicitations from local businesses.
23. The prosecutors did recognize that there are times when provisions of the Criminal Code may come into conflict with Constitution Article 21. But their examples had nothing to do with residences. Instead, they cited the regulation of demonstrations on public roads and "generally open spaces," when courts must balance free speech rights against other interests, such as public safety.
24. The prosecutors also described an especially pernicious effect of the flyer deliveries, which they saw as acts of harassment intended to cause emotional harm. To bolster this claim, they cited internal Tent Village literature that actually stated the flyers were intended to be part of their "SDF operations" (*SDF kōsaku*), a term that suggested their action was akin to a military action.
25. Summary of Defense Closing Statement (*benron yōshi*), submitted to court November 4, 2004, 5–6.
26. Kojima, "Trial Proceedings," 74–76; *Shūkan Kinyōbi 533* (November 19, 2004), 4.
27. The closing statements of the three defendants are reproduced in *The Tachikawa Antiwar Flyer Case* [*Tachikawa Hansen Bira Jiken*] (Tokyo: Akashi Shōten, 2005), 249–59.
28. *Tachikawa Antiwar Flyer Case*, 250.
29. *Tachikawa Antiwar Flyer Case*, 251.
30. *Tachikawa Antiwar Flyer Case*, 252.
31. *Tachikawa Antiwar Flyer Case*, 253.
32. *Tachikawa Antiwar Flyer Case*, 257.
33. *Tachikawa Antiwar Flyer Case*, 257.

Chapter 12

1. Mainstream news coverage of the trial had been intermittent and fragmentary, so the *Asahi* report served as a useful review that prepared readers for the judgment expected on December 16. *Asahi Shimbun*, December 14, 2004. The *Mainichi* published another pre-judgment summary of the case on the morning of December 16. Readers would see this reminder at the breakfast table or while commuting to work. *Mainichi Shimbun*, December 16, 2004.
2. *Asahi Shimbun*, December 14, 2004.
3. See judicial statistics compiled by the Supreme Court, at https://www.courts.go.jp/app/sihotokei_jp/search, annual report for 2004, chart No. 32.
4. Mori Inoue, "Looking Back on the Year Following the Arrests" [Taiho kara no ichinen wo furikaeru], in *The Tachikawa Antiwar Flyer Case* [*Tachikawa Hansen Bira Jiken*] (Tokyo: Akashi Shōten, 2005), 41.
5. *Mainichi Shimbun*, December 14, 2004.
6. *Tokyo Shimbun*, December 17, 2004.
7. The Japanese expressions are "*muzai wo kachitotta zo*!" and "*futō hanzai wo yurusanai*!" Tachikawa Antiwar Flyer Suppression Support Group [Tachikawa Hansen Bira Dan'atsu Kyūenkai], *The Complete Record 2004–2009* [*Zenkiroku 2004–2009*] (Tokyo, 2009), 24.
8. *Tokyo Shimbun*, December 17, 2004.
9. *Mainichi Shimbun*, December 17, 2004. Japan's court opinions ordinarily begin with a brief statement of the verdict (*shubun*) followed by a summary of facts, an explanation of the grounds for the decision, and a conclusion. See also Inoue, "Looking Back," 41.
10. Obora told a reporter that during the early part of Hasegawa's presentation, he thought the defendants had lost. *Tokyo Shimbun*, December 17, 2004.
11. Constitution Article 22(1) reads, "Every person shall have freedom to choose and change his residence and to choose his occupation to the extent that it does not interfere with the public welfare." It is interpreted to apply to commercial speech.
12. All quotations are translations of the judgment text. Versions published by newspapers the next day varied slightly, but did not differ in content.
13. *Mainichi Shimbun*, December 17, 2004.
14. *Mainichi Shimbun*, December 17, 2004.
15. Mitsuru Munakata, *When Voices Against War Leave Town—The Tachikawa Antiwar Flyer Suppression Case* [*Machi Kara Hansen no Koe ga Kieru Toki—Tachikawa Hansen Bira-ire Dan'atsu Jiken*] (Tokyo: Jushinsha, 2005), 228. Munakata writes that the reporters were accompanied by four or five television cameras and that by this point, more than 10,000 petitions had been signed.
16. *Mainichi Shimbun*, December 17, 2004.
17. Tachikawa Antiwar Flyer Suppression Support Group, *Complete Record*, 24.
18. Inoue, "Looking Back," 42.
19. The speaker was Keiichi Muraoka, a professor of criminal procedure law at Hitotsubashi University.
20. *Mainichi Shimbun*, December 17, 2004.
21. *Asahi Shimbun*, December 17, 2004.
22. The police statement appeared on the front page of the *Asahi*. The SDF quotation is from the *Asahi*, which identified the speaker as a GSDF public relations official. The *Asahi* and the *Tokyo Shimbun* also carried brief comments from a spokesperson for the Hachioji prosecutors' office, December 17, 2004.
23. *Tokyo Shimbun*, December 17, 2004. During his career as a prosecutor, Tsuchimoto had reached one of the ladder's highest rungs as a government advocate in cases before Japan's Supreme Court.
24. Ken'ichiro Okada, who joined defense counsel meetings and assisted in research on legal issues as a graduate student at the time, spoke with defense counsel on the day

of judgment. Okada writes that, although counsel were delighted with the not guilty verdict, they expected the District Court's "punishable illegality" reasoning to be overturned on appeal so they would have to find other grounds to support it. Okada is currently a law professor at Kōchi University. E-mail from Ken'ichiro Okada, January 26, 2021.

25. Yutaka Osawa, *Homepage for Peace* [Heiwa no Peiji], blog, December 18, 2004, http://osawa-yutaka.my.coocan.jp/heiwa-top.htm.
26. Tachikawa Support Group, *Complete Record*, 24. Munakata, *Voices Against War*, 232. Munakata lamented that although the Tent Village had won in court, the Iraq deployment continued. When he watched the television news that evening, he was disappointed to find no report on the judgment; instead he saw news reports on the SDF deployment. Munakata, *Voices Against War*, 230–31.
27. For the full text of the statement, see Shizu Yamamoto, "Reversal of the Judgment in the Tachikawa Antiwar Flyer Delivery Trial" [Tachikawa hansen bira-ire saiban de gyakuten hanketsu], Japan Institute of Constitutional Law [Hogakukan Kempō Kenkyūjo], http://www.jicl.jp/old/now/saiban/backnumber/tachikawa2.html. The three leaders (*yobikakenin*) were Yasuhiro Okudaira, Toshihiro Yamauchi (Ryukoku University), and Takaaki Matsumiya (Ritsumeikan University).
28. Code of Criminal Procedure, Article 373. Colin P.A. Jones and Frank S. Savitch, *The Japanese Legal System* (St. Paul, MN: West Academic Publishing, 2018), 275.

Chapter 13

1. The specific items distributed by Arakawa are listed at Ryūichi Ozawa, "Victory for Conscience and Common Sense" [Ryōshin to Ryōshiki no Shōri], *Hō to Minshushugi 412* (October 2006), 54. This article also reports many specific details of the arrest and detention.
2. "Average Annual Incomes for Tokyo's 23 Wards," *City Cost*, May 27, 2016, https://www.city-cost.com/blogs/City-Cost-News/w2Rgw.
3. Over the years, a large proportion of the residents have moved into multistory apartments and condominiums.
4. Arakawa provided these details in his statement at the first trial hearing, May 20, 2005. The text is published in Society to Protect the Freedom to Deliver Flyers [Bira Haifu no Jiyū wo Mamoru Kai], *Trial Materials from the Katsushika Flyer Distribution Suppression Case* [*Katsushika bira haifu dan'atsu jiken—shiryōshū*], vol. 1, 52. (Arakawa statement at 49–58.)
5. Ozawa, "Victory for Conscience," 55.
6. A summary of the events of December 23 appears in the Defense Counsel Opinion, *Trial Materials*, vol. 1, 5–7 and in Ozawa, "Victory for Conscience," 54–55.
7. *Trial Materials*, vol. 1, 52.
8. Detainees were not allowed to place calls themselves.
9. Arakawa statement in *Trial Materials*, 49–51; Ozawa, "Victory for Conscience," 55.
10. The URL for the Japan Relief Network website is http://kyuenkai.org/.
11. The police station is located in nearby Kameari. Protesters would repeat the performance daily, often accompanied by a sound car with a bullhorn.
12. The lawyers met with their new client for more than one hour. Author interview with Minoru Nishida, May 29, 2018.
13. Author interview with Nishida, May 29, 2018. Ozawa, "Victory for Conscience," 55.
14. Author interview with Nishida, May 29, 2018. Ozawa, "Victory for Conscience," 55.
15. According to Attorney Nishida, "If a judge rules against an attorney, there is no complaint. But if a judge rules against the prosecutors, he can expect trouble." Nishida interview, May 29, 2018.
16. Fax message from Attorney Kotō to Tent Village members and other defense counsel, December 24, 2004.

17. Yutaka Osawa, *Homepage for Peace* [*Heiwa no Peiji*], blog, December, 26, 2004, http://osawa-yutaka.my.coocan.jp/heiwa-top.htm.
18. Ozawa, "Victory for Conscience," 55.
19. Tachikawa Antiwar Flyer Suppression Support Group [Tachikawa Hansen Bira Dan'atsu Kyūenkai], *The Complete Record 2004–2009* [*Zenkiroku 2004–2009*] (Tokyo, 2009), 26.
20. There was a fourth task: retaining additional attorneys to assist in the work to come.
21. All quotations and other details regarding the February 27 event are from Osawa, *Homepage for Peace*, March 1, 2005.
22. The publishing house is *Iwanami Shinsho*. Toshihiro Yoshida, *Refusing to Cooperate in War* [*Sensō Kyōryoku Kyōhi*] (Tokyo: Iwanami Shinsho, 2005). (By contrast, Munakata's book was put out by a tiny publishing house that later went out of business.)
23. Osawa, *Homepage for Peace*, March 1, 2005. The U.S. Embassy incident is also described in Yoshida, *Refusing to Cooperate in War*, 178–79.
24. Osawa, *Homepage for Peace*, March 1, 2005.
25. Brief reviews of Mitsuru Munakata, *When Voices Against War Leave Town—The Tachikawa Antiwar Flyer Suppression Case* [*Machi Kara Hansen no Koe ga Kieru Toki—Tachikawa Hansen Bira-ire Dan'atsu Jiken*] (Tokyo: Jushinsha, 2005) and the book produced by Tent Village supporters, *The Tachikawa Antiwar Flyer Case* [*Tachikawa Hansen Bira Jiken*] (Tokyo: Akashi Shōten, 2005) are posted at Osawa, *Homepage for Peace*, July 19, 2005.
26. Other supplementary material includes a comprehensive chronology of the case and the full texts of statements delivered in court by the three defendants on November 4.
27. Tachikawa Support Group, *Complete Record*, 26.
28. All quotations in this section are from the government's Statement of Reasons for Appeal (*kōso shuisho*), submitted to court on May 30, 2005.
29. Minor Offenses Act [Keihanzaihō], Law no. 39 of 1948. Case summary from Hidenori Tomatsu and Masanori Shiyake, *Constitutional Law Cases and Comments* [*Kempō Hanrei*] (Tokyo: Yūhikaku, 2007), 202.
30. The train station was Kichijōji, in western Tokyo. The defendant was protesting the conviction of the defendant in the well-known *Sayama* case. See summary in Tomatsu and Shiyake, *Constitutional Law Cases and Comments*, 204.
31. For a recent review of the Supreme Court's record in English, see Keigo Obayashi, "Free Speech Jurisprudence in Japan," in *Hate Speech in Japan: The Possibility of a Nonregulatory Approach*, eds. Shinji Higashi and Yuji Nasu (Cambridge: Cambridge University Press, 2021), 341. See also, Shigenori Matsui, *The Constitution of Japan* (Oxford and Portland, OR: Hart Publishing, 2011).
32. Details of the national tour, including a map with commentary, at Tachikawa Support Group, *Complete Record*, 28–29. (One motto for the national tour: "We want to learn from you!")

Chapter 14

1. The authors were third- and fourth-year students participating in a seminar-style course taught by a constitutional law professor at Waseda University. "Shadows on City Streets: What We Saw as Courtroom Spectators" [Tsuisekisha no machi—saiban bōchō kara mieta koto], *Hōgaku Seminar* 615 (March 2006), 56–59.
2. The witness testified that he was just following orders and had not otherwise confirmed Horikoshi's movements.
3. Kenji Kato, "The Progress of the Horikoshi Case and Issues in the Criminal Trial" [Horikoshi jiken no keika to keiji saiban no mondaiten], *Hō to Minshushugi* 408 (May 2006).

4. Shirō Okubo, "The Current Stage of the Trial and Points at Issue" [*Soshō no gendankai to sōten*], *Hōgaku Seminar* 615 (March 2006), 54.
5. Tokyo Southern District Law Office [Tokyo Nanbu Hōritsu Jimusho], *Trials and Human Rights* [*Saiban to Jinken*] (Tokyo: Nihon Hyōronsha, 2009), 147.
6. *Trials and Human Rights,* 147–48.
7. "The first principle is that this regulation must not be abused; it is interpreted to be as limited as possible." Directive of Administrative Chief Kiyoshi Asai, October 21, 1949, quoted in Okubo, "Current Stage," 54.
8. Okubo, "Current Stage," 52.
9. "Shadows on City Streets," 57. Professor Okubo is also dubious. Okubo, "Current Stage," 52.
10. Defendants from the three cases were joined on stage by Katsuhisa Fujita, a retired high school teacher who was prosecuted for disrupting a graduation ceremony by distributing copies of a magazine article on the Tent Village case. Defense counsel who spoke included Tent Village counsel Uchida and Kenji Kato, the attorney who served as administrative chief of the Horikoshi defense team.
11. *Suppression Under National Public Law—The Horikoshi Case Record of Battle, 2004–2013* [*Kokkōhō Dan'atsu Horikoshi Jiken Tatakai no Kiroku 2004–2013*] (Tokyo: Society to Prevent Suppression Under National Public Law and Protect Freedom of Speech, 2013), 9–10.
12. Because there was little coverage of the case in the mainstream news media, regular reporting by *Shūkan Kinyōbi*, a leftwing newsweekly, was very important in disseminating news on trial developments.
13. Akira Uozumi et al., *Very Strange! Police, Prosecutors, Courts—The Freedom of Civil Society is in Danger* [*Okashii zo, Keisatsu, Kensatsu, Saibansho—Shimin Shakai no Jiyū ga Abunai*] (Tokyo: Tsukuru Shuppan, 2005).
14. *Record of Battle*, 8.
15. "Introducing the Tokyo High Court" [Tokyo kōtō saibansho no shōkai], *Courts in Japan* [Saibansho], https://www.courts.go.jp/tokyo-h/about/syokai/index.html. In 2020, 187 judges were assigned to the Tokyo High Court.
16. The court building houses more than 150 courtrooms employed by the Tokyo High Court and lower courts in the Tokyo district. According to Tent Village supporters, of the 100 or so people who joined the queue to draw straws for entry to the hearing, about 40 were undercover police. Some pulled good straws and then walked away. As a result, many spectators' seats were empty.
17. Nakagawa continued on the Tokyo High Court until he reached the mandatory retirement age of 65 in 2011. Following his retirement as a judge, he commenced work as a private attorney, a common practice.
18. Colin P.A. Jones and Frank S. Ravitch, *The Japanese Legal System* (St. Paul, MN: West Academic Publishing, 2018), 275.
19. Tachikawa Antiwar Flyer Suppression Support Group [Tachikawa Hansen Bira Dan'atsu Kyūenkai], *The Complete Record 2004–2009 [Zenkiroku 2004–2009]* (Tokyo, 2009), 31. The prosecutors waived cross-examination of the defendants.
20. The prosecutors did claim there were actually a total of 84 arrests for "postings" at residences over that period leading to 24 prosecutions, but they did not explain the 60 cases where they declined prosecution or what standard was applied to select the seven sample cases from the remaining 24.
21. Tachikawa Support Group, *Complete Record,* 32; Argument Summary [*benron yōshi*], October 3, 2005, chart at 10.
22. Tachikawa Support Group, *Complete Record,* 32.
23. Shizu Yamamoto, "Reversal of the Judgment in the Tachikawa Antiwar Flyer Delivery Trial" [Tachikawa hansen bira-ire saiban de gyakuten hanketsu], Japan Institute of Constitutional Law [Hōgakukan Kempō Kenkyūjo], http://www.jicl.jp/old/now/saiban/backnumber/tachikawa2.html. Tachikawa Support Group; *Complete Record,* 32.

24. The *Mainichi* even placed the iconic phrase "fortress of human rights" [*jinken no toride*] in a headline. As spectators departed the courthouse, Tent Village supporters displayed the customary "Unfair Decision!" banner in front of the courthouse for the cameras and the crowd outside.
25. *Asahi Shimbun*, December 9, 2005.
26. This key sentence was carried on the front page of the evening editions of the *Asahi*, *Mainichi*, and *Yomiuri*. Wording differs slightly among the different papers. December 9, 2005.
27. Jones and Savitch note that counsel do not always receive these summaries, so news reporters are sometimes better informed than the attorneys. *Japanese Legal System*, 274.
28. Tokyo High Court Judgment of December 9, 2005, *Hanrei Jihō* No. 1949, 169; *Hanketsu Jihō* Vol. 56, 102.
29. Kōji Adachi, "Is Posting at Multifamily Residences the 'Crime of Trespassing on Premises'?" [Shūgojutaku no posting ha 'teitaku shinyūzai' ka], *Hōgaku Seminar* 616 (April 2006), 6.
30. Tokyo High Court Judgment of December 9, 2005.
31. Tokyo High Court Judgment of December 9, 2005.
32. *Asahi Shimbun*, December 9, 2005.
33. *Yomiuri Shimbun*, December 9, 2005.
34. Fujita's case was perhaps the strangest of all the political prosecutions of this period. He was charged with the crime of "forcible obstruction of business" for his actions during a high school graduation ceremony. Fujita was a retired teacher who had taught at the school and was invited to attend. When he passed out copies of a magazine article describing the Tent Village and Horikoshi cases and exhorted guests to remain seated during the playing of the national anthem, he was quickly escorted out of the building. Prosecutors indicted him nine months later. The case is described at Masatoshi Uchida, *Is this a Crime? Thinking About "Arrests for Handing Out Flyers"* [Kore ga hanzai? "Bira kubari de taiho" wo kangaeru] (*Iwanami Booklet, No. 655*, 2005), 9–12.
35. December 9 meeting details from Osawa, *Homepage for Peace*, December 9, 2005, http://osawa-yutaka.my.coocan.jp/heiwa-top.htm.
36. Osawa, *Homepage for Peace*, December 9, 2005.
37. *Record of Battle*, 10–11 (trial summary). In February 2005, Judge Mōri replaced Yūjirō Nakatani as chief judge. He presided over courtroom proceedings commencing with the seventh hearing, held on March 22, 2005. *Suppression Under National Public Law*, 40. Japan's judges are typically rotated at intervals of approximately three years.
38. *The Appeal of the National Public Law Case and the Supreme Court [Kokkōhō Jiken Jōkokushin to Saikōsaibansho] Hōritsu Jihō Zōkan* (Tokyo Nihon Hyōronsha, 2011), 201–02. The court also mentioned that the police used a "videocamera with ordinary functionality."
39. This is usually called *shōzōken*, the "right to one's likeness." The case is commonly known as the *Kyoto-fu gakuren jiken*, Judgment of the Supreme Court, Grand Bench, December 24, 1969. *Keishū* 23, no. 12, 1625. Hidenori Tomatsu and Masanori Shiyake, *Kenpō Hanrei*, 5th ed. (Tokyo: Yuhikaku, 2008), 48–50. Lawrence W. Beer, *Freedom of Expression in Japan* (Tokyo: Kodansha, 1984), 298.
40. *The Appeal and the Supreme Court*, 203.
41. *The Appeal and the Supreme Court*, 204–05.
42. The court also added, "there has been no decision on this type of case since the Supreme Court decision in the *Sarufutsu* case." *The Appeal and the Supreme Court*, 219.
43. The two scholars were Takaaki Matsumiya and Masato Ichikawa, both of Ritsumeikan University.
44. Society to Protect the Freedom to Deliver Flyers, "Flyers Filled with Thoughts About Peace" [Heiwa e no Omoi—Bira ni Komete] (Tokyo, 2010), 6; *Tokyo Shimbun*, August 28, 2006.

45. *Asahi Shimbun*, August 28, 2006. Quotations are from news accounts. The court released its full opinion on October 11, 2006. It was published by the Katsushika support group in November 2006 (Trial Materials, vol. 4, 1–35).
46. John Owen Haley, *The Spirit of Japanese Law* (Athens, GA: University of Georgia Press, 2006), 157. Haley's discussion of the "sense of society" in this work is limited to civil cases.
47. *Asahi Shimbun*, August 28, 2006.
48. *Asahi Shimbun*, August 28, 2006. Tsuchimoto was also quoted to this effect in the *Mainichi*.
49. *Mainichi Shimbun*, August 28, 2006.
50. *Asahi Shimbun*, August 28, 2006.
51. *Mainichi Shimbun*, August 28, 2006.
52. Despite mass protests and opposition from nearly every quarter, the Diet adopted such a law in June 2017. See, e.g., Colin P.A. Jones, "Japan's New Conspiracy Law Expands Police Power," *Asia-Pacific Journal* 15, issue 16, no. 1 (August 15, 2017). If it had been in place during the Iraq War era, Katsuko Kato and others would have been subject to arrest and prosecution for planning the Tent Village flyer deliveries even though they did not actually enter the SDF property or handle the flyers themselves. Law No. 57 of 2017 (June 21, 2017).

Chapter 15

1. Tachikawa Antiwar Flyer Suppression Support Group [Tachikawa Hansen Bira Dan'atsu Kyūenkai], *The Complete Record 2004–2009* [*Zenkiroku 2004–2009*] (Tokyo, 2009), 75.
2. Yutaka Osawa posted the texts of nine editorials. Yutaka Osawa, *Homepage for Peace* [*Heiwa no Peiji*], blog, December 16, 2005, http://osawa-yutaka.my.coocan.jp/heiwa-top.htm.
3. The broadcast aired on March 26, 2006. Tachikawa Support Group, *Complete Record,* 64.
4. Tachikawa Support Group, *Complete Record,* 64. According to the *Complete Record,* Tent Village supporters held demonstrations outside the Supreme Court compound on nine occasions between April 12, 2006 and January 16, 2008, 64–65.
5. Shizu Yamamoto, "We Will Not Be Silent" [*Watakushitachi ha chinmoku shinai*], in *In Order to Avoid a Silent Society—168 Appeals to the Supreme Court* [*Chinmoku no shakai ni shinai tame ni—saikōsai ni ateta 168tsū no jōshinsho*] (Tokyo: Jushinsha, 2006), 252.
6. There is a detailed description of the petition campaign at Tachikawa Support Group, *Complete Record,* 36.
7. Kato's petition is in *168 Appeals to the Supreme Court,* 29–33. The book divides the petitions into four categories: "from military base towns," "this is freedom of expression," "this is why we oppose war!" and "the police are very strange!" There are petitions from a wide variety of authors, including activists who stopped flyer distribution due to the Tent Village prosecution, individuals with memories from the war, law students, and at least one anonymous SDF member who criticized the SDF for filing a criminal complaint.
8. Regarding "research judges," see Masako Kamiya, "Chōsakan: Research Judges Toiling at the Stone Fortress," *Washington University Law Review* 88, no. 6 (2011), 1601.
9. Regarding the events of May 31, 2005, see Tachikawa Support Group, *Complete Record,* 38.
10. Kato describes the supporters' visits to the Supreme Court compound. Katsuko Kato, "History and Daily Life and Then Antiwar, Part 2" [Rekishi to nichijō to, soshite hansen to—2], *War and Sex* [*Sensō to Sei*] 27 (Spring 2008), 160.
11. *168 Appeals to the Supreme Court,* 3.

12. "First Supplementary Appellate Brief" [Jōkoku shuisho hojūsho (1)], December 22, 2006, 2.
13. "First Supplementary Appellate Brief," 6.
14. The 115 signatures were gathered as of January 6, 2006. The attorneys' request to meet with the research judges to explain the document was denied. Kato, "History and Daily Life," Part 2, 160; Tachikawa Support Group, *Complete Record*, 64.
15. Jones and Ravitch cite provisions allowing appellate courts to reject appeals without hearings. Colin P.A. Jones and Frank S. Ravitch, *The Japanese Legal System* (St. Paul, MN: West Academic Publishing, 2018), 114.
16. Tachikawa Support Group, *Complete Record*, 40.
17. The two responses are reproduced in Tachikawa Support Group, *Complete Record*, 41.
18. *Shimbun Akahata*, October 12 and October 14, 2007. (The Japanese term for the JGSDF Intelligence Security Corps (ISC) is *Rikujō jietai jōhō hozentai.*) See also, *Complete Record*, 42.
19. "Second Supplementary Appellate Brief" [Jōkoku shuisho hojusho (2)], December 25, 2007, 4.
20. "Second Supplementary Appellate Brief," 10.
21. "Second Supplementary Appellate Brief," 13.
22. "Second Supplementary Appellate Brief," 11.
23. For courtroom testimony, see Chapter 9.
24. For courtroom testimony, see Chapter 9.
25. "Second Supplementary Appellate Brief," 11–12.
26. The national bar association statement is titled "Opinion Concerning Ground Self-Defense Force Monitoring of Citizens" (Rikujōjieitai ni yoru shimin kanshi ni tsuite no ikensho), October 23, 2007, available at https://www.nichibenren.or.jp/document/opinion/year/2007/071023.html.
27. *Asahi Shimbun*, March 22, 2008.
28. Kato's words were published as a postscript to an entry in her diary series in the quarterly publication *War and Sex* [*Sensō to Sei*]. Kato, "History and Daily Life," Part 3, 157–58.
29. Kato, "History and Daily Life," Part 3, 158.
30. Lawrence Repeta, "Reserved Seats on Japan's Supreme Court," *Washington University Law Review* 88, no. 6, (2011), 1713–44.
31. Because the Supreme Court chief justice serves not only as a judge but also as the administrative chief of Japan's entire judicial system, he tends to be busy with personnel, budgeting, and other managerial issues, leaving insufficient time to review cases. Jones and Ravitch, *Japanese Legal System*, 109–16.
32. Construction was completed in 1974. "Fifty Years of the Supreme Court, as Seen Through Photographs" [Shashin de miru saikōsaibansho no 50 nen], *Courts in Japan* [*Saibansho*], https://www.courts.go.jp/vc-files/courts/file2/20916003.pdf. Susumu Yamaguchi and Yu Miyaji, *Shadow Fighting at the Supreme Court* [*Saikōsai no Antō*] (Tokyo: Asahi Shinsho, 2011), 40–46.
33. For references to the "Stone Fortress," see, e.g., Yamaguchi and Miyaji, *Shadow Fighting*, 40–6, and Kamiya, "Research Judges."
34. Kato, "History and Daily Life," Part 3, 155.
35. The Grand Bench courtroom, site of en banc proceedings by all 15 justices, is far more grandiose. Yamaguchi and Miyaji, *Shadow Fighting*, 41–43.
36. Tachikawa Support Group, *Complete Record*, 44.
37. The Supreme Court is Japan's only court in which judges file dissenting opinions.
38. Major newspapers all included this statement in their reports on April 12, 2008.
39. *Mainichi Shimbun*, April 12, 2008.
40. For a recent discussion in English, see Keigo Obayashi, "Free Speech Jurisprudence in Japan," in *Hate Speech in Japan,* eds. Shinji Higashi and Yuji Nasu (Cambridge: Cambridge University Press, 2021). For a summary of the Supreme Court's many

rejections of claims to constitutional protection for free speech, see Shigenori Matsui, *The Constitution of Japan*, (Oxford and Portland, Oregon: Hart Publishing, 2011), 196–211.

41. The texts of Constitution Articles 12 and 13 read as follows (italics added):
    Article 12. The freedoms and rights guaranteed to the people by this Constitution shall be maintained by the constant endeavor of the people, who shall refrain from any abuse of these freedoms and rights and shall always be responsible for utilizing them for the *public welfare*.
    Article 13. All of the people shall be respected as individuals. Their right to life, liberty, and the pursuit of happiness shall, to the extent that it does not interfere with the *public welfare*, be the supreme consideration in legislation and in other governmental affairs.
42. See, e.g., Shōjirō Sakaguchi, "The Tachikawa Antiwar Flyer Case—Review of the Supreme Court Judgment," [Tachikawa hansen bira jiken—saikōsai hanketsu hihan], *Sekai*, July 2008, 48, and Norikazu Kawagishi, "Freedom of Expression is a House Built on Sand," [Sajō no rōkaku ni tatsu hyōgen no jiyū] *Hōgaku Seminar* 643 (August 2007).
43. Japanese scholars borrowed the "strict scrutiny" concept from American jurisprudence, but the Supreme Court rarely finds an opportunity to apply it, so in Japanese law the meaning is unclear.
44. Judgment of the Supreme Court, Second Petty Bench, April 11, 2008. *Keishū,* vol. 68, no. 5, 1217.
45. *Asahi Shimbun*, April 15, 2008 (English edition). (This is the Asahi's translation of its original Japanese editorial that appeared on April 12, 2008.)
46. *Asahi Shimbun*, April 15, 2008 (English edition). The film was screened in the conference hall of the national bar association in central Tokyo.
47. *Nihon Keizai Shimbun,* April 12, 2008.
48. *Yomiuri Shimbun*, April 12, 2008.

Chapter 16

1. *Yomiuri Shimbun*, December 12, 2007.
2. According to defense counsel, however, there was no evidence to show who placed these signs at the property. The condo association had no record of such an action. Author interview with Minoru Nishida, May 29, 2018.
3. Society to Protect the Freedom to Deliver Flyers, "Flyers Filled with Thoughts About Peace" [Heiwa e no Omoi—Bira ni Komete] (Tokyo, 2010), 61.
4. The judgment appeared a little over two months after a national election that saw the LDP driven from office only the second time since the party was formed in 1955.
5. *Thoughts About Peace*, 8.
6. Minoru Nishida, "What Did the Supreme Court Try to Protect?" [Saikōsai ha nani wo mamorō to shita no ka], *Hō to Minshushugi* 444 (December 2009), 68.
7. The Occupation's hardline stance against allowing government workers the right to bargain collectively and to strike is described in Eiji Takemae, *The Allied Occupation of Japan* (New York and London: Continuum, 2002), 330–32. National Public Employees Law [Kokka kōmuin hō], Law No. 120 of 1947.
8. Lawrence Repeta, "Reserved Seats on Japan's Supreme Court," *Washington University Law Review* 88, no. 6 (2011), 1728–41.
9. The text of the court's judgment is reproduced in *The Appeal of the National Public Law Case and the Supreme Court* [*Kokkōhō Jiken Jōkokushin to Saikōsaibansho*] *Hōritsu Jihō Zōkan* (Tokyo: Nihon Hyōronsha, 2011), 195–220, 219.
10. *Suppression Under National Public Law—The Horikoshi Case Record of Battle, 2004–2013* [*Kokkōhō dan'atsu horikoshi jiken tatakai no kiroku 2004–2013*] (Tokyo: Society to Prevent Suppression Under National Public Law and Protect Freedom of Speech, 2013), 13.

11. *Asahi Shimbun*, March 29, 2010. The text of the court's judgment is reproduced in *The Appeal and the Supreme Court,* 221–33.
12. Quotations are from the front-page report of the *Asahi Shimbun*, March 29, 2010.
13. Judge Nakagawa's comments are reported in the *Asahi* and *Mainichi Shimbun,* March 29, 2010.
14. See the *Asahi, Mainichi*, and *Tokyo Shimbun,* March 29, 2010.
15. *Yomiuri Shimbun*, March 29, 2010.
16. The text of the court's judgment is reproduced at *The Appeal and the Supreme Court,* 248–55.
17. *Record of Battle*, 16–19. There was an especially notable gathering on June 30, 2012. In the end, supporters managed to gather approximately 180,000 signatures.
18. *Record of Battle*, 44.
19. Judgment of the Supreme Court, Second Petty Bench, *Keishū*, vol. 66, no. 12, 1337, https://www.courts.go.jp/app/hanrei_jp/detail2?id=82801.
20. Judgment of the Supreme Court, Second Petty Bench, *Keishū*, vol. 66, no. 12, 1722, https://www.courts.go.jp/app/files/hanrei_jp/802/082802_hanrei.pdf.
21. Quotations from the judgment summary published in the *Asahi Shimbun,* December 8, 2012.
22. The *Sarufutsu* cases involved somewhat different acts from the Horikoshi and Ujihashi cases. For a description of the facts of *Sarufutsu* and two other cases decided by the Supreme Court that day, see Lawrence W. Beer, *Freedom of Expression in Japan* (Tokyo: Kodansha, 1984), 236–37.
23. *Asahi Shimbun*, December 8, 2012.

Conclusion

1. Masatoshi Uchida describes other cases in *Is this a Crime? Thinking About the "Arrests for Handing Out Flyers"* (*Kore ga hanzai? "Bira kubari de taiho" wo kangaeru*) (*Iwanami Booklet, No. 655,* July 5, 2005).
2. Yasuhiro Okudaira, "The Present Stage of Freedom of Expression and the 'Safe, Secure State'" ["Anzen, Anshin" Kokka to Hyōgen no Jiyū no Gendankai], *Hōritsu Jihō Zōkan*, October 31, 2016, 2.
3. Manabu Ishizaki, "Freedom of Expression and Civil Society" [Seijiteki hyōgen no jiyū to shimin shakai], *Hō to Minshushugi 430,* July 2008, 28.

BIBLIOGRAPHY

Abe, Shunsuke. "Lawyers in Call to End Practice of Handcuffs, Ropes in Courtrooms." *Asahi Shimbun*, August 15, 2021. https://www.asahi.com/ajw/articles/14407268.

Adachi, Kōji. "The Criminal Law Issues in the Case" [*Jiken no keijihōteki mondaiten*]. *Hōgaku Seminar* 596 (August 2004), 65–67.

Adachi, Kōji. "Is Posting at Multifamily Residences the "Crime of Trespassing on Premises"?" [Shūgojutaku no posting ha 'teitaku shinyūzai' ka?]. *Hōgaku Seminar* 616 (April 2006), 6–7.

AFP Tokyo. "Koizumi Pays Surprise Visit to Yasukuni Shrine." January 2, 2004. http://www.taipeitimes.com/News/world/archives/2004/01/02/2003086040.

Amnesty International. "Who We Are." https://www.amnesty.org/en/who-we-are.

Andrews, William. *Dissenting Japan*. London: Hurst, 2016.

Anonymous. "Arrest and Prosecution for Antiwar Graffiti on a Public Park Outhouse" [Kōen toire de hansen rakugaki de taiho/kiso]. In *Very Strange! Police, Prosecutors, Courts: The Freedom of Civil Society Is in Danger* [*Okashii zo, Keisatsu, Kensatsu, Saibansho—Shimin Shakai no Jiyū ga Abunai*], eds. Akira Uozumi et al. Tokyo: Tsukuru Shuppan, 2005.

Arimoto, Mayu. "Is There Attorney–Client Privilege in Japan?" *LLM Law Review*, June 16, 2018. http://www.llmlawreview.com/2018/06/16/is-there-attorney-client-privilege-in-japan.

Ashibe, Nobuyoshi. "The United States Constitution and Japan's Constitutional Law: Human Rights and Judicial Power." In *Constitutional Systems in Late Twentieth-Century Asia*, ed. Lawrence W. Beer. Seattle, WA: University of Washington Press, 1992.

Beer, Lawrence W. *Freedom of Expression in Japan*. Tokyo: Kōdansha, 1984.

Beer, Lawrence W., and Hiroshi Itoh. *The Constitutional Case Law of Japan, 1970 through 1990*. Seattle, WA: University of Washington Press, 1996.

Benenson, Peter. "The Forgotten Prisoners." *Guardian*, May 28, 1961. https://www.theguardian.com/uk/1961/may/28/fromthearchive.theguardian.

Brown, Alexander. *Anti-Nuclear Protest in Post-Fukushima Tokyo: Power Struggles*. New York: Routledge, 2018.

Burukitch, Kanako. "Protest Rally at the American Embassy 2003." [*amerika taishikan kōgi kōdō 2003*], 2003. http://www.mkimpo.com/diary/2003/american_embassy_03-03-01.html.

CBS News. "Bush Has Yen for Japan Help." *CBS News*, October 18, 2003. https://www.cbsnews.com/news/bush-has-yen-for-japan-help.

Dower, John W. *Embracing Defeat: Japan in the Wake of World War II*. New York: W. W. Norton, 1999.

Emmerson, John K. *Arms, Yen, and Power*. North Clarendon, VT: Tuttle, 1971.

Foote, Daniel H. "Confessions and the Right to Silence in Japan." *Georgia Journal of International and Comparative Law* 21 (1991), 415–488.

Foote, Daniel H. "The Benevolent Paternalism of Japanese Criminal Justice." *California Law Review* 80 (1992), 317–390.

Foote, Daniel H. "From Japan's Death Row to Freedom." *Pacific Rim Law and Policy* 1, no. 1 (1993), 11–103.

Foote, Daniel H. "Introduction and Overview." In *Law in Japan: A Turning Point*, ed. Foote, Daniel H. Seattle, WA: University of Washington Press, 2007, xix–xxxix.

Fukurai, Hiroshi. "A Step in the Right Direction for Japan's Judicial Reform." *Hastings International and Comparative Law Review* 36, no. 2 (2013), 517–566.

Haley, John O. *Authority Without Power*. New York: Oxford University Press, 1991.

Haley, John O. "Waging War: Japan's Constitutional Constraints." *Constitutional Forum* 14, no. 2 (2005). https://papers.ssrn.com/sol3/papers.cfm?abstract_id=821504.

Haley, John O. *The Spirit of Japanese Law*. Athens, GA: University of Georgia Press, 2006.

Haley, John O. "Article 9 in the Post-*Sunakawa* World: Continuity and Deterrence Within a Transforming Global Context." *Washington International Law Journal* 26, no. 1 (January 2017), 1–16.

Haley, John O. "Punish or Prevent: The Night and Day of Criminal Justice." *Virginia Journal of Criminal Law* 7 (2019), 119–172.

Havens, Thomas R.H. *Fire Across the Sea: The Vietnam War and Japan 1965–1975*. Princeton, NJ: Princeton University Press, 1987.

Higuchi, Yōichi, Tōru Nakajima, and Yasuo Hasebe, eds. *The Dignity of Constitutionalism: Themes from the Constitutional Philosophy of Yasuhiro Okudaira* [*Hō no Songen—Okudaira Kempōgaku no Keishō to Tenkai*]. Tokyo: Nihon Hyōronsha, 2017.

Horikoshi, Akio. "The First Indictment in 37 Years Under the National Public Employees Law for Delivering Political Flyers" [Seitō bira haifu de 37 nenburi no kokkōhō ihan kiso]. In *Very Strange! Police, Prosecutors, Courts: The Freedom of Civil Society Is in Danger* [*Okashii zo, Keisatsu, Kensatsu, Saibansho—Shimin Shakai no Jiyū ga Abunai*], eds. Akira Uozumi et al. Tokyo: Tsukuru Shuppan, 2005.

Human Rights Watch. "Call to Eliminate Japan's "Hostage Justice" System by Japanese Legal Professionals." April 10, 2019. https://www.hrw.org/news/2019/04/10/call-eliminate-japans-hostage-justice-system-japanese-legal-professionals#.

Inoue, Hisashi, et al. *Constitution Article 9 Is Still Fresh* [*Kempō Kyūjō Ima Koso Shun*]. Iwanami Booklet 639. Tokyo: Iwanami Shōten, 2004.

Inoue, Mori. "Looking Back on the Year Following the Arrests" [Taiho kara no ichinen wo furikaeru]. In *The Tachikawa Antiwar Flyer Case* [*Tachikawa Hansen Bira Jiken*], ed. Tachikawa Antiwar Flyer Suppression Support Group [Tachikawa Hansen Bira Dan'atsu Kyūenkai], 26. Tokyo: Akashi Shōten, 2005.

Ishizaki, Manabu. "Freedom of Expression and 'Distortions' in Constitutionalism" [Rikkenshugi no 'yugami' to hyōgen no jiyū]. *Hōgaku Seminar* 596 (August 2004), 60–61.

Ishizaki, Manabu. *Examining Democracy* [Demokurashii Kentei]. Tokyo: Ōtsuki Shōten, 2006.

Ishizaki, Manabu. "Political Freedom of Expression and Civil Society" [Seijiteki hyōgen no jiyū to shimin shakai]. *Hō to Minshushugi* 430 (July 2008), 28–33.

Japan Federation of Bar Associations. "Opinion Concerning Ground Self-Defense Force Monitoring of Citizens" [Rikujōjieitai ni yoru shimin kanshi ni tsuite no ikensho], October 23, 2007. https://www.nichibenren.or.jp/document/opinion/year/2007/071023.html.

Japan Federation of Bar Associations. *It's Time to Think About Freedom of Expression and the Right to Know* [*Ima Hyōgen no Jiyū to Shiru Kenri wo Kangaeru*]. Proceedings from the 52nd Human Rights Conference, Tokyo, November 5, 2009.

Japan Federation of Bar Associations. *2016 Attorneys' White Paper* [*Bengoshi Hakusho 2016*]. Tokyo: Japan Federation of Bar Associations, 2016.

Japan Lawyers Association for Freedom [Jiyū Hōsōdan]. *The Jiyū Hōsōdan Story* [*Jiyū Hōsōdan Monogatari*]. 2 vols. Tokyo: Nihon Hyōronsha, 2002.

Japan Revolutionary Communist League [Nihon kakumeiteki kyōsanshugisha dōmei]. "We Won't Allow the Unfair Arrests for the Tachikawa Antiwar Flyer Deliveries" [Tachikawa hansen bira-ire futō taiho wo yurusanai]. *Kakehashi*, blog, March 22, 2004. https://jrcl.info/web/frame040322a.html.

Japan Revolutionary Communist League [Nihon kakumeiteki kyōsanshugisha dōmei]. "We Oppose the Iraq Deployment! We Denounce the Unfair Indictments and Long Detentions!" [Iraku hahei hantai! Futō kiso to chōki kōryu kyūdan]. *Kakehashi*, blog, May 3, 2004. https://jrcl.info/web/frame0453c.html.

Jesty, Justin. "Tokyo 1960: Days of Rage and Grief." *MIT Visualizing Cultures*, 2012. https://visualizingcultures.mit.edu/tokyo_1960/anp2_essay05.html.

Johnson, David T. *The Japanese Way of Justice: Prosecuting Crime in Japan*. New York: Oxford University Press, 2002.

Jones, Colin P.A., and Frank S. Ravitch. *The Japanese Legal System*. St. Paul, MN: West Academic Publishing, 2018.

Kamiya, Masako. "Chōsakan: Research Judges Toiling at the Stone Fortress." *Washington University Law Review* 88, no. 6 (2011), 1601–1629.

Kapur, Nick. *Japan at the Crossroads: Conflict and Compromise After Anpo*. Cambridge, MA: Harvard University Press, 2018.

Kato, Katsuko. "Urgent Interview: We Won't Allow Suppression of Antiwar Flyer Deliveries!" [Kinkyū intabyū—Hansen bira ire he no dan'atsu wo yurusanai!]. *War and Sex* [*Sensō to Sei*] 22 (Spring 2004) 10–29.

Kato, Katsuko. "Why We Hand Out Flyers to Self-Defense Force Members" [Watakushitachi ha naze jieikan ni bira wo kubaru no ka]. In *The Tachikawa Antiwar Flyer Case* [*Tachikawa Hansen Bira Jiken*], ed. Tachikawa Antiwar Flyer Suppression Support Group [Tachikawa Hansen Bira Dan'atsu Kyūenkai], 15. Tokyo: Akashi Shōten, 2005.

Kato, Katsuko. "History and Daily Life and Then Antiwar, Part 2" [Rekishi to nichijō to, soshite hansen to 2]. *War and Sex* [*Sensō to Sei*] 27 (Spring 2008), 154–161.

Kato, Katsuko, ed. *Blown by the Wind: The 101 Years of En Suda* [*Kaze ni fukaretsu—Suda En hyakuichinen*]. Self-published pamphlet, 2017.

Kato, Kenji. "The Progress of the Horikoshi Case and Issues in the Criminal Trial" [Horikoshi jiken no keika to keiji saiban no mondaiten]. *Hō to Minshushugi* 408 (May 2006).

Kawagishi, Norikazu. "Freedom of Expression Is a House Built on Sand" [Sajō no rōkaku ni tatsu hyōgen no jiyū]. *Hōgaku Seminar* 643 (August 2007).

Kingston, Jeff. *Japan's Quiet Transformation*. London: Routledge, 2004.

Kingston, Jeff. "Justice on Trial: Japanese Prosecutors Under Fire." *Asia-Pacific Journal* 9, issue 10, no. 1 (March 7, 2011), 3496. https://apjjf.org/2011/9/10/Jeff-Kingston/3496/article.html

Kojima, Hirotatsu. "Trial Proceedings Until We Won the Not Guilty Verdict" [Muzai hanketsu wo kachitoru made no saiban shinri]. In *The Tachikawa Antiwar Flyer Case* [*Tachikawa Hansen Bira Jiken*], ed. Tachikawa Antiwar Flyer Suppression Support Group [Tachikawa Hansen Bira Dan'atsu Kyūenkai]. Tokyo: Akashi Shōten, 2005.

Kyodo News Digital Co., Ltd. "Average Annual Incomes for Tokyo's 23 Wards." *City-Cost*, May 27, 2016. https://www.city-cost.com/blogs/City-Cost-News/w2Rgw.

"Law Scholars' Declaration Against Suppression of the Tachikawa Self-Defense Force Surveillance Tent Village" [Tachikawa Jietai Kanshi Tento-Mura he no Dan'atsu ni Kōgi suru Hōgakusha Seimei], March 3, 2004. In *The Tachikawa Antiwar Flyer Case* [*Tachikawa Hansen Bira Jiken*], ed. Tachikawa Antiwar Flyer Suppression Support Group [Tachikawa Hansen Bira Dan'atsu Kyūenkai]. Tokyo: Akashi Shōten, 2005.

Matsui, Shigenori. *The Constitution of Japan*. Oxford and Portland, OR: Hart, 2011.

McNeill, David. "Japan's Crime Problem? Too Many Police, not Enough Criminals." *Irish Times*, April 6, 2018. https://www.irishtimes.com/news/world/asia-pacific/japan-s-crime-problem-too-many-police-not-enough-criminals-1.3451997.

McNeill, David. "Death Row Miscarriage Case Puts Spotlight on Japanese Justice." *Irish Times*, February 19, 2019. https://www.irishtimes.com/news/world/asia-pacific/death-row-miscarriage-case-puts-spotlight-on-japanese-justice-1.3798279.

Ministry of Foreign Affairs of Japan. "Three Non-Nuclear Principles." December 11, 1967. https://www.mofa.go.jp/policy/un/disarmament/nnp/index.html.

Minowa, Noboru, and Uchida, Masatoshi. *Constitution Article 9 and Exclusive Self-Defense* [*Kenpō Kyūjō to Senpu Bōei*]. Tokyo: Nashinoki, 2004.

Miyazawa, Setsuo. "The Politics of Increasing Punitiveness and the Rising Populism in Japanese Criminal Justice Policy." *Punishment and Society* 10, no. 1 (January 2008), 47–77.

Munakata, Mitsuru. *When Voices Against War Leave Town: The Tachikawa Antiwar Flyer Suppression Case* [*Machi Kara Hansen no Koe ga Kieru Toki—Tachikawa Hansen Bira-ire Dan'atsu Jiken*]. Tokyo: Jushinsha 2005.

Nakajima, Hiroaki. "Reporting that Cheers the "Not Guilty Verdict" but Excuses Suppression" [Dan'atsu wo menzai suru 'muzai hanketsu' banzai hōdō]. In *The Tachikawa Antiwar Flyer Case* [*Tachikawa Hansen Bira Jiken*], 129. Tokyo: Akashi Shōten, 2005.

Narusawa, Muneo. "The Overseas Dispatch of Japan's Self-Defense Forces and U.S. War Preparations." *Asia-Pacific Journal* 12, no. 31 (July 28, 2014). https://apjjf.org/2014/12/31/Narusawa-Muneo/4158/article.html.

National Personnel Authority. *Annual Report FY2018 (April 2018–March 2019)*. https://www.jinji.go.jp/en/recomme/annual2018/index.html.

National Police Agency. "Developments Concerning the Japan Communist Party" [Nihon kyōsantō no dōkō], *The White Paper on Police (Keisatsu Hakusho)*, 2021. https://www.npa.go.jp/hakusyo/r03/honbun/index.html.

Newman, Nic, Richard Fletcher, Antonis Kalogeropoulos, David A.L. Levy, and Rasmus Kleis Nielsen. *Reuters Institute Digital News Report 2018*. Reuters Institute for the Study of Journalism. https://www.digitalnewsreport.org/survey/2018.

Nishida, Minoru. "What Did the Supreme Court Try to Protect?" [Saikōsai ha nani wo mamorō to shita no ka]. *Hō to Minshushugi* 444 (December 2009).

Obayashi, Keigo. "Free Speech Jurisprudence in Japan." In *Hate Speech in Japan: The Possibility of a Nonregulatory Approach*, eds. Shinji Higashi and Yuji Nasu. Cambridge: Cambridge University Press, 2021.

Obora, Toshiyuki. "Statement of Opinion" [Iken chinjutsu], May 6, 2004. In Yutaka Osawa, *Homepage for Peace* [*Heiwa no Peiji*], blog, May 8, 2004.

Obora, Toshiyuki. "75 Days in Detention for Dropping Antiwar Flyers in Mailboxes at Self-Defense Force Housing" [Jieitai kansha he no hansen-bira tōkan de 75-nichikan no kōryu]. In *Very Strange! Police, Prosecutors, Courts: The Freedom of Civil Society Is in Danger* [*Okashii zo, Keisatsu, Kensatsu, Saibansho—Shimin Shakai no Jiyū ga Abunai*], eds. Akira Uozumi, et al. Tokyo: Tsukuru Shuppan, 2005.

Office of the Historian. "George W. Bush." 2003. https://history.state.gov/departmenthistory/travels/president/bush-george-w.

Office of the United Nations High Commissioner for Human Rights. "International Covenant on Civil and Political Rights." *General Assembly Resolution* 2200A(XXI), December 16, 1966. https://www.ohchr.org/en/professionalinterest/pages/ccpr.pdf.

Okubo, Shirō. "The Current Stage of the Trial and Points at Issue" [Soshō no gendankai to sōten]. *Hōgaku Seminar* 615 (March 2006), 52–55.

Okudaira, Yasuhiro. "Once Again Under Threat: Freedom of Expression" [Ima futatabi odokasareru hyōgen no jiyū]. *Hōgaku Seminar* 615 (March 2006), 46–51.

Okudaira, Yasuhiro. *A Brief History of the Peace Preservation Law* [*Chian Ijihō Shoshi*]. Tokyo: Chikuma Shobō, 1977; reprint, Tokyo: Iwanami Shōten, 2006.

Okudaira, Yasuhiro. *Living the Constitution* [*Kenpō wo Ikiru*]. Tokyo: Nihon Hyōronsha, 2007.

Okudaira, Yasuhiro. "The 'Safe, Secure' State and the Present Stage of Freedom of Expression" ["Anzen, Anshin" Kokka to Hyōgen no Jiyū no Gendankai]. *Hōritsu Jihō Zōkan*, October 31, 2016.

Onishi, Nobuhiro. "Statement of Opinion" [Iken chinjutsu], May 6, 2004. In Yutaka Osawa, *Homepage for Peace* [*Heiwa no Peiji*], blog, May 8, 2004.

Onishi, Norimitsu. "After 8-Year Trial in Japan, Cultist Is Sentenced to Death." *New York Times*, February 28, 2004. https://www.nytimes.com/2004/02/28/world/after-8-year-trial-in-japan-cultist-is-sentenced-to-death.html.

Onishi, Norimitsu. "Pressed by Police, Even Innocent Confess in Japan." *New York Times*, May 11, 2007. https://www.nytimes.com/2007/05/11/world/asia/11japan.html.

Onishi, Norimitsu. "Majority Party in Japan Retains Power in Parliament." *New York Times*, July 12, 2004. https://www.nytimes.com/2004/07/12/world/majority-party-in-japan-retains-power-in-parliament.html.

Osawa, Yutaka. *Homepage for Peace* [*Heiwa no Peiji*], blog, http://osawa-yutaka.my.coocan.jp/heiwa-top.htm.

Osawa, Yutaka. "Final Comment" [Owari ni]. In *The Tachikawa Antiwar Flyer Case* [*Tachikawa Hansen Bira Jiken*], ed. Tachikawa Antiwar Flyer Suppression Support Group [Tachikawa Hansen Bira Dan'atsu Kyūenkai]. Tokyo: Akashi Shōten, 2005.

Ozawa, Ryūichi. "Victory for Conscience and Common Sense" [Ryōshin to Ryōshiki no Shōri]. *Hō to Minshushugi* 412 (October 2006), 54–58.

Penn, Michael. *Japan and the War on Terror.* London: I. B. Tauris, 2014.

Prime Minister of Japan and His Cabinet. "Press Conference by Prime Minister Junichiro Koizumi." *Speeches and Statements by Prime Minister*, December 9, 2003, provisional translation. http://japan.kantei.go.jp/koizumispeech/2003/12/09press_e.html.

Prime Minister of Japan and His Cabinet. "Prime Minister Encourages Japan Air Self-Defense Force (JASDF) to be Dispatched to Iraq." *What's Up Around the Prime Minister*, December 24, 2003. http://japan.kantei.go.jp/koizumiphoto/2003/12/24komaki_e.html.

Repeta, Lawrence. "Reserved Seats on Japan's Supreme Court." *Washington University Law Review* 88, no. 6 (2011), 1713–1744.

Repeta, Lawrence. "'Personal Information,' Media Control, and Government Power: Legislative Battles in Japan, 1999–2003." *Meiji Law Journal* 22 (March 2015), 9–35.

Repeta, Lawrence. "Nationalism and the Law: Japan's Tale of Two Constitutions." In *Asian Nationalisms Reconsidered*, ed. Jeff Kingston. London: Routledge, 2016.

Repeta, Lawrence. "The Struggle to Protect Individual Rights in Postwar Japan: Seven Decades of Progress." In *The Cambridge History of Japan*. Vol. 3, *The Modern Japanese Nation and Empire*, ed. Laura Hein. London: Cambridge University Press, forthcoming in 2023.

Repeta, Lawrence, and Colin P.A. Jones. "State Power Versus Individual Freedom: Japan's Constitutional Past, Present, and Possible Futures." In *Japan: The Precarious Future*, eds. Frank Baldwin and Anne Allison. New York: New York University Press, 2015.

Rich, Motoko. "Carlos Ghosn Emerges to Say He Was "Wrongly Accused and Unfairly Detained."" *New York Times*, January 7, 2019.

Rosen, Dan. "Policing Political Speech: Japan's Mistrust of the Marketplace." *Michigan State International Law Review* 22 (2014), 799–814.

Sakaguchi, Shōjirō. "The Tachikawa Antiwar Flyer Case: Review of the Supreme Court Judgment" [Tachikawa hansen bira jiken—saikōsai hanketsu hihan]. *Sekai* (July 2008).

Sasayama, Naoto. "A Great, Historic Case: Suppression Under National Public Law in the Horikoshi Case, Report from the First Court Hearing" [Rekishiteki daijiken—kokkōhō dan'atsu Horikoshi jiken dai-ikkai kōhan no hōkoku]. *Jiyū Hōsōdan report* [Jiyū Hōsōdan tsūshin] 1139 (September 1, 2004). https://www.jlaf.jp/old/tsushin/2004/1139.html.

Society to Prevent Suppression Under National Public Law and Protect Freedom of Speech. *Suppression Under National Public Law: The Horikoshi Case Record of Battle, 2004–2013* [*Kokkōhō dan'atsu horikoshi jiken tatakai no kiroku 2004–2013*]. Tokyo: Society to Prevent Suppression Under National Public Law and Protect Freedom of Speech [Kokkōhō Dan'atsu wo Yurusazu Genron no Jiyū wo Mamoru Kai], 2013.

Society to Prevent Suppression Under National Public Law and Protect Freedom of Speech. *Trial Materials from the Suppression Under National Public Law Case* [*Kokkōhō dan'atsu jiken—saiban shiryō*]. Vol. 1. Tokyo: Society to Prevent Suppression Under National Public Law and Protect Freedom of Speech. [Kokkōhō Dan'atsu wo Yurusazu Genron no Jiyū wo Mamoru Kai], 2004

Society to Protect the Freedom to Deliver Flyers. *Flyers Filled with Thoughts About Peace [Heiwa e no Omoi—Bira ni Komete]*. Tokyo: Society to Protect the Freedom to Deliver Flyers [Bira Haifu no Jiyū wo Mamoru Kai], 2010.

Society to Protect the Freedom to Deliver Flyers. *Trial Materials from the Katsushika Flyer Distribution Suppression Case* [*Katsushika bira haifu dan'atsu jiken—shiryōshū*]. Tokyo: Society to Protect the Freedom to Deliver Flyers [Bira Haifu no Jiyū wo Mamoru Kai], 2005–2009.

"Suppression of Antiwar Flyers—Our Battle" [Hansen bira dan'atsu—Watakushitachi no tatakai]. *War and Sex* [*Sensō to Sei*] 24 (Summer 2005), 6–39.

Supreme Court of Japan. "Fifty Years of the Supreme Court, as Seen Through Photographs" [Shashin de miru saikōsaibansho no 50 nen]. *Courts in Japan* [*Saibansho*]. https://www.courts.go.jp/vc-files/courts/file2/20916003.pdf.

Supreme Court of Japan. "Introducing the Tokyo High Court" [Tokyo kōtō saibansho no shōkai]. *Courts in Japan* [Saibansho]. https://www.courts.go.jp/tokyo-h/about/syokai/index.html.

Tachikawa Antiwar Flyer Suppression Support Group [Tachikawa Hansen Bira Dan'atsu Kyūenkai], ed. *The Complete Record 2004–2009* [*Zenkiroku 2004–2009*]. Tokyo: Tachikawa Antiwar Flyer Suppression Support Group [Tachikawa Hansen Bira Dan'atsu Kyūenkai], 2009.

Tachikawa Antiwar Flyer Suppression Support Group [Tachikawa Hansen Bira Dan'atsu Kyūenkai], ed. *The Tachikawa Antiwar Flyer Case* [*Tachikawa Hansen Bira Jiken*]. Tokyo: Akashi Shōten, 2005.

Takada, Sachimi. "Statement of Opinion" [Iken chinjutsu], May 6, 2004. In Yutaka Osawa, *Homepage for Peace* [*Heiwa no Peiji*], blog, May 8, 2004.

Takada, Sachimi. "Jail Diary: 75-Day Fight from Inside the Walls" [Gokū-chu Nikki: Kabe no naka de tatakatta 75-nichikan]. In *The Tachikawa Antiwar Flyer Case* [*Tachikawa Hansen Bira Jiken*], ed. Tachikawa Antiwar Flyer Suppression Support Group [Tachikawa Hansen Bira Dan'atsu Kyūenkai]. Tokyo: Akashi Shōten, 2005.

Takahashi, Saul, ed. *Civil and Political Rights in Japan*. London: Routledge, 2019.

Takemae, Eiji. *The Allied Occupation of Japan*. New York: Continuum, 2002.

The Appeal of the National Public Law Case and the Supreme Court [*Kokkōhō Jiken Jōkokushin to Saikōsaibansho*]. *Hōritsu Jihō Zōkan*. Tokyo: Nihon Hyōronsha, 2011.

Tokyo Southern District Law Office [Tokyo Nanbu Hōritsu Jimusho]. *Trials and Human Rights* [*Saiban to Jinken*]. Tokyo: Nihon Hyōronsha, 2009.

Tomatsu, Hidenori, and Shiyake, Masanori. *Constitutional Law Cases and Comments*. Tokyo: Yūhikaku, 2007.

Tomatsu, Hidenori, and Shiyake, Masanori. *Kenpō Hanrei*. 5th ed. Tokyo: Yūhikaku, 2008.

Trans-Pacific GI/SDF Rights Hotline. [Beihei Jieikan Jinken hotline], February 15, 2006. https://www.jca.apc.org/gi-heisi.

Uchida, Masatoshi. *Born in the Year of Defeat* [*Haisen no Toshi ni Umarete*]. Tokyo: Ohta Shuppan, 2001.

Uchida, Masatoshi. *Is This a Crime? Thinking About "Arrests for Handing Out Flyers"* [*Kore ga hanzai? "Bira kubari de taiho" wo kangaeru*]. Iwanami booklet 655. Tokyo: Iwanami Shōten, 2005.

Uozumi, Akira, et al. *Very Strange! Police, Prosecutors, Courts: The Freedom of Civil Society Is in Danger* [*Okashii zo, Keisatsu, Kensatsu, Saibansho—Shimin Shakai no Jiyū ga Abunai*]. Tokyo: Tsukuru Shuppan, 2005.

Upham, Frank. "Japan v. Kawamoto: Judicial Limits on the State's Power to Indict." *Law in Japan: An Annual* 13 (1980), 137–149.

Upham, Frank. *Law and Social Change in Postwar Japan*. Cambridge, MA: Harvard University Press, 1987.

Usaki, Masahiro. "Restrictions on Political Campaigns in Japan." *Law and Contemporary Problems* 53, no. 2 (1990), 133–156.

Vanoverbeke, Dimitri. *Juries in the Japanese Legal System: The Continuing Struggle for Citizen Participation and Democracy*. London: Routledge Law in Asia, 2015.

Ward, Max M. *Thought Crime: Ideology and State in Interwar Japan*. Durham, NC: Duke University Press, 2019.

Waseda Law Department, Nakajima Tetsu Seminar. "Shadows on City Streets: What We Saw as Courtroom Spectators" [Tsuisekisha no machi—saiban bōchō kara mieta koto]. *Hōgaku Seminar* 615 (March 2006), 56–59.

Watanabe, Shun-ichi J. "The Historical Analysis of the "Kunitachi Machizukuri Movement": Its Nature and the Role of Professor Shiro Masuda." Paper presented at the *15th International Planning History Society Conference*. http://www.usp.br/fau/iphs/abstractsAndPapersFiles/Sessions/36/WATANABE.pdf.

Winkler, Christian G. *The Quest for Japan's New Constitution: An Analysis of Visions and Constitution Reform Proposals, 1980–2009*. London: Routledge, 2011.

"World Peace Now 3.20." March 20, 2004. http://www.mkimpo.com/diary/2004/wpn_04-03-20.html.

Wright, Dustin. "'Sunagawa Struggle' Ignited Anti-U.S. Base Resistance Across Japan." *Japan Times*, May 3, 2015. https://www.japantimes.co.jp/community/2015/05/03/issues/sunagawa-struggle-ignited-anti-u-s-base-resistance-across-japan.

Wright, Dustin. "The Sunagawa Struggle: A Century of Antibase Protest in a Tokyo Suburb." PhD diss., University of California at Santa Cruz, June 2015.

Yamaguchi, Susumu, and Miyaji, Yu. *Shadow Fighting at the Supreme Court* [*Saikōsai no Antō*]. Tokyo: Asahi Shinsho, 2011.

Yamamoto, Shizu. "Reversal of the Judgment in the Tachikawa Antiwar Flyer Delivery Trial" [Tachikawa hansen bira-ire saiban de gyakuten hanketsu]. Japan Institute of Constitutional Law [Hogakukan Kempō Kenkyūjo], 2006. http://www.jicl.jp/old/now/saiban/backnumber/tachikawa2.html.

Yamamoto, Shizu. "We Will Not Be Silent" [Watakushitachi ha chinmoku shinai]. In *In Order to Avoid a Silent Society: 168 Appeals to the Supreme Court* [*Chinmoku no shakai ni shinai tame ni—saikōsai ni ateta 168tsū no jōshinsho*], ed. Tachikawa Antiwar Flyer Suppression Support Group [Tachikawa Hansen Bira Dan'atsu Kyūenkai]. Tokyo: Jushinsha, 2006.

Yoshida, Toshihiro. *Refusing to Cooperate in War* [*Sensō Kyōryoku Kyōhi*]. Tokyo: Iwanami Shinsho, 2005.

INDEX

Page numbers in *italics* indicate figures in the text, and references following "n" refer endnotes.